NEWS AND EXCHANGE RATE DYNAMICS

The translation of this work has been funded by SEPS
SEGRETARIATO EUROPEO PER LE PUBBLICAZIONI SCIENTIFICHE

SEPS
SEGRETARIATO EUROPEO PER LE PUBBLICAZIONI SCIENTIFICHE

Via Val d'Aposa 7 – 40123 Bologna – Italy
tel +39 051 271992 – fax +39 051 265983
seps@alma.unibo.it – www.seps.it

News and Exchange Rate Dynamics

MASSIMO TIVEGNA
University of Teramo and LUISS Guido Carli, Rome

GRAZIA CHIOFI
Banca Nazionale del Lavoro
Wholesale & International Banking Division, Rome

ASHGATE

Published by

Ashgate Publishing Limited
Gower House
Croft Road
Aldershot
Hants GU11 3HR
England

Ashgate Publishing Company
Suite 420
101 Cherry Street
Burlington, VT 05401-4405
USA

Ashgate website: http://www.ashgate.com

British Library Cataloguing in Publication Data
Tivegna, Massimo
News and exchange rate dynamics
1. Foreign exchange rates - Italy 2. Foreign exchange rates - Italy - Statistics 3. Lira, Italian - Statistics 4. Mass media - Italy 5. Press - Italy 6. Foreign news - Italy
I. Title II. Chiofi, Grazia
332.4'56'0945

Library of Congress Cataloging-in-Publication Data
Tivegna, Massimo.
[News e dinamica dei tassi de cambio. English]
News and exchange rate dynamics / Massimo Tivegna and Grazia Chiofi.
p. cm.
Includes bibliographical references and index.
ISBN 0-7546-3901-0
1. Foreign exchange rates--Italy. 2. Foreign exchange rates--Italy--Statistics. 3. Lira, Italian--Statistics. 4. Mass media--Italy. 5. Press--Italy. 6. Foreign news--Italy. 7. Foreign exchange rates--Econometric models. I. Chiofi, Grazia. II. Title.

HG3871.I8T5813 2004
332.4'56'0945--dc22

2004048449

ISBN 0 7546 3901 0

Printed and bound in Great Britain by MPG Books Ltd, Bodmin, Cornwall

Contents

List of Figures

List of Tables

The Authors

Massimo Tivegna, born in Rome in 1945, is a Professor of Political Economy and Econometrics in the Faculty of Political Sciences at the University of Teramo and at LUISS Guido Carli, in Rome. He taught at the University of Rome "Tor Vergata", at the University of Perugia and at the University of Pennsylvania. He worked in the Bank of Italy, the Confederation of Italian Industry (Confindustria) and, as a consultant, at Wharton Econometric Forecasting Associates (WEFA) in Philadelphia, Istituto Mobiliare Italiano (IMI), the General Accounting Office of the Treasury in Italy and recently at Banca di Roma.

Grazia Chiofi, born in Rome in 1971, works in the Wholesale & International Banking Division of Banca Nazionale del Lavoro. She graduated at the University of Rome "Tor Vergata" and has been teaching part-time Econometrics ever since at Tor Vergata and at LUISS Guido Carli.

Mario Sarcinelli is a Lecturer in Monetary Economics at the University of Rome "La Sapienza" and in Global Banking at LUISS Guido Carli. He was Deputy Director General at the Bank of Italy, where he spent a large part of his career, and later Minister of Foreign Trade, Director General of the Treasury, Operations Vice President at the EBRD and Chairman of Banca Nazionale del Lavoro.

Introduction to the English Edition

This book contains the first and basic results of an ongoing research activity on the economic, financial and non-financial determinants of exchange rate fluctuations at a moderately high frequency with twice daily data observations. The initial motivations of this project were to establish a cardinal metrics of the impact of a broad family of news on exchange rates movements. The first results are described in this book. The ultimate goal is to explain the formation of market sentiment on one particular currency and the way it changes overtime in response to the accumulation of new information. The question here is to investigate whether the differential response of exchange rates to the same type of scheduled and unscheduled news and the context where that happens can be used to monitor market sentiment and predict its shifts. An intermediate by-product is the construction of news-based trading rules, built using extensions of the work described in this book.

News was collected into two broad families: scheduled news concerning the discrepancy between published macroeconomic data (by Governments or Central Banks) and the values expected by financial markets; unscheduled news consists of an economic or institutional event, a declaration or a disclosure, which can be either totally unexpected or – even though expected to occur – has an unknown timing, an unknown content or both.

All the news was collected in a relational data bank which we called *Newsmetrics* and is a companion to this book. The bank is available over the Internet according to information provided elsewhere in the book.

Scheduled news concerning generally macroeconomic announcements by Governments or Central Banks from the United States, Germany, Japan and Italy, between 1994 and 1997 are collected here. Among these countries, the United States has an annual calendar of statistical releases. Financial markets have long been following the 8.30 A.M. Eastern Standard Time (EST) ritual when the most important US macroeconomic data are published, generating a cluster of volatility in every world financial market open at that time, both before and after the announcement.

The unknown timing of unscheduled news makes it likely that its impact is not embodied into observed prices. The acquisition and the analysis of the latest available information is the core of the daily activity in currency trading. Such a keen attention to the latest piece of available information – not necessarily macroeconomic information – stands in sharp contrast to standard theories of asset pricing that hinge only on the relationship between prices and a set of "fundamental" macroeconomic variables. However the most recent experience of foreign exchange markets seem to suggest that market participants are more willing to follow the information coming from the latest news rather than forecasting the future developments of "fundamentals". The empirical results obtained so far indicate that the family of unscheduled news has the highest explanatory power.

Newsmetrics is updated continuously to feed the research work mentioned above. The collection of events of course takes into account the arrival of the Euro. Our empirical results, though, do not show any sensible difference between unscheduled news and movements in the DM-$ or in the Euro-Dollar. Interestingly, €-$ is moved by German scheduled news as in previous times, the Euroland macroeconomic announcement do not appear to be – up to this time – statistically significant.

The English translation of the book comes out four years after the Italian edition. As such the book deals with two currencies – the German Mark and the Italian Lira – which belong to the archeology of financial markets. But the basic methodology to assess how exchange rates respond to news has still an ongoing validity which can explain the fluctuations of the Euro *vis-à-vis* the US Dollar. The Italian Lira experience (with its overwhelming importance of political news and the frequent episodes of over-reaction) can be valuable in explaining today's behavior – for example – of the Brazilian Real, of the Mexican Peso or of some Eastern Europe currencies.

Subsequent steps in the study of news and exchange rates, following the lead of this book, were in the direction of investigating the simultaneous nature of the relationships between interest rates, the Dow Jones Industrial Index and exchange rates through multivariate GARCH estimation. The explanatory power of news did not change substantially but some simultaneous parameters changed, of course. The resulting models – one in the Japanese-European Time Zone and another in the American Time Zone, the same zoning of the global trading day adopted in this book – showed a remarkable tracking performance, beating the traditional random walk, and appeared immediately as a viable trading tool. The above results are contained in a published article: Massimo Tivegna "News and Dollar Exchange Rate Dynamics", Rivista Italiana degli Economisti 2002, pages 3-48. The paper is also available on the web site where the data bank is located.

Given the tracking properties of the model and the multivariate GARCH estimation of the generating process of its error terms, some uses as a signal-generating device for trading the €-$ rate were made at a leading financial institution in Italy.

The news-based structural model of exchange rates described in this book and in the above paper has some useful properties to generate buy and sell signals for trading. The relationships between various families of news and exchange rate variations makes it possible to generate values of say the €-$ conditional on the occurrence of a particular news. The GARCH volatility obtained in the estimation process can be used to build confidence bands around point forecasts of conditional simulations (on news occurrence) or baseline simulations (in this case without the occurrence of any news).

The model can thus generate a set of technical bands and a trading signal according to where the exchange rate happens to be shortly after the forecast. The arrival of an unscheduled news is of course unknown, but truly unexpected events are not common. It happens more frequently that market positioning early in European time reflects short term expectations, sentiment or even polarization, a frequent phenomenon especially between late 2002 and 2003, because of the Iraq war. This is fully reflected in the position of the exchange rate within the technical bands (as the above market phenomena are unscheduled news) so that a trading signal can be extracted from this position.

Another trading rule is going long or short the €-$ (for instance) according to whether the model predicts an appreciation or a depreciation of the exchange rate. Various model-based trading rules were tried and some of them produced very good profit rates and Sharpe ratios. A paper was presented at various financial conferences: Massimo Tivegna "Day Trading the Euro-Dollar with a News-based Model of Exchange Rates. Descriptive Results", unpublished but available on the web site of the data bank.

All the above research carried out after the completion of this book is based on the work described in it especially on the methodology to detect unscheduled news and on the division of the twenty-four hours global trading day into two parts. These two features are at the base of our foreign exchange models and their trading use.

This book should be of interest also for two other broad categories of readers: economic and financial historians and communication scholars. The first group may appreciate some methodological aspects of the political and financial history, at daily frequency, of the United States, Italy, Germany and Japan between 1994 and 1997. This is concentrated in Chapter 2, but is also present in other parts the book. The second group will probably appreciate the attempt to construct a communication model for traders based on empirical tests of some of their decoding schemes, mostly Shannon-Weaver and the semiotic-informational model. Most of this material is concentrated in the last Chapter. The Introduction to the Italian Edition offers some examples and further remarks on this latter topic.

This English translation of the book would not exist without the friendly insistence and the organising support of Luciana Delfini, the editor of the book in Italian. The Segretariato Europeo per le Pubblicazioni Scientifiche, a non-profit Italian organisation, financed the translation of this book. The translator, Silvia Pulino, did an excellent job, especially when describing some very cryptic aspects of Italian public life and in the more technical parts of the book.

The research work that went into the Italian edition of the book was generously supported by the University of Teramo, the Italian National Research Council (CNR) and the Italian Ministry for University and Scientific and Technological Research (MURST).

Our life partners endured the time spent on this book, in both languages.

Roma, December 2003

Introduction to the Italian Edition

Mario Sarcinelli

With the vast amount of information that economic operators and the public in general have to interpret nowadays, communication has acquired an extraordinary importance, unimaginable even a few years ago. The global economy is above all the economy of information. Communication, while always an art to some extent, is now becoming a science, as evidenced by the creation of so many University majors in this discipline in Italy. This book is but an example of this phenomenon: it uses the tools of economic analysis and econometrics in order to explain the variations in exchange rates, by examining the international markets' reactions to the various forms of macroeconomic and political news.

Macroeconomic News

While corporate communication is highly professional, macroeconomic communication has fewer scientific points of reference and, at least in Italy, it still follows old paths. This is particularly true for the institutional information contained in official documents of the economic policy Authorities, such as the "Final Considerations" of the Governor of the Bank of Italy, not to mention the Economic and Financial Planning Document produced by the Minister of the Treasury. Shortly after the end of the public reading of the final considerations, we see the emergence of different interpretations on many points of the text, which – when not inspired by a specific political or sector interest – can be attributed to a different economic model of reference or to an unequal perception of the cyclical situation or of the temporal lapse in which the proposed economic policy can produce effects.

Another form of economic news is represented by "disclosures", which can be of two types. The first type is similar to the disclosures relative to sales, profits, capital operations, acquisitions, etc., which publicly held companies are obliged to make. In Italy, the production of information on the state of the economic system is in the hands of policy-makers and their statistical offices, particularly in the areas of growth, inflation and balance of payments. This type of periodical information constitutes what we call "scheduled news". The difference between actual and expected news, which strongly influences the reactions of financial markets, is of interest to a large part of the economic research performed at leading international banking institutions and it can determine a rapid reassessment of market sentiment. Indeed, the greatest beneficiaries of the research on which news is relevant to the market are probably the people whose business it is to explain market positioning and sentiment. This is certainly the first attempt in Italy to construct a database of news – hence the name *Newsmetrics* – and to use it to provide an econometric estimate of the response of exchange rates to news.

A second form of disclosure, with greater regulatory significance, is represented by the statements made by policy-makers, which contain evaluations of current trends and economic and monetary policy proposals. Given the *ex ante* uncertainty over its contents and timing, and the *ex post* uncertainty over its interpretation (think of how the traders interpret, real time, President Greenspan's testimony before Congress), this information has greater effects on the prices of financial activities. Indeed, this research confirms that "unscheduled" news produce greater exchange rate fluctuations and the sharpest peaks of volatility.

This book is full of this type of news. An example is given by the long sequence of statements preceding and following the presentation of the proposed Budget in Italy, with corrective measures called for by some political parts and with lobbying on the contrary by others (e.g. sections 2.4, third quarter, and 2.6, third quarter). In Germany, another example is given by the statements by Bundesbank President Tietmeyer – and by many other Bundesbank council members – regarding the German monetary policy objectives in early 1997, following the attempts to weaken the European currencies relative to the Dollar towards the end of 1996 as a response to French pressure (see sections 2.2, fourth quarter, and 2.3, first quarter).

Announcement Effect

The interpretation of this news can be made more difficult by the fact that it often contains another type of communication, the "message". Even though it is at times obscure, the message is intended to produce an "announcement effect" among economic and financial agents. The statements by US Treasury Secretary Rubin regarding the opportunities offered to the United States by a strong Dollar are a perfect example of this mix of political disclosure and announcement. A sample of this is provided by news 912, 1387, 1685 and 2074 of *Newsmetrics*. Sometimes the announcement effect can be caused unintentionally: such is the case, perhaps, of Prime Minister Prodi's statement, upon his return from a meeting with Spanish Premier Aznar, that he intended to introduce in the 1997 Budget a one-off tax of 30,000 billion Lire in order to meet the Maastricht parameters of that year (see section 2.6, third quarter).

Also, election results can produce a positive (the possibility or probability of implementing certain policies) or negative (difficulties in implementing them) announcement effect. The victory of the Polo delle Libertà in the 28 March 1994 elections produced an unequivocally positive effect on the markets, as was to be expected from the first victory in post-war Italy of an expressly conservative coalition. The Ulivo prevailed in the April 21, 1996 elections producing an equally positive effect, surprisingly, according to the parameters used to evaluate the previous result. This is probably due to the presence in both election results of "political moderation" (in the person of the Premier) and of a promise (later unfulfilled by both governments) of greater stability in political life.

Examples of negative effects are those produced by the disappointing electoral results of the Polo in the regional elections towards the end of November 1994, as that was the governing coalition, and the victory of the "No" in the referendum over television regulatory regime in June 1995 (for the Dini government, see section 2.5, second quarter). The most significant foreign example of an electoral announcement effect is certainly that of Jospin's victory in the French elections of May 1997, which the markets interpreted as having a negative impact on the future existence of the Euro (see section 2.3, second quarter). This happened shortly after an episode which the markets had read as a promise of a weak Euro: the unfortunate dispute between German Minister of Finance Weigel, who wanted to use the gold reserves of the Bundesbank to help the country meet the Maastricht parameters, and President Tietmeyer who opposed the initiative (see section 2.3).

Unexpected Events

The difficulty of decoding events is heightened in the case of unscheduled news, because they also include, in addition to the communication phenomena described above, truly unexpected and usually – though not always – unpredictable events.

The earthquake that hit Kobe, Japan on 17 January, 1995 was certainly unpredictable, and it probably was partly responsible for the repatriation of capital and the resulting increasing weakness of the Dollar against the Yen in that period. The writ of summons against Prime Minister Berlusconi in November 1995 was also unpredictable, at least in its timing. Other news, while having greater elements of predictability, are also able to move the markets: for instance, the repeated provocative statements by the Honorable Bossi regarding the political dynamics within the coalition sustaining the Berlusconi government, in early August 1995, produced the marked weakening of the Lira on August 11, and the corresponding increase in the discount rate.

The difficulties, however, do not end here. Many of the news contained in this book seem hard to decode *ex ante* and at the time they take place, even if they have precise effects *ex post*. To this group belong all the Italian judiciary news, such as the proposals by Minister Biondi on an extension of preventive prison in the Spring of 1994 (section 2.4, third quarter), the Biondi-Mani Pulite conflict (*ibidem*), the Mancuso-Mani Pulite contrast (section 2.5, second quarter); as well as the negative statements regarding Italy's ability to enter the Euro in September 1995 and their effect on the DM/$ (section 2.1, third quarter).

Market Sentiment, Polarization and the Euro

An important contribution of this book is the precise description, with a wealth of examples, in section 8.5, of two terms much used by foreign exchange traders and analysts: "market sentiment" and "market polarization". These two concepts are particularly useful in explaining the Euro's recent history.

The analyses in this book refer to a period that goes from the second quarter of 1994 to the end of 1997, when the Euro experience had not yet begun, even though one of the categories of news that is potentially relevant to the exchange rate fluctuations explicitly refers to the new currency (Chapter 5).

The diagnoses of the continued depreciation of the Euro in the first two years of its existence have focused, on one hand, on the growth differential between the American and the European economy (with the consequent increase in the expected yield of stock market investment in the United States and the resulting diversion of funds), and, on the other hand, on an apparent divergence of opinions over the long-term development model for the countries participating to the European Monetary Union (EMU), as exemplified by the contrasting positions taken by economic policy-makers on the effects of a devaluation of the European currency.

The first diagnosis can easily explain the 1999 depreciation, but it is harder to use it to justify the continuing depreciation in 2000, given that the growth differential between the USA and the EMU had lessened and that the American stock market had lost strength. In the terms used in this book (Chapter 8), the market sentiment emerging during 1999, when the US economy had grown much more than the European economy, then became a "polarization" of the bullish trend of the Dollar in 2000: in this year all the good news of European growth, which should have caused a strengthening of the Euro, was systematically ignored, together with all the symptoms of slowdown in the American economy, which should have produced the same effect. Thus, while the bullish opportunities in the US stock markets were rigorously accompanied by a weakening of the Euro, the somewhat bearish situation one year later did not produce a symmetrical effect on the European currency.

The second diagnosis fares somewhat better. Only rarely during 1999 did the Directors of the European Central Bank show a united front. When they did, in April of that year, responding to President Duisenberg's request of a greater union, the Euro appreciated. The understanding improved slightly in 2000, even if toning down the stereotypical repetition of the strength of the European economy and the potential for revaluation of the Euro (negatively regarded by the markets as a "mantra"). However, the polarization was already in place and the European currency often weakened after such statements. German Chancellor Schroeder's statements made on 4 September and later confirmed by his representative on 6 September in case he had not been properly understood, brought to the fore the subject of the divergent views. Thus the Euro continued to depreciate.

Economic Theory and Communication Science

It is clear at this point that, in the explanation of short-term exchange rate fluctuations, economic and financial analysis can benefit from the use of different theoretical models belonging to the science of communication: from the various versions of the original Shannon-Weaver mathematical model (1949), with its concepts of signal and noise, to Eco's semiotic-informational model (1965), with its possibility to isolate the nature of the "signal symbols" that the markets find in policy-makers' statements; from contextual models such as those by Schramm and Slama-Cazacu, which can help understand the different reactions of the market to apparently identical news, to the "Johary window" (see Chapter 4 in Morcellini-Fatelli (1994) and other references in the Bibliography), which to economists suggests game theory with asymmetric information. The interface with communication models is not explicit in the book, but it underlies the cause-effect relationship between news and exchange rate variation studied with econometric methods, even if the author does refer to these communication models in the first and the last chapters.

A final word: this book describes an innovative line of research in economics and finance that underlines multi-disciplinarity. It can, therefore, be useful to financial market operators and analysts, who are currently bombarded by heterogeneous news. They are certainly hungry for a methodology which can offer them a better and more coherent interpretation of market events. Will this book help them better organize their mental and electronic archives? I hope so.

List of Abbreviations (*)

AN	Alleanza Nazionale, National Alliance , an Italian party
ANFIA	Italian Union of Italian Car Manufacturers
ARCH	AutoRegressive Conditional Heteroskedasticity
ATZ	American Time Zone
BBC	British Broadcasting Corporation
BCE	European Central Bank
BIL	Billions
BIS	Bank for International Settlements
BLS	Bureau of Labour Statistics
BoJ	Bank of Japan
BOT	Buoni Ordinari del Tesoro, Italian Treasury Bills
BTP	Buoni del Tesoro Poliennali, Italian Bonds
BUBA	Bundesbank
CB	Conference Board
CC	Citta' Campione, sample cities for flash estimates of Italian inflation
CCD	Christian Democratic Centre, an Italian party
CCT	Certificati di Credito del Tesoro, Italian Treasury Certificates
CDU	Christian Democratic Union, an Italian party
CDU-CSU	The Christian Democratic Party of Germany
CET	Central European Time
CGIL	Confederazione Generale Italiana del Lavoro, the socialist trade union in Italy
CISL	Confederazione Italiana Sociale del Lavoro, the catholic trade union in Italy
CNR	Italian National Research Council
CPI	Consumer Price Index
CSM	Consiglio Superiore della Magistratura, Upper Council of Magistrates
CTZ	Italian Treasury Certificates with Option
DJ	Dow Jones
DL	Department of Labour
DM	German Deutsche Mark
DM-$	DM-$ exchange rate
DoC	Department of Commerce
DPEF	Document for Public Budget Planning
ECB	European Central Bank
ECOFIN	Council of Ministers of the European Union
EMI	European Monetary Institute

EMU	European Monetary Union
ENEL	Ente Nazionale Energia Elettrica, Italy's Electricity Board
EPA	Economic Planning Agency of Japan
ERM	European Exchange-Rate Mechanism
EST	Eastern Standard Time
ETZ	European Time Zone
EU	European Union
FED	Board of Governors of the Federal Reserve System
FFSS	Italy's Railways Company
FI	Forza Italia, Berlusconi party
FIML	Full Information Maximum Likelihood
FMI	International Monetary Fund
FOMC	Federal Reserve Open Market Committee
FT	Financial Times
G-10	G7 plus Sweden, Switzerland and Australia at the BIS
G3	United States, Germany and Japan
G7	Canada, France, Germany, Japan, Italy, United Kingdom, United States
GARCH	Generalized AutoRegressive Conditional Heteroskedasticity
GDP	Gross Domestic Product
GE	Germany
HK	Hong Kong
HT	Herald Tribune
IFO	IFO Institute for Economic Research, Munich, Germany
ILOR	Local Income Tax
IME	European Monetary Institute
IMF	International Monetary Fund
INPS	National Pension Institute in Italy
IRAP	Regional Tax on Economic Activity
IRI	Istituto per la Ricostruzione Industrale, State Industrial Holding in Italy
IRPEF	Personal Income Tax in Italy
IRPEG	Corporate Income tax in Italy
IRS	Institute for Social Research in Italy
ISCO	Institute for Business Cycles Analysis in Italy
ISTAT	Italy's Central Statistical Office
IVA	Value Added Tax
LDP	Liberal Democratic Party of Japan
Lit-DM	Lira-DM exchange rate
M3	M3 monetary aggregate
MITI	Foreign Trade Ministry of Japan
MLD	Billions
MMS	Money Market Services
MoF	Ministry of Finance of Japan
MQ3S	Three Stages Least Squares

MURST	Italian Ministry for University and Scientific and Technological Research
NAIRU	Non Accelerating Inflation Rate Unemployment
NAPM	National Association of Purchasing Managers
NY	New York
OCSE	Organisation for Economic Co-operation and Development
OECD	Organisation for Economic Co-operation and Development
P/T	Repo rate in Italy
PCE	Personal Consumption Expenditure
PCI	Consumer Price Index
PDS	Partito Democratico della Sinistra, Italy's former communist party
PIL	Gross Domestic Product
PPI	Partito Popolare Italiano, Italian Popular Party
PRC	Reconstructed Communist Party
RAI	Italy's public TV company
SME	European Monetary System
SNB	Swiss National Bank
SPD	German Social Democratic Party
STET	Italy's State Telephone Company
SURE	Seemingly Unrelated Regressions Estimator
TRF	Severance Pay
TUS	Discount Rate
UE	European Union
UIC	Italian Office for Foreign Exchange
UIL	Unione Italiana del Lavoro, Social Democratic trade union in Italy
UME	European Monetary Union
US	United States
VAR	Vector Auto Regression
WSJ	Wall Street Journal
WTO	World Trade Organisation

(*) This refers to both the book and the data bank *Newsmetrics*.

How to access *Newsmetrics* and contact the authors of this volume:

Newsmetrics, the data bank underlying this book and denoted throughout by news number, is contained in four Microsoft Excel files named thus: 1994.xls, 1995.xls, 1996.xls and 1997.xls. The information is numbered continuously from 1 (a news item occurring on 28 March 1994) to 5165 (a news item occurring on 31 December 1997). These files may be accessed from three locations, the first two hosted by the University of Teramo, Italy:

1. http://www.unite.it/Insegnamenti/econometria_tivegna.htm.
   This is the homepage of Massimo Tivegna. Click 'Prof. Massimo Tivegna', then 'Materiale didattico'. The four Microsoft Excel files may then be accessed and downloaded.

2. The research page of the Department of Systems Theory:
   http://www.unite.it/Ateneo/Dipartmento/teoria_sistem/euro_tivegna.htm

3. http://www.fin-newsmetrics.it.
   These MS Excel files contain a part of the whole *Newsmetrics* with event number, date, event description and two codes (the latter described in the book). The entire databank has additional news codes and quantitive information on several items.

Further information may be obtained on: info@fin-newsmetrics.it or by emailing the authors Massimo Tivegna on mc1223@mclink.it and Grazia Chiofi on GRAZIA.CHIOFI@bnlmail.com or gchiofi@yahoo.com

Chapter 1

Newsmetrics: Measurement of News Impact in the Foreign Exchange Market

1.1 Theories of Exchange Rate Determination

The literature regarding the economic determinants of exchange rates (intended in this work as the price of a unit of foreign currency in terms of the domestic currency) is significant and goes considerably back in time. The first contributions can be found in the period between the two wars, when currencies fluctuated freely; however, the explosion of studies on this subject dates back to 1973, with the suspension of the Bretton Woods agreement and the return to a free fluctuation of exchange rates.

Since then, exchange rate modelling has developed along two main strands of macroeconomic theory: the Keynesian direction, where we find the Mundell-Fleming exchange rate determination model, and the monetarist direction, which provides the theoretical base for the monetary approach to exchange rate determination. The two schemes have been widely supplemented by the various mechanisms of expectation formation produced over time by the economic literature.[1]

Mundell-Fleming

According to the first scheme, exchange rates are a function of economic activity, domestic prices and interest rates in the two countries connected by the exchange rate: they vary positively with the first variable (which can be expressed in relative terms by the flows of industrial production or of aggregate demand) and with the second variable (relative prices or inflation rates expressed in a common currency). Both these variables have a direct influence on the "domestic country's" balance of payments (an increase in both has a negative effect) and thus influence the exchange rate (resulting in its depreciation, i.e. an increase in the domestic currency units for each unit of foreign currency).

On the other hand, the part of the balance of payments related to capital flows – largely prevalent in currency demand and supply – is sensitive to the relative interest rates between the "domestic" country, that is the country of the currency to be exchanged (for instance the Lira in the case of Italy) and the "foreign" country (for instance Germany in the Lira-Deutschmark exchange): a relative increase in the Italian interest rates produces an increase in the capital inflows towards Italy increasing the international demand for Lire and therefore resulting in an appreciation of its exchange rate.

Under this scheme, then, the exchange rate is the reduced form of a small structural model of this type:

$$GB = TB + CB \tag{1.1}$$

$$TB = f_1\left[\underset{(+)}{\frac{Y}{Y^*}}, \alpha\underset{(+)}{\left(\frac{P}{P^*S}\right)}, \ldots\ldots\ldots\right] + \varepsilon_{SM} \tag{1.2}$$

$$CB = f_2\left[\beta\underset{(+)}{\left(i - \frac{S}{S_{-1}}i^*\right)}, \ldots\ldots\ldots\right] + \varepsilon_{SMC} \tag{1.3}$$

in which all the variables – with the exception of the accounting balances, namely GB, the global balance of payments, TB, the trade balance, and CB, the balance of capital movements – are expressed in logarithmic form; the variables with an asterisk indicate foreign variables; *Y* represent economic activity variables, *P* inflation rates, *i* interest rates, *S* exchange rates (e.g. Lit-DM), α is an impact coefficient of the inflation differential in the short term, b represents both a risk aversion coefficient and an elasticity, ε_{SM} and ε_{SMC} are normally distributed stochastic errors with a zero mean and a generally non-constant variance. The expected coefficient signs are indicated below the variables. The reduced form of this model – with a balance of payment at equilibrium – would therefore be:

$$\Delta S = g\left(\underset{(+)}{\frac{Y}{Y^*}}, \underset{(+)}{\frac{P}{P^*}}, \underset{(-)}{i - i^*}\right) + h\left(\varepsilon_{SM} - \varepsilon_{SM}\right) \tag{1.4}$$

The error term is given by a linear combination of the individual stochastic errors of the two structural equations (1.2) and (1.3), according to a functional form $h(\bullet)$, whose parameters are a function of those tying the trade balance to relative inflation and capital movements to the interest rate differential. Generally, the error terms in (1.4) maintain the same distribution as the original errors ε_{SM} and ε_{SMC}, distribution that in any case is typically heteroscedastic, and can thus be modelled with ARCH or GARCH techniques, or with analogous families of models.[2] It is also possible that changes in the risk aversion parameter β, implicit in the coefficient relating the rate differential to the capital flows in (1.3), or variations in the velocity with which the inflation differential exerts its influence on the trade balance captured by the coefficient α [3], may cause alterations in the distribution symmetry, resulting in anomalous movements of appreciation or depreciation of the exchange rate. Central bank interventions in the foreign exchange markets may cause some shifts in the mean of $h(\bullet)$.[4]

Thus, it is on this term $h(\bullet)$ that the market sentiment is concentrated, which can lead to substantial deviations in the exchange rate dynamics relative to forecasts based on the so-called "fundamentals", i.e. the arguments in $g(\bullet)$ in equation (1.4). We will refer to this point again repeatedly throughout the book, a point that represents the main stimulus leading to the development of *Newsmetrics*, the news database described in this work.

The Monetary Model

The monetary exchange rate model has been proposed in the literature by the monetarist school, primarily of North-American origin. According to this approach, the exchange rate is still a function – always in relative terms, domestic versus foreign country – of the three variables we have seen in Mundell-Fleming's Keynesian model in function (1.4) (economic activity, inflation, interest rates), with the addition of a relative monetary growth. What changes now is the effect of variations in two of the explanatory variables on the exchange rate, as we will see later: an increase in the domestic rates results in a depreciation, not an appreciation, and an increase in the domestic economic activity results in an appreciation and not a depreciation of the exchange rate as in the Mundell-Fleming model.

This effect is solidly built in traders' minds, as is evident from reading the market comments that appear in international financial newspapers. The relative interest rate differential effect, on the other hand, will appear highly counter-intuitive. The reason why in this paragraph we want to contrast the two models and the opposite exchange rate dynamics implied by them in response to variations in the same "fundamentals", is to establish from the outset that different market traders may have different expectations regarding the reaction of exchange rates to variations in the same "fundamentals". Thus, since the markets follow heterogeneous schemes of interpretation, it is possible that, in the presence of an identical macroeconomic news item, different traders react in a different manner at any given time[5]. In addition, equation (1.4) shows that even those who follow the same market interpretation model – and therefore form expectations based on the same scheme – must in any case interpret the extent to which the stochastic function $h(\bullet)$ weighs on their understanding of the exchange rate dynamics. Thus, we see that heterogeneity can exist both among traders using different interpretation models and traders using the same model but with different view of the stochastic part of their model ($h(\bullet)$ in the Mundell-Fleming case).

Also the monetary equation to determine the exchange rate is the reduced form of a small structural model, with variables expressed in logarithmic form. The analysis of this model enables us to understand why the same macroeconomic variables can produce opposite effects on exchange rate dynamics. The key assumptions of the monetary model are the purchasing power parity even in the shortterm, (1.5), and the currency demand equations, both in the domestic and the foreign country, (1.6) and (1.7):

$$S_t = p - p^* + \varepsilon_s \tag{1.5}$$

$$m^d - p = \alpha_1 y - \alpha_2 i + \varepsilon_m \tag{1.6}$$

$$m^{d*} - p^* = \alpha_1 y^* - \alpha_2 i^* + \varepsilon_{m*} \tag{1.7}$$

in which parameters a1, a2 >0 are assumed to be equal in the domestic country and in the foreign country (note the simplification) while in both countries md represents the currency stock level demanded by the economy and provided by the central bank to satisfy its needs:[6]

$$m^d = m^s = m \tag{1.8}$$

$$m^{d*} = m^{s*} = m \tag{1.9}$$

By simple substitution in equations (1.5) – (1.9) we obtain the reduced form

$$S = (m - m^*) - \alpha_1(y - y^*) + \alpha_2(i - i^*) + (\varepsilon_m - \varepsilon_{m*} + \varepsilon_s) \tag{1.10}$$

From (1.10) we can immediately see that an increase in domestic economic activity goes hand in hand with an appreciation of the exchange rate, while an increase in the domestic interest rates produces devaluation. This results from the fact that both Y and i are two arguments of the currency demand. An increase in Y under the assumption of a constant velocity of circulation (in parameter a1), is equivalent to an increase in the demand for currency for transaction purposes which, at the same level of currency supply, is consistent with a decrease in the price level and an appreciation of the exchange rate, by purchasing power parity. The interest rate is also present in the currency demand; thus, an increase in the interest rate decreases the currency demand, thus creating an excess of money in circulation – when central bank supply remains constant – which can cause a price increase, and therefore a devaluation of the exchange rate.[7]

Interest and Exchange Rates

Lets examine more closely the relationship between interest rates and exchange rates. As shown above, in the Mundell-Fleming Keynesian model a relative increase in the domestic interest rate produces a univocal revaluation of the exchange rate in the domestic country; in the monetary model, on the contrary, such an increase causes devaluation. The potential for different effects, however, especially in the Italian and American institutional context, can be even greater, depending on the reactions of the financial markets to interest rate variations; there can also be a juxtaposition of effects when a reputation effect is at work in traders' minds,[8] especially in the presence of formal fluctuation ranges such as those of the European Exchange-Rate Mechanism (ERM),[9] or of pre-announced target exchange rates.[10]

In the Italian context, which is characterized by a high public debt, the markets have generally shown a negative reaction (selling Lira spot or buying Deutschmark forward) to interest rate increases, whether government or market driven, or to macroeconomic developments that could push interest rates in the same direction, such as an increase in inflation.[11] The reason here can be traced back to an increase in the risk premium of Italian assets.

Another atypical reaction of the exchange rates to variations in the interest rate – at least within the two schemes presented here – is the one observed in the American markets over the last few years, whereby an increase of the interest rate (actual or expected) is perceived by the markets as bearish for the Dollar, while a decrease (actual or expected) is considered bullish. Here too the monetary scheme appears to be at work, but there is no trace of this (nor of the related subject of the relationship between currency and inflation) in the markets' comments. Traders simply acknowledge the "sympathy" between US securities markets and the Dollar, in the terms illustrated above.

The probable reason for this atypical relationship between, for instance, a decrease in interest rates and the strengthening of the Dollar, is to be found in the positive impact the former has on securities in the long term – or on the prices of the futures related to them – and therefore on the yield of Dollar-denominated securities in the portfolio through the capital gain thus generated. In this case we would find ourselves in the Mundell-Fleming scheme, because the yield on American securities already purchased increases as a consequence of the decrease in short-term interest rates. Hence the rally of the Dollar when a decrease in interest rates is expected, and the consequent increase in the expected yield of securities.

Finally, the atypical effect of an increase in US interest rates on the Dollar manifests itself in the stock market. Even now the expectation of an increase in interest rates causes the stock markets to fall, and consequently the US currency to weaken – through capital outflows or decreased capital inflows, because of the enormous weight, also internationally, of the American market. *Newsmetrics* gathers data regarding the main events in the American stock market; the strong effect on the exchange rate is documented through the empirical findings of this work.

News Models

Given the many elements of uncertainty in both models – captured primarily in the stochastic structure of the two reduced forms (1.4) and (1.10) – and the multiple noise factors that can affect the relationship between interest rates and exchange rates, it is not surprising that the econometric estimate of the two specifications seen above – and of many empirical variations on them – has produced disappointing results.[12]

Over the years, then, the equilibrium approach of the two classical forms seen above has given way to "disequilibrium" models that are closer to the actual *modus operandi* of currency traders. This stems from an asset-pricing financial culture, whereby the price of a currency is determined precisely by the expectations regarding its fundamental determinants.[13] Several authors – among whom most prominently MUSSA [1979], DORNBUSCH [1980], FRENKEL [1981], and ISARD [1983] – propose models in which exchange rate variations are influenced primarily by the discrepancies between the values of fundamentals as expected by the markets – incorporated in the expected exchange rates for the immediate future – and those announced by the statistical institutions responsible for their development. These discrepancies represent one part of the news considered in this work.

The exchange rate equation to be estimated in "news mode", then, follows a base specification of the following type, always maintaining the logarithmic variations:

$$S_t + 1 - E_t\,(S_t + 1) = \alpha + \sum_{j=1}^{m} \beta_j [Z_j,\, t + 1 - E_t\,(Z_j,\, t + 1)] + \varepsilon_t \qquad (1.11)$$

where S is the exchange rate; the Zs, in m number, are the values of the fundamental variables, those present in equations (1.4) and (1.10), if referring to the models presented here; E is the trader expectation at time t; ε_t is an error term which, in the daily data used in this study, is I.I.N. $(0\ ,\ \sigma^2_t\ )$ with a variance that follows a GARCH model[14] of the type:

$$\sigma^2_t + \omega + \alpha\varepsilon^2_{t\text{-}1} + \beta\sigma^2_{t\text{-}1} \qquad (1.12)$$

In the econometric estimates of equation (1.11), $E_t\ [S_{t+1}]$ is usually represented by the forward exchange rate or by the lagged dependent variable, after a translation on the temporal axis. This equation may also be linearly integrated by other arguments.

In the short and very shortterm – the time frame of our analysis of data collected daily in two time zones – the exchange rate dynamics is ruled by the use of technical analysis tools.[15] In our exchange rate equations, estimated in Chapter 7, the base specification (1.11) is integrated by regressors that are representative of the technical analysis filters most commonly used.[16] In addition, for the greater part the news examined by *Newsmetrics* is unexpected and is therefore is not captured by the term within square brackets in equation (1.11).

Even if it refers only to the exchange rate, equation (1.11) may be modified and applied to other financial instruments. In fact, the news approach has been much used for the stock markets[17] – in parallel with the more traditional event studies approach (see CAMPBELL-LO-MACKINLEY [1997], Chapter 4), for fixed income securities,[18] and for futures related to various financial instruments.[19]

After HOFFMAN-SCHLAGENHAUF [1985]'s eclectic beginning – estimating exchange rate models in news form, according to the two theoretical formulations presented here, as well as others – the literature on the impact of news on the exchange rate generally followed a monetary scheme. EDWARDS [1982, 1983] suggests a news scheme derived from a structural model of this kind. The news in this case consist of the deviations between the expected and actual values of the variables that appear in the structural form of a monetary model that is analogous to the one we developed above, (1.5) – (1.13). The expected values are projected with a VAR model with no restrictions that simulates the process whereby traders' expectations develop. The results confirm the explanatory power of the news.

Several authors followed Edwards' approach[20] with mixed results, using purely auto-regressive models in order to generate expected values on a single variable,[21] or expected values of multiple variables, modelling the economy with a VAR approach or looking for a slightly more structural explanation of the news.[22] The theoretical approach used in this literature is always the monetary model, with the exception of BRANSON [1983] who uses the portfolio balance approach.

The late 1970s/early 1980s ritual of weekly announcements regarding the trends of the main monetary aggregates of the US economy generated a literature, always based on the news approach, that relates (generally through interest rates and inflation) the exchange rate dynamics to the deviations between the monetary targets announced by central banks and the actual monetary dynamics.[23] The conclusion of this latter group of contributions is that traders expect the correction in the opposite direction of an overshooting of the monetary target, and therefore the exchange rate will appreciate as a result, instead of depreciating as would be expected in a monetary model as a consequence of a wider monetary circulation.

A final group of contributions, which largely inspires this study, estimates the equation (1.11) by using the differences between the values expected by the markets (and collected by specialized organizations,[24] headed by the Money Market Service of Belmont, California) and the actual published values of the explanatory variables in the various exchange rate models – which, as we have seen earlier, can be the same but often with opposite signs – in order to explain the daily[25] and intra-daily[26] exchange rate variations.

The results obtained so far are very encouraging and they identify the statistically significant effects of different macroeconomic variables – trade balance, production and consumer inflation, variations in employment, retail sales, durable goods orders, etc. – to explain the daily and intra-daily exchange rate fluctuations. In the empirical verifications recounted in Chapter 7 we have studied the effects on exchange rate variations (of the Lira and the Dollar) of the deviations of the economic variables from their expected values, and of the occurrence of unexpected events of various kinds, described in this work.

It is important to underline, as a comment to the results of this literature, that the effect of specific news on the exchange rate varies in time in relation to the market sentiment of the moment and to the different importance assigned by the markets, at different times, to this type of event: for instance, from the studies mentioned above we can see that the importance of announcements regarding the trade balance is very high between 1984 and 1987, when the revaluation of the Dollar, which reached its highest point in 1985, and the subsequent overvaluation lasting for a few years even into the period of devaluation, caused a marked deterioration in the United States' commercial position. Thus any news on this variable that is worse than expected, or in any case worse than the current situation, sends to the markets an unequivocal message of devaluation, either because it increases the probability of an immediate intervention on the part of the monetary authorities, or because that is the direction in which the exchange rate will move anyway given the increase in Dollar supply produced by the deficit.[27] [28]

While the news literature has yielded mixed results from the statistical point of view, it has nonetheless highlighted both the limits of traditional exchange rate determination models[29] and, more importantly, the markets' actual *modus operandi*. Thus we can quote the considerations formulated in a recent economics and international finance textbook, HALLWOOD-MACDONALD [1994], pp. 251-2, which contains an excellent collection of all the recent results in this sector:

> The above results (*on the empirical effectiveness of news*) suggest that the news approach to the determination of the exchange rate is reasonably well supported by the data, and future research on this topic should usefully extend the range of news terms considered and the methods of generating the news. Nevertheless, a difficulty remains: the volatility of exchange rates appears to be greater than the volatility of the conventional news items. How can this be explained? It may be possible to supplement the news approach in a number of ways.
>
> First of all it is quite possible that non-quantifiable news elements, such as political announcements and rumours, dominate the quantifiable elements which researchers use in their news models.
>
> Second, a high relative volatility of exchange rates may be due to the presence of rational speculative bubbles.

A third rationalization for the greater volatility of exchange rates relative to the news is that market participants may be using a different economic model from that prescribed by international economists.

The first point, according to which markets often tend to overshoot the values implicit in their fundamentals, is a commonly observed fact and has been amply verified empirically, for example DAVIDSON [1985] and FLOOD-ROSE [1993]. In this study, which refers to the experience of the Lira and the Dollar in the years from 1994 to 1997, we supplement the explanations provided by economic news with those provided by political and economic policy news, which have been particularly abundant and have been indicated in the reference quoted above as potentially dominant relative to the economic explanations. The effects of the various announcements made by the Economic Policy Authorities in the United States, Germany, Japan and Italy – the countries considered in *Newsmetrics*,[30] have been highly relevant.

In this work – especially in Chapters 2 and 7 – we find confirmation that the weight of political news has had a significant role in exchange rate fluctuations, and that the weight and the sign of the various families of news, economic and political, are not constant in time, both because of the repeated distributive alterations of the error terms in the reduced forms of the two models of reference (1.4), (1.10) and (1.11) – objectively produced by the markets or subjectively attributed to the markets by traders – and because of the various "sensitivities" that the political cycle transmits to the markets over time.

This is how we interpret the third consideration expressed by Hallwood and MacDonald. They state that various interpretative models can exist in the traders' minds that may be different from those proposed by international economists. It is in this spirit that we have made reference to schemes that are typically present in traders' backgrounds – the Mundell-Fleming model of Keynesian inspiration and the monetary model – with a view to underlining the diversity of the models used by traders and the development in various stages of a market sentiment that can cause even significant deviations in the exchange rate behaviour relative to the prevailing (or considered prevailing) interpretative models. In addition, the actual exchange rates, even while moving within the same interpretative model, may undergo parametric variations that alter the stochastic part of the model in (1.4), (1.10) and (1.11). Finally, the purely economic determinants may not suffice to explain the hyper-volatility of exchange rates in certain phases and it is therefore also necessary to introduce in the explanatory scheme volatility-generating political and market variables. In this study we grapple with all these elements.

1.2 Newsmetrics

Newsmetrics is a textual and numerical database of events related to the Italian Lira, the US Dollar, the German Deutschmark and the Japanese Yen markets.

Naturally, the description of the events is the main source of textual news, but it is not the only one. *Newsmetrics* also contains several statements from the Monetary and Economic Policy Authorities (e.g. government heads, economic ministers, party leaders, etc.) as well as a vast selection of traders' comments on market events and on the orientation of policy-makers. Statements and comments are considered "events" for the purposes of this work.

Not only do exchange rates react to statements and events of a political, economic policy and financial nature,[31] but they also react to the continuous flow of statistical information regarding the macroeconomic situation. If anything, the economic and financial literature on the impact of news on exchange rates has primarily studied the response of exchange rates to the publication of data on the macroeconomic situation. Thus, *Newsmetrics* is also an archive of the quantitative data relative to the Italian and the international situation, used by the financial markets for analytical purposes; however, they are not organized in the traditional historical series form, but rather with reference to the day in which the statistical event was released. Whenever available, the data point is also associated to corresponding value expected by the markets.

The period examined by *Newsmetrics* goes from 28 March, 1994 (victory of the *Polo delle Libertà* coalition in the first Italian political elections held with the new majority electoral system) to the end of 1997. While the starting point has a strong political characterization for Italy – and the reason for it will become evident – the end point is not marked by an event of similar importance. Two factors have led us to conclude the study at the end of 1997: (1) the need to provide documented support for the news archive, since some scientific works that use a statistical sample falling between these two dates make a reference to it;[32] (2) the opportunity to have some critical feedback on the work, given the apparent lack of published databases of this kind.

As indicated above, *Newsmetrics* refers primarily, but not exclusively, to the foreign exchange markets. A not insignificant portion of the study is devoted to events in the foreign currency markets that for some time now have also weighed significantly on the exchange rate dynamics examined in this study, particularly since the autumn of 1997 with the financial crisis of the major Far Eastern countries.

There is also substantial space for the political events that have heavily influenced the dynamics of the Lira, especially from 1994 to November 1996, with the return of the Lira to the European Exchange-Rate Mechanism (ERM).

In this work quantitative (or scheduled) news refers to the macroeconomic news relative to the nature of the phenomena (for instance inflation rate, currency balance, etc.) that are periodically provided by the appointed statistical organizations, while qualitative (or unscheduled) news refers to events of a political and institutional nature that are not directly measurable (with the exception of discretional variations in the official interest rates and the interventions on the foreign currency markets, which we include in this category and which obviously have a quantitative dimension), such as political events, provisions and trends of economic and monetary policy, official and officious announcements, events of an institutional nature, information on the market climate, and qualitative descriptions of quantitative economic events of particular relevance.

The entire database is contained in the web site mentioned at the beginning of the volume.

The items in the archive consist of reformulations of the headlines usually present in the first two pages of *Il Sole XXIV Ore*, with additions from the body of the newspaper article, and headlines and texts of articles extracted from *The Financial Times*, *The International Herald Tribune* (limited to a few months in 1997), and the Internet edition of the *The Wall Street Journal*, from August 1997.[33] The majority of these articles or headline reformulations entered in the database are factual in nature and can be traced back directly to the primary source of the news (for example from the newsflashes of Reuters, Bloomberg, Associated Press, Radiocor, Ansa, etc.), but as we will see there are plenty of items describing the opinion and climate of the foreign exchange markets, extracted from the daily columns and specialized articles on this subject.

In addition to factual news – both qualitative and quantitative – *Newsmetrics* gathers almost daily the comments from foreign currency markets, in summarized form (e.g. codes MGE, MJA, MUS), generally taken from *The Financial Times*, *The International Herald Tribune* and *The Wall Street Journal*, which are particularly useful to zero in on the markets' climate, their volatility and the consequently different responses to apparently similar events, even when occurring within short periods of time.

Newsmetrics offers detailed statements from policy-makers, especially from Bundesbank Governor Tietmeyer, and the council members of the German Central Bank. Clearly this is not coincidental, given their role both in the "verbal management" of the Deutschmark exchange rate and the German monetary orthodoxy evident in the choice of countries that should constitute the initial core of the European Monetary Union (EMU). Substantial space is devoted also to statements of Fed Chairman Greenspan – by far less talkative than Tietmeyer – and those of the Japanese Authorities. The statements of Bank of Italy Governor Fazio are regularly collected in *Newsmetrics*, but their relevance is very different from that of his G3 colleagues' statements, in the same way that the Bank of Italy's tradition of communication and the way in which news is broadcasted and commented by the media and perceived by the markets are different.

All news that refers to two different categories of events considered by the database are assigned a double code (see the *Newsmetrics* web archive). These codes permit the selection of news with any relational database software.

At the base of the entire design of the archive is an experience of foreign exchange markets, strengthened by an extended empirical verification of the explanatory power of the news collected. This experience has been accumulated in previous consulting activities and various interviews with foreign exchange traders in Italy and in other countries. The empirical foundation has been built through a series of intermediate statistical verifications, described in a note to Chapter 7. The statistical significance of the individual news categories contained in this study was subsequently tested with various econometric techniques at different times: in Chapter 7 of this volume, in TIVEGNA [1996], in FORNARI-MONTICELLI-PERICOLI-TIVEGNA [1999], and in TIVEGNA [2000].

1.3 Uses of Newsmetrics

Naturally the primary use of the archive is to help order in one's own analytical "black box" the elements that appear most significant in explaining the Lira, the Dollar, the Deutschmark and the Yen exchange rates. However, the majority of the news in the database can also help explain the anomalous fluctuations in the government bond markets, the stock markets, and the corresponding futures markets. The archive will be useful not only for financial analysts but also for economic and financial journalists for a review of past events, in order better to understand what is currently happening, and to quickly situate them in the international context in which they occurred. The historical reconstruction of the events of the Lira and Dollar markets will further assist them in this endeavour.

Newsmetrics will probably be useful in empirical research on price formation in financial activities and in studies of the empirical determinants of volatility of derivative instruments.

Another potentially promising and intellectually stimulating research application that has influenced the range of events collected by *Newsmetrics* is the study of the information decoding processes (political, economic and financial) used by traders and strategists in their multi-currency investment activities, applying communication theory techniques – especially those based on mathematics and semiotics (SHANNON-WEAVER [1949] and ECO ET AL [1965] respectively).[34]

Finally, why "*Newsmetrics*"? The first application of the events recorded in this database was the "drafting" of a news classification based on the degree of their influence on the Lira exchange rate in TIVEGNA [1996]. The ultimate goal of the line of analysis undertaken at the time was to build a sort of "Richter scale" of the events to help understand why certain news carries more weight than others and why its weight or "metrics", changes over time.

1.4 Development of the Study

At the time of bringing together the various research activities that have contributed to the creation of our database, we asked ourselves how we could make our work accessible and interesting to a circle of users beyond a strictly academic one. The result is a study that is developed at three levels: the gathering of micro-events, the statistical verification of their explanatory power, and the "micro-historical" reconstruction of the entire period in which these "daily events" took place.

We felt that by gathering in the same pages the daily news and the longer-term trends of the foreign exchange markets we could provide an effective tool to contextualize the former and to explain the latter, also as the sum of single events.

Chapter 2 of this book is dedicated to the "historical" reconstruction of the foreign exchange market, which, while keeping in sight the daily frequency of the basic information units, has also a perspective on what connects the micro-events.

Chapters 3 to 6 describe the criteria for identification, collection and organization of the events contained in *Newsmetrics*.

In Chapter 3, dedicated to the Italian news, the collection of events is traced back to the activity of the governments in place between 1994 and 1997. Chapter 4 describes the qualitative and quantitative characteristics of the American, German and Japanese news.

The creation of the European Monetary Union (EMU) has represented – in the years covered by our database – a fundamental economic policy commitment for most European countries and for Italy in particular. While originally we had not explicitly isolated this category of news, we realized – in the subsequent empirical verifications of our analysis and with the passing of time – that a great part of the dynamics not only of the Lira but also of the Deutschmark against the Dollar needed an explicit consideration of the events linked to the implementation of the EMU; Chapter 5 presents the selection criteria for these events, with a few historical digressions.

An original characteristic of our archive of events is probably given by the collection of statements issued in various circumstances by the leading policy-makers of the United States, Germany and Japan, either to "talk the Dollar up or down" (in accordance with a fashion affirmed in the first half of the 1980s, thanks also to its frequent use on the part of USA Treasury Secretary Baker, its creator according to the media), or to express their own personal beliefs, or to give the markets "unbiased" information regarding the monetary and fiscal policy trends. Chapter 6 describes the characteristics and per capita quantity of this oratorical activity.

Chapter 7 sets out to achieve two ambitious goals: to attempt a general taxonomy of exchange rate market-moving events, obviously taking the inputs for the analysis from *Newsmetrics*, and to perform a statistical verification of the explanatory power of the news categories identified in this study.

The eighth and final chapter contains various ideas for debate on the research described herein and formulates some hypotheses on how to use this research for the analysis of foreign exchange markets and for trading. The chapter also contains a description of the communication model that can be applied to foreign exchange markets that can further clarify the criteria of our news collection, especially that which we define as "market news" and which in the database appears with the codes MGE, MUS, MJA.

Notes

1 There are many reference texts in this field. Among the most recent ones, we find COPELAND [1994] Chapters 5-10, and HALLWOOD-MACDONALD [1994], Chapters 5, 8, 9, 10. ISARD [1995], MacDONALD-TAYLOR [1995], TAYLOR [1995] contain excellent surveys of the development of this literature.

2 There is a vast body of literature on the application of heteroscedastic models to financial series. BOLLERLSEV-CHOU-KRONER [1992] provides a good critical overview from the point of view of applications, and BOLLERSLEV-ENGLE-NELSON [1994] from the point of view of statistical theory.

3 It is common knowledge that the law of single price is a long-term phenomenon and, therefore, the effect of relative prices on the exchange rate may be limited, and in any case smaller than that of the economic activity differential Y-Y*, and, above all, smaller than that of the interest rate differential. There is a vast body of literature on the long-term validity of the purchasing power parity theory. See GIOVANNETTI [1992] for a recent review.

4 In recent times the mere prospect of a central bank intervention has affected exchange rates, and the joint and publicized interventions of the G-3 central banks have had greater success, as was the case of the Dollar on 15 August, 1995. See DOMINGUEZ-FRANKEL [1993] and CATTE-GALLI-REBECCHINI [1992].

5 Also ALMEKINDERS-ROVERS [1994], in their survey of news literature, maintain that traders are quite uncertain as to which model can best explain the events they witness, p.40.

6 In the monetary model there are only two financial activities: currency – for transaction purposes – and securities, to which the interest rates i and i* refer.

7 In the monetary models that produce this effect, economic activity is always assumed to be at near full employment of the production factors, so that an excess of currency produces an increase in prices, also through a possible pressure exerted by demand. It should be noted, moreover, that an increase in interest rates should exert a downward pressure on domestic demand, and in particular on stocks and on the more interest rate-sensitive goods. This can cause a contraction in the demand for transaction currency, aggravating the problem of excess currency in the economy and consequently that of inflation.

8 This literature is based on game theory, and is usually present in the studies of international coordination of economic policies that were popular in the 1980s. See BUITER-MARSTON [1985] and MACDONALD-MILBOURNE [1991].

9 The relevant literature is the one on target zones. See SVENSSON [1992].

10 Such as those underpinning the pegging of domestic currencies to the dollar.

11 From what has been observed above, this reaction could be determined – according to the monetary model of exchange rate determination – by the markets' fear of an excess of monetary stock in circulation, with the consequent depreciation of the Lira. On the other hand, this does not appear to be the tone of market-place comments when Italian

interest rates increase, partly because the monetary growth has remained under control for some years.

12 Especially after the well-known paper by MEESE-ROGOFF [1983]. For a summary, see BAILLIE-McMAHON[1989], Chapter 8.

13 The relationship between the fundamentals and the exchange rates can follow one of the two models illustrated above, or others. But the actual exchange rate dynamics is determined by the difference between the expected and actual values of these fundamentals.

14 See note 2.

15 See ALLEN-TAYLOR [1990].

16 For applications of technical analysis to the currency markets see DUNIS-FEENY [1989].

17 PEARCE-ROLEY [1985], HARDOUVELIS [1987], McQUEEN-ROLEY [1993], MITCHEL-MULHERIN [1994], LI-HU [1998]

18 ROLEY [1983], BECKER-FINERTY-KOPECKY [1995], KARFAKIS-KIM [1995], ELMENDORF-HIRSHFELD-WEIL [1996], JONES-LAMONT-LUMSDAINE [1998], BALDUZZI-ELTON-GREEN [1998].

19 JOHNSON-SCHNEEWEIS[1994], EDERINGTON-LEE[1993, 1995, 1996].

20 In reality he has been preceded by his thesis advisor Jacob FRANKEL (1981) who introduces an expected interest rate, produced by an auto-regressive model, into an efficiency equation of the exchange rate. It is worth noting here that the regression of an auxiliary variable obtained from a different statistical procedure may result in distortions of the corresponding coefficient and in loss of efficiency. See PAGAN [1984].

21 COPELAND [1984], EDWARDS [1982], BOMHOFF-KORTEWEG [1983].

22 BRANSON [1983], EDWARDS [1983], MACDONALD [1983 a and b], FIORENTINI [1994] CIFARELLI [1986, 1990].

23 URICH-WACHTEL [1981], CORNELL [1982,1983], ENGEL-FRANKEL [1984], SMITH-GOODHART [1985], GOODHART-SMITH [1985], ROLEY-WALSH[1985], PERUGA[1996].

24 Also some of the monetary news studies examined above use the values of expected monetary growth developed by these organizations.

25 DERAWI-GREGOROWICZ [1988], HARDOUVELIS [1988], IRWIN [1989], HOGAN-MELVIN-ROBERTS [1991], HARVEY [1993], DOUKAS-LIFELAND [1994], HIN HOCK LEE [1995], EDISON [1996].

26 ITO-ROLEY[1988], GOODHART-HALL-HENRY-PESARAN[1993], HOGAN-MELVIN[1994], BASTAENS-VAN DEN BERG[1996], ALMEIDA-GOODHART-PAYNE[1998].

27 This is an implication of the portfolio balance model for the exchange rate determination. HALLWOOD-MACDONALD [1994], Chapter 10.

28 A similar effect may be found in TIVEGNA [1996]'s empirical verifications relative to the Lira-Deutschmark exchange rate. Here inflation carries a different weight in the two periods under analysis: the Berlusconi government, when inflation tends to decrease at first and then stabilizes, and the Dini government, when inflation flares up from February 1995, followed immediately by an increase in the discount rate. Consistently with these two different market sentiments, the news on inflation are not significant in the Berlusconi period, while they are in the Dini period.

29 In so far as the empirical verifications of various monetary models are concerned. For a summary, see the considerations of BAILLIE-MCMAHON [1989], Chapter 8, PENTECOST [1993], Chapters 2 and 4.

30 Chapter 6 focuses on such announcements.

31 The Italian experience in the period under consideration shows the sensitivity of exchange rates to short-term political events, and occasionally we see signs of it with respect to other countries in the international press (just recently Brazil, for example).

There are no studies in the international literature that explicitly address the short- and very short-term sensitivity. There are some studies on the impact of political risk on the stock markets, AGMON-FINDLAY [1992], DIAMONTE-LIEW-STEVENS [1996], ERB-HARVEY-VISKANTA [1986], and on the effects of American presidential elections always on the same variable, ALLVINE-O'NEIL [1980], HOBBS-RILEY [1984]. In any case, the methodology of these studies is very different from the one adopted here. As for the foreign exchange markets, see the results of DOMINGUEZ [1993] and DOMINGUEZ-FRANKEL [1993].

32 At the moment, works that make reference to *Newsmetrics* include: TIVEGNA [1996], FORNARI, MONTICELLI, PERICOLI, TIVEGNA[1999], TIVEGNA[2000]. Starting from the literature on the effect of unexpected events in the the foreign exchange markets, TIVEGNA [1996] supplements the study of the impact of economic news with that of political news, of particular relevance in the explanation of the fluctuations of the Lira in 1994 and 1995. The goal of this study is achieved by means of a very detailed reconstruction of the daily political and economic events that have punctuated the Berlusconi and later the Dini governments. This reconstruction is used to estimate equations on daily data that try to measure the specific weight of individual events in the determination of the day's variations of the exchange rate. In that study the base specification, under which it is primarily the movements of the Dollar against the Deutschmark that determine those of the Lira relative to the latter, is supplemented with the effects of the various announcements relative to the Italian economy (including public finances, inflation, economic activity, interest rates, and economic policy trends in the very short term) and with the effects of the innumerable episodes of micro and macro political conflict that have characterized the two periods analysed in the study. Such episodes, generically defined as "political noise", have been reclassified according to fundamental factor that generated them. They constitute *Newsmetrics*' first nucleus. FORNARI-MONTICELLI-PERICOLI-TIVEGNA [1999] to build a vectorial GARCH model that explains the DM-$, Lira-$ exchange rates, and alternatively the yield on BTPs (long-term treasury bills) and the price of BTP futures on the same instrument. This study devotes particular attention to the impact of news on volatility, and it calculates the characteristics of the model's impulsive response to shocks on variance. TIVEGNA [2000] proposes multi-equation models of the DM-$ and Yen-$ exchange rates in two partitions of the global trading day of the foreign exchange market.

33 From early September 1997, the update of the database is carried out via the Internet. Thus the number and variety of the news increases, as does its length, although always within the 254-character limit allowed by the management software DBASE5.

34 For a survey, see MORCELLINI-FATELLI [1996], Chapter 4. For a summary statement of the main theoretical strands, see also WINDHAL-SIGNITZER-OLSON (1992)) and from a historical perspective, see ROGERS (1994).

Chapter 2

The Foreign Exchange Market in 1994-1997: Events, Trends and Economic Policies

2.1 The Dollar in 1995: Depreciation and Attempts at Stabilisation

The First Quarter

At the end of a swinging 1994, the Dollar maintains its value against the Deutschmark and the Yen; in January, the year 1995 opens with a series of favorable US economic news (531, 541, 542)[1] and inflation data (549, 554), highlighted also by the comments of US Central Bank (the Fed) President Greenspan on Wednesday, 25 January (600), Figure 2.1, upper panel.

The widespread concerns regarding an excessive economic exposure to Mexico (531, 583, 599,613, 617, 651, 656), which is experiencing a deep financial crisis begun in early December 1994, push the American currency in the opposite direction. This is openly manifest on Thursday, 12 January, when rumours that a major US bank is over-exposed to neighbouring Mexico (559) cause a marked weakening of the Dollar against the Deutschmark and the Yen.

In a Mundell-Fleming model, the moderate fall of the Dollar in January could be explained by the robustness of US macroeconomic fundamentals, compensated in part by the expectation of an interest rate increase (531, 577, 583, 600), which is indeed lifted by the Fed on Wednesday, 1 February (624, 625, 628).

In Europe the Deutschmark benefits from its safe haven role, in the wake of political uncertainty in Italy – beginning of Dini government – and in Spain (546, 550, 558, 656).

On Tuesday, 17 January a devastating earthquake hits the important industrial city of Kobe and the Prefecture of Osaka (567). Following this event, the Yen's weakening phase – under way for some time – is temporarily arrested, remaining substantially stable against the Dollar until the first ten days of February.

The potentially positive effect on the Dollar of the US interest rate rise in early February begins to falter on Friday, 3 February because of an unexpected worsening of the US unemployment rate (633, 634, 635, 636, 637).

From 13 to 17 February the Dollar loses approximately 3.3 pfennings. This weakening can be traced back to the expectation of a probable

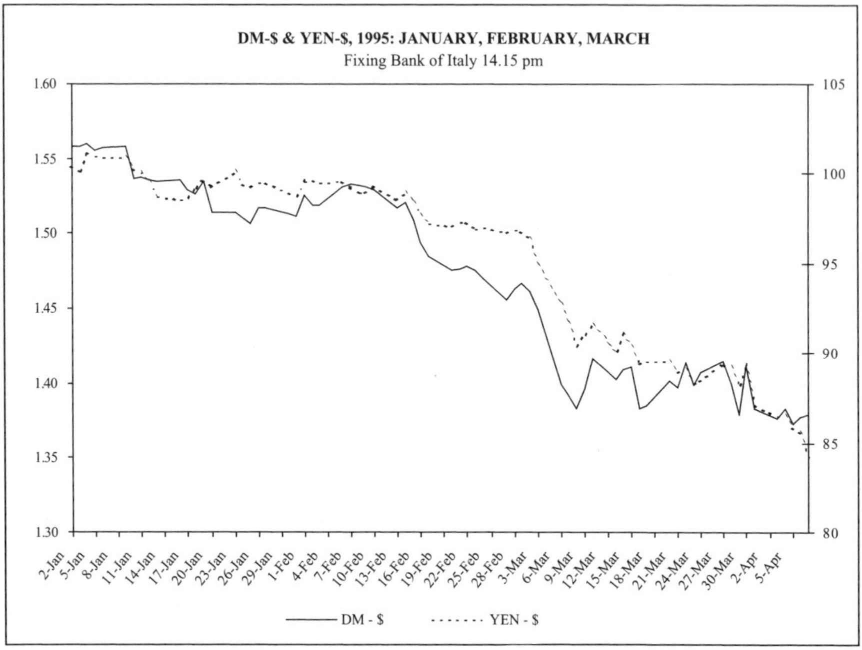

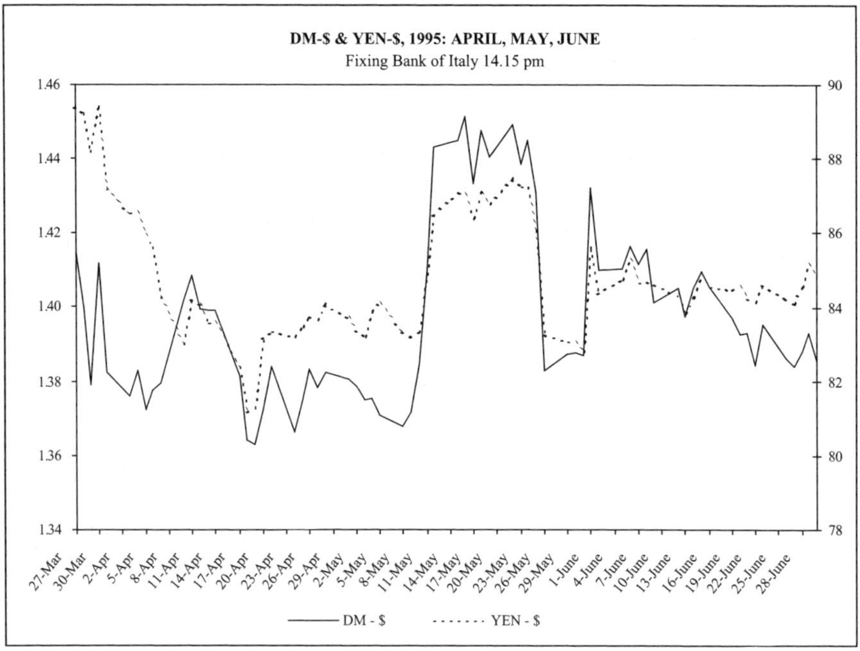

Figure 2.1 DM-$ & Yen-$, 1995: January, February, March – April, May, June

economic slowdown, and is caused by several factors: (a) fear of the consequences of an excessive trade union militancy in Germany (648), which could result in pre-emptive action on the part of the Bundesbank; (b) renewed worries about the effects of the Mexican crisis (651, 656), from Tuesday 14 and for the rest of the week; (c) weak US industrial production figures (653).

The Deutschmark, for its part, is further strengthened in Europe by political uncertainty in Italy and Spain (656, 663), on Thursday 16 and Friday 17.

In his twice-yearly report to Congress on economic policy, on Wednesday, 22 Februray, Greenspan confirms the markets' fears, noting that the US economy will slow down considerably in 1995 relative to 1994, settling at a growth level of 2-3% (675, 677). During the remainder of February the Deutschmark continues to appreciate against the Dollar because of the vote in favor of strike action by German union IG Metall (676), because of the continuing political turmoil in Italy and Spain (688) and even – albeit a remote and limited event – because of the demise of Barings, the British merchant bank (692).

A series of central bank interventions – first on an individual basis by the Fed, on Thursday, 2 March (707), then in a co-ordinated effort by fifteen Central Banks the following Friday 3, and then again on Wednesday 8 (713, 722) – is not enough to stop the fall of the Dollar, which on the contrary becomes more pronounced between the end of February and the beginning of March. Slightly better results are obtained by a series of verbal interventions, by Greenspan (723), by Bundesbank officials, by members of the German Government and by the French Minister of Finance (724), on Wednesday, 8 March, and finally by US Treasury Secretary Rubin and by Governor Tietmeyer (728), on Thursday 9. See Figure 2.1, upper panel.

On Friday, 10 March the announcement of better-than-expected US unemployment figures (731,734,735, 749, 752, 753) contributes to stabilize the Dollar for the entire month, after the fall in February. This equilibrium is determined by opposing forces: mediocre short-term results pushing in the direction of depreciation – such as the moderate growth contained in the figures of the Fed's "beige book" on Wednesday 15 (753), and the durable goods release on Friday 24 (782); and the constant support of verbal interventions pushing towards appreciation – such as those by Alphandery and Issing, on Wednesday 15 (750, 751), and by Tietmeyer and Trichet on Monday 20 and Tuesday 21 (763, 768, 769). See Figure 2.1, upper panel.

In terms of tangible monetary policy interventions, the Bundesbank leaves rates unchanged in the meeting of Thursday, 16 March (758), and so does the Fed in the meeting of Tuesday and Wednesday 28-29 (797). Then it is the German Central Bank's turn to surprise the markets by cutting interest rates on Thursday 30, causing a merely temporary strengthening of the Dollar (802, 803).

The Second Quarter

The US and Japan Central Banks make another attempt to shore up the weakening Dollar in the beginning of April, with short-lived success (a week), with co-ordinated interventions supported by official statements on Monday, 3 April and Wednesday, 5 April (812, 813, 814, 815, 819, 823), Figure 2.1 lower panel. The decision to intervene directly with actions supporting the exchange rate, rather than indirectly through an interest rate increase, may have been determined by the difficulty of increasing interest rates in a sluggish US economy.

There is some turmoil in Japan caused by the strong revaluation of the Yen, especially in the beginning of 1995 (827), even after the temporary effect of the co-ordinated interventions of the Japanese Central Bank and the Fed. The government announces expansionary measures as a way to substitute external demand, presumably penalized by the exchange rate revaluation (826, 828, 836, 854, 855), with domestic demand. The much-awaited reduction of the Japanese interest rate to 1%, on Wednesday, 14 April, seems to have no effect on the exchange rate (853).

This is the last measure prior to the Washington meeting of G7 Finance Ministers and Central Bank Governors, on Tuesday, 25 April. In the days immediately preceding the meeting, traders, as usual, "tread water" (870, 875, 883, 888). Then, despite the meeting's absolute lack of official definitions and the series of weak US economic announcements in the month of April (887, 891), surprisingly the American currency appreciates somewhat for a few days (892, 900).

This anticipates the more robust strengthening of the currency that begins on Monday, 8 May, for no clear motive, and even – given traders' apparent operating model – despite a very negative announcement on the US unemployment rate (919, 920, 921). The events taking place immediately before this rally are as follows: (a) the interruption of commercial negotiations between the US and Japan on Saturday, 6 May (924, 933), a type of event that usually produces an appreciation of the Yen; (b) the pro-Dollar declarations of two Bundesbank Directors on Tuesday 9 (928); (c) a recovery in the European currencies, including the Lira, relative to the Deutschmark (932, 942); (d) pro-Dollar declarations from Tietmeyer (943, 945); and lastly (e) US macroeconomic results that are unfavorable to the Dollar, on Thursday 11 (939). However, a rally of more than 7 pfennings in four days – peaking on Friday 12 (948, 949, 950) – requires a far more solid explanation than this. Equally hard to explain is the drop of the US currency on Wednesday and Thursday, 24 and 25 May. On 24 May the US durable consumer goods show very poor results (975, 976), and the following day there are rumours of financial trouble at a Mexican financial institution (983). These two events have typically a low impact on Dollar movements.

This "hump" in the graph of the Dollar, quite visible in Figure 2.1, lower panel, could be caused by hidden interventions of the Central Banks. The modern orthodoxy of supporting interventions determines the need to implement them in correspondence with events and market climates that can maximize their effect. It is therefore possible that they may have taken place at the same time as the events and statements described above, which, even if by themselves they are not enough to cause the sudden revaluation of the Dollar, may have contributed to rendering the interventions more effective.

The month of June begins with the expectation of a series of co-ordinated interventions by the G3 central banks, on Wednesday, 31 May (994, 995, 996, 997), which produce a strong impact. In time, however, the effect fades and the Dollar weakens again, although at a more moderate pace than in February and March, essentially because of the still weak US economic situation (1005, 1007, 1014, 1015).

The rest of the month passes without any significant events, apart from the G7 meeting in Halifax over the weekend of 17-18 June (1049, 1058). The meeting does not produce announcements or policy statements of relevance for the currency markets, even if the Dollar is slightly stronger in the days immediately preceding the meeting, perhaps in expectation of its outcome, settling then at around 85 Yen against the Dollar until the end of July. The unexpectedly positive conclusion of the car trade dispute between the United States and Japan on Wednesday, 28 June (1084, 1085, 1090) produces a noticeable rally of the American currency, which then remains above the 85-Yen mark for some time. On 7 June Clinton exercises for the first time his veto on a National Budget Act voted by a Republican-controlled Congress (1024, 1025). This is the first act in a long and extremely tough contest between the Presidency and the Congress over the US Federal Budget, which will lead to the suspension of many governmental activities between the end of 1995 and the beginning of 1996.

The Third Quarter

After an initial negative economic announcement in the United States (1096), on Thursday, 6 July the Fed reduces the Federal Funds target by 0.25 percentage points (1103, 1107, 1108, 1112). Then, on the following Friday 7, a series of positive announcements improve the US economic situation (1115, 1137, 1138, 1140), with the creation of 215,000 new jobs, well beyond expectations (1116, 1117). A few hours after this last release, in the morning (New York time), the Fed and the Bank of Japan effect a series of co-ordinated interventions that cause a strong appreciation of the Dollar (1119). Figure 2.2, upper panel.

The cut in interest rates by the Fed on 6 July seems to have a negative direct effect on the Dollar – as predicted by economic theory – but a positive indirect effect, by way of the bond market (1107). This effect appears to prevail in the following days, also because of the intervention on the currency market mentioned earlier.

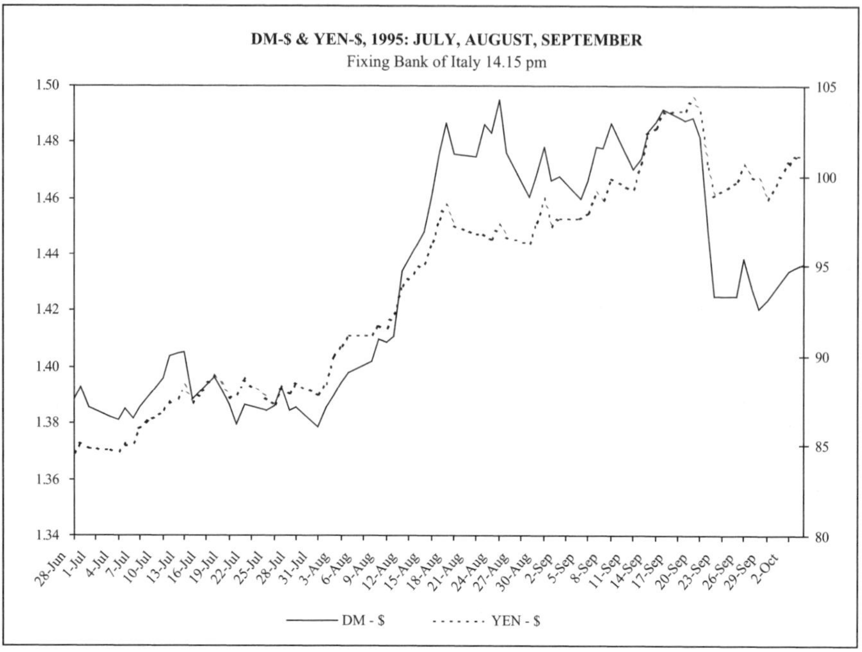

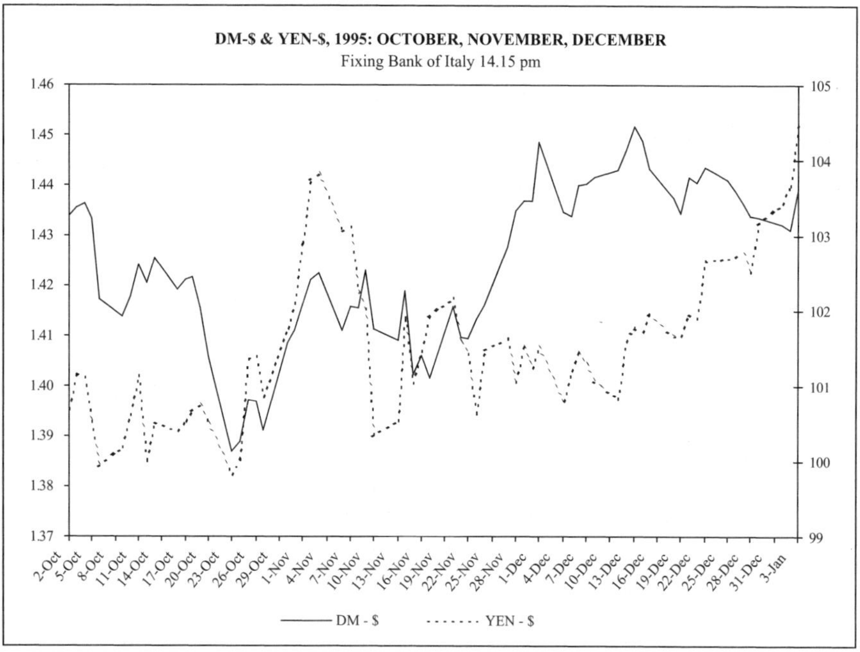

Figure 2.2 DM-$ & Yen-$, 1995: July, August, September – October, November, December

The appreciation of the exchange rate following an interest rate cut may be surprising.[2] We see in this episode one of the first examples of a "new" modus operandi of the US financial market. An increase (decrease) in the interest rates depresses (revives) the stock and bond markets and, through these, it may cause a devaluation (revaluation) of the exchange rate through the outflows (inflows) of funds from (to) the stock and bond markets or through the decreased inflows (outflows) towards these markets. In the American case, then, interest rate variations do not result in univocal effects on the exchange rate, rather they depend on the positive or negative effect that they have on stock and bond prices.

We can see the same mechanism at work in the markets' reaction to Greenspan's testimony before Congress on Wednesday, 19 July, when he rules out further cuts in the US interest rates, thus causing a retrenchment in the US financial markets and a fall of the Dollar (1150, 1151, 1157).

During the month of July the Dollar remains fundamentally stable, albeit with wide fluctuations. The hospitalization of Russian President Yeltzin on Tuesday, 11 July (1126), weakens the Deutschmark, while the Bundesbank's failure to announce cuts in the German interest rate on Thursday 13 later strengthens it (1130, 1133, 1134). Figure 2.2, upper panel.

A marked rally of the Dollar, after the pronounced devaluation experienced in the first half of 1995, takes shape as of the end of July with a series of almost simultaneous events occurring primarily in Japan. The Japanese Central Bank intervenes on Monday, 24 July, with no apparent immediate effect (1167). Then, on Tuesday 25, a positive release on US consumer confidence polarizes the markets' attention, as it seems to confirm the positive forecasts of the Fed – expressed at the time of Greenspan's Congress appearance on 19 July (see above) – regarding a US economic recovery in the second half: the Dollar rallies significantly (1172), especially considering the Dollar's insensitivity to this variable.

Between Monday, 31 July and Wednesday, 2 August various events mark a turning point for the Dollar, especially against the Yen:

- On 31 July Clinton declares that the Federal Budget will be balanced earlier than expected (1187);
- On 31 July the financial trouble of a major Japanese financial institution raises the possibility of a new flow of funds towards Japan to cover possible losses (1188);
- On 2 August the Japanese Government passes measures to liberalise investments of major national financial institutions in foreign securities, with the declared objective of weakening the Yen (1195, 1198, 1199);
- On 2 August the Fed and the Bank of Japan intervene on the foreign exchange market to bolster the joint effect of all these events (1195, 1197, 1199).

This is another example of an intervention on the currency markets directed at reinforcing spontaneous trends. This will be an increasingly frequent model in the subsequent – although not numerous – examples of central bank intervention.

From then on the American currency will continue to revalue until 17 August, after unexpected – and therefore quite effective – joint interventions of the US and Japanese Central Banks on Monday, 7 August (1212, 1213, 1214), and of the G3 Central Banks on Tuesday, 15 August (1235, 1237). Thereafter the US currency continues to fluctuate at much higher levels than those that had prevailed since the beginning of April.

The interventions of 7 and 15 August represent further important examples of interventions aimed at reinforcing spontaneous trends in the market.

On Thursday, 24 August the Bundesbank reduces interest rates (discount and Lombard) by 0.50 percentage points (1258, 1261, 1262), after allowing a reduction of the repo on Wednesday, 9 August (with no consequences for the exchange rate since it was expected and in line with median expectations, 1219), after a slowdown in the monetary growth – Tuesday, 22 August (1250) – and almost at the same time as the positive inflation figures of Friday 25 (1265).

This is not the last interest rate cut of the summer. Japan, in the middle of a stagnation caused by the major revaluation of the Yen and by the growing difficulties in the banking and financial sectors, reduces the discount rate to its post-war historical minimum of 0.5%, on Friday, 8 September (1299), preceding this measure with interventions on the foreign exchange market on Wednesday and Thursday 6-7 (1292, 1296) and also reinforcing the effect on the exchange of the interest rate cut with further, almost simultaneous interventions (1299).

And this represents another example of an intervention intended to reinforce existing or induced trends.

Then the Bundesbank reduces the repo slightly on Wednesday, 13 September, with an immediate positive effect on the Dollar (1312). The Bank of Japan, for its part, intervenes again the same day to weaken the Yen, supporting this action with "verbal interventions" (1311, 1313, 1317), which will be discussed at length in Chapter 6. See Figure 2.2, upper panel.

From September 1995, back from the summer recess, the first statements regarding the construction of the European Monetary Union (EMU) begin to appear. It is difficult to imagine a more sensational opening than that of Thursday, 21 September, when German Minister of Finance Weigel made his now famous statement: "Italy, founding member of the European Economic Community, will not form part of the initial group of EMU countries" (1332, 1339, 1340). This statement – which was not denied, but offered in confidence to a commission of the German Bundestag – provokes not only the collapse of the Lira but also a strong and undesired revaluation of the Deutschmark (as confirmed by the declarations of Buba Council Member Sievert the following 25 September; 1353), which gains back in September and October all that it had lost against the Dollar with the joint initiatives of August. On Monday, 25 September Tietmeyer, with similar considerations on the matter, contributes to this undesired revaluation of the Deutschmark, which will not return to the 20 September levels until the end of March 1996.

The constant positive pressure on the Deutschmark is induced by a widespread uncertainty regarding the extent to which it is really possible to implement EMU respecting the scheduled time and agreed terms, while maintaining the Maastricht criteria and a suitable strategy (1346, 1361). The German comments represent a veritable shock for the markets, stifling for some time the pull in the opposite direction produced by other events, such as the USA Federal Open Market Committee (FOMC)'s decision, at the Wednesday, 27 September meeting, not to cut interest rates (1358).

The Fourth Quarter

The stance taken on EMU by policy-makers, particularly German ones (1365, 1352), together with some episodes of political turmoil, gives further impetus to exchange rate fluctuations in Europe. There is additional uncertainty regarding the Monetary Union on Thursday, 5 October, with a marked weakening of the ECU determined by Dutch uneasiness over the use of this accounting unit within EMU (1383). See Figure 2.2, lower panel.

The following day, Friday 6, the speculative attacks on the French Franc culminate with the Bank of France's imposition of restrictive measures (1391, 1392), which appear as the logical conclusion to the German "monetary *machismo*": after Italy, what is the next weak link in the European monetary construction? Obviously, France.

In Europe there continues to be political uncertainty in France, Sweden and Italy, from Monday 16 to Tuesday 24 October (1405, 1408). In this period the revaluation of the Lira – which had paralleled the rally of the Dollar – stops, primarily because of the removal from office of Minister of Justice Mancuso and the Polo's subsequent attempt at passing a no-confidence vote against Dini. Concurrently with this latter event, the Lira undergoes a drastic devaluation. In the case of the Mancuso crisis it is even possible to wonder whether the Lira devaluation may not have caused the strengthening of the Deutschmark against the Dollar (see par. 2.2.2).

In the last quarter of 1995 the American economy grows at a moderate pace (1453, 1454, 1456, 1457, 1458, 1459, 1460, 1461, 1469). A similar trend is observed in Germany (1471), while the Japanese economy undergoes a pronounced slowdown, again due to the revaluation of the Yen (1452). In December the symptoms of a national banking crisis worsen; these symptoms have been evident for some time and will constitute a constant in the future economic events of the Asian country. While Japan, with interest rates at a historical minimum of 0.50%, no longer has the possibility of effecting further cuts, Germany and the United States still have room for downward corrections which indeed they use: Germany on

Thursday, 14 December (1563, 1564), and the United States on Wednesday, 20 December (1580).

The Dollar had previously experienced fluctuations produced primarily by market dynamics, and by reactions to macroeconomic news considered of some relevance, for instance after Friday, 27 October following a better-than-expected third quarter growth (1451). Figure 2.2, lower panel.

The Deutschmark continues to fluctuate at high levels, sustained by the unfortunate oratory of Germany's Minister of Finance, until the end of November when, on Monday 27, the strong expectations of a German interest rate cut intensify further, with the consequent welcome weakening of the currency against the Dollar (1521, 1527).

During the month of November, after months of smouldering, the Federal Budget controversy between the US Presidency and the Congress escalates, with an implicit "theoretical" possibility that the US Government may default on its own debt, leading in December – and then again in early 1996 – to the closure of several Federal offices, including those responsible for the publication of economic statistics. See: 1416, 1417, 1455, 1481, 1486, 1501, 1502, 1552, 1571.

These are the terms of the controversy: the US Congress, dominated by the Republicans, has succeeded – with the help of conservative Democrats – in forcing an amendment comporting the balancing of the Federal Budget within 2002. A violent argument on the ways to reach this result erupts between Republicans – who want to achieve this objective with fewer taxes and less social spending – and Clinton, who wants more taxes and more social spending. The drama and the suspense of this battle reach a climax when the Federal Government debt reaches its legal limit, finding itself – in theory – unable to meet payments due on short-term obligations and to maintain the expense of a functioning central public administration. Hence the theoretical possibility of default.

Congress is willing to raise the Federal debt ceiling with partial decrees, improperly introducing in them clauses that commit the Federal Government to implementing the taxation measures favored by the Republican majority. Clinton obviously exerts his veto on all these measures, and is not overruled by Congress as the measures are bordering on the illegal. The Government, however, finds itself short of funds and must therefore suspend some governmental services.

I would not hesitate to term this situation "surreal", a feeling obviously shared by the financial markets, which fortunately refrain from precipitating a new collapse of the Dollar – although this would have been more justified than the devaluation in early 1995.

Yet, there are some exceptions: the Yen, for instance, experiences a strong appreciation on Wednesday, 8 November (1476), when – hunting among reserves data – traders realise that during the month Japan has disinvested, imagining perhaps catastrophic scenarios for the Federal Government debt. On Monday, 18 December the market comments blame this for the marked fall in Wall Street stocks and bonds, and the consequent depreciation of the Dollar (1572).

2.2 The Dollar in 1996: The Long-overdue Rally

The First Quarter

At the beginning of 1996 the Dollar is at 1.4323 against the Deutschmark and at 103.42 against the Yen. While the rally against the Yen has basically exhausted itself, after the marked depreciation of the first quarter in 1995, the Deutschmark is even stronger against the Dollar relative to the end of 1994. At the beginning of 1996 the German economy is at a standstill, both because of the revaluation relative to the Dollar and because of widespread domestic unemployment (1606).

Thus it is hardly surprising that the German Monetary Authorities should begin the year with the explicit objective of weakening their currency. Evidence of this may be found in the four successive cuts in the spot and forward rates (the repo rate) which followed the official interest rate cut on 14 December, 1995. The repo reduction operation is conducted over a four-week period, from Wednesday 10 to Wednesday, 31 January (see 1646, 1704, 1743), driving the interest rate down from 3.75% to 3.30%. This policy is supported, over the same period, by a series of announcements by Bundesbank Governor Tietmeyer and Bank Council Members Koebnick and Jochimsen, on 15, 16 and 23 January (1664, 1667, 1701), aimed at maximising the effect of the interest rate cuts. The result on the DM-$ exchange rate is significant, going from 1.43 at the end of 1995 to 1.49 at the end of January. See Figure 2.3, upper panel.

In February, however, the German currency strengthens again for reasons that are probably independent from the will of German policy-makers and from the economic situation. This revaluation may have been the result of the decrease in US Federal Funds rate on Wednesday, 31 January (1742,1743,1750,1751), the uncertain growth of the American economy – tied also to the serious weather conditions in the East Coast (1668) – and the reluctance of international investors to invest in the United States caused by the absence of current data on the economic situation and by residual fears of default on the US debt (1690). It is worth remembering that from December 1995 to mid-January (1668) the federal offices do not provide regular information on the American situation. The only organisations that can do it are the Fed, for industrial production, and the National Association of Purchasing Managers (NAPM) with its indices.

From Monday, 12 February to Friday 16, the strengthening of the Deutschmark is also helped by the collapse of the Lira, determined by the Hon. Maccanico's failure to form a post-Dini government that can complete the Italian semester of European Union presidency (1753, 1769, 1773, 1778,

Figure 2.3 DM-$ & Yen-$, 1996: January, February, March – April, May, June

1785, 1789, 1795). There may be a repetition of a phenomenon already observed towards the end of October 1995, during the crisis initiated by the "forced resignation" of the Hon. Mancuso: the weakness of the Lira contributes to the international strengthening of the Deutschmark.

The February strengthening of the Deutschmark, probably still undesired, is interrupted on at least two occasions, on Wednesday, 28 February and Friday, 1 March, with a movement of funds towards the Dollar in the expectation of a cut in the German official interest rates (1845, 1857).[3] However, interest rates remain disappointingly unchanged after the two regular meetings of the Bundesbank, on Thursday 14 and Thursday 28 March (1937). On the Yen front, the Japanese Central Bank produces in a single week – from 20 to 23 February – a series of interventions to weaken its own currency, without achieving any noticeable success, Figure 2.3 upper panel.

On Tuesday, 26 March, Fed President Greenspan makes a significant statement in one of his periodic speeches before Congress:

> Keeping the Dollar's key role in the international context is very important for the growth of the American economy and for the living standards of our citizens. Therefore the US Authorities are not indifferent to the international value of the Dollar.

The markets do not react immediately to this explicit declaration of intent, but this is probably the beginning of a revaluation process that will last for the following year and a half, continuously supported by Treasury Secretary Rubin ("*A strong Dollar is in the best interest of the United States*").[4]

The Second Quarter

The American economy speeds up its expansion in the second half of 1996 (1874, 1879, 1880, 1962) while the slowdown of the German economy becomes more pronounced (1870, 1871, 2010, 2026). Concerns regarding the serious unemployment issues are prompted by the German economy's insufficient growth rate and are expressed on Monday, 1 April by the Minister of Labour, causing (according to statements released by this source) an unusual and significant appreciation of the Dollar (1943 and Figure 2.3, lower panel). This is a thorough demonstration of one of the most popular interpretative models among traders: the model that views the growth differential between the USA and Germany as having a decisive role in the appreciation of the Dollar, through the widening gap between interest rates and the inflow of funds towards the US financial market.

On Wednesday, 10 April the monthly results of March for German unemployment are published (1968, 1969), the first in a long series of subsequent records. This announcement is followed by a robust appreciation of the Dollar. The German Monetary Authorities reinforce this trend with a series of specific pro-Dollar statements – Tietmeyer on Monday, 14 April

(1981), on the following Thursday 18 (1995) and then again, some time later, on Monday, 10 June (2167, 2168), Zeitler on Thursday, 25 April (2016) and lastly Sievert on Tuesday, 21 May (2110) – but above all with a cut in the discount rate to its historical low on Thursday, 18 April (1991, 1992, 1994). The Deutschmark reacts to these stimuli accordingly, depreciating by 3.5% between the beginning of April and the end of May. See Figure 2.3, lower panel.

The appreciation of the Dollar is determined by other reasons in addition to the German stimuli: after the meeting of G7 Ministers of Finance and Central Bank Governors over the weekend of 20-21 April in Washington, a Dollar-friendly statement is released, producing the desired effect (2000, 2005). This statement is probably reinforced later by the conclusion, on Thursday, 25 April, of the long, painful negotiation on the US Federal Budget (2018) mentioned earlier, which hints of a significant decrease in Uncle Sam's pressure on the bond market in the mediumterm.

In 1996 the relationship between the evolution of the US domestic financial markets and the value of the Dollar becomes more pronounced. We see two eloquent examples of this "new" relationship between Tuesday, 7 May (2061, 2064) and Tuesday, 14 May (2082) – with a weakening of the Dollar followed by a sensible appreciation – and then again on Wednesday, 29 May and Friday 31 (2133, 2143). See Figure 2.3, lower panel.

During May and June the trend of positive news regarding the US economic situation (2046) and negative news regarding the European situation continues. On 15 May, the Brussels EU Commission publishes bearish forecasts regarding the European economy for 1996 and 1997 (2087). On Tuesday, 21 May Germany records negative GDP growth in the first quarter of 1996 (2108), "in the red" for the second time since the fourth quarter of 1995: according to international tradition this situation spells economic recession in the technical sense. Then, on 5 June, the federal statistical offices are able to revise upwards the GDP for the fourth quarter, thus "patching" a difficult situation (2156).

On 20 June OECD projections indicate the possibility that France and Germany may miss the Maastricht 3% target in 1997 (2210, see also 2092), while not only in Germany but also in France unemployment is almost at a record high (2226, 2279).

In Japan there is a "mysterious" GDP increase in the first quarter, 12.7% on an annualized basis, announced on Tuesday, 18 June (2200), but ten days later, on Thursday 28 (2247), it is announced that the unemployment rate for May is at the highest level since 1953. On Tuesday, 25 June (2229) the Japanese Government approves the introduction, effective as of 1 April, 1997, of a sales tax, which will be largely responsible for the Japanese recession of 1997-1998.[5] Lastly, on Friday, 14 June comes the announcement that the Japanese Sumitomo Bank has sustained extremely severe losses in speculations on copper futures. The Yen immediately appreciates, reflecting an interpretative model of the event already observed at the beginning of August, 1995 (event number 1188): the financial trouble of a financial institution may cause a large flow of funds towards the Yen in order to cover potential operating losses in this currency (2189, 2190). See Figure 2.3, lower panel.

The events in Japan generate also a temporary strengthening of the Deutschmark that, having returned to the previous levels, appreciates again on Thursday, 27 June when the Bundesbank fails to cut interest rates at its periodic meeting. This revaluation is reinforced by statements from Tietmeyer, who considers that the German economy is recovering ("even if not spectacularly") and therefore a request to cut interest rates is not justified (2241, 2242). See Figure 2.3, lower panel.

The Third Quarter

The good performance of the American economy during the summer quarter conditions the interpretative models and the investment strategies of the financial players. Particularly poignant is the anguished wait for the Fed's decisions relative to the interest rate movements (for instance 2318, 2324). This translates into a meticulous analysis of all the US economic releases and of their implications in terms of the Fed's interest rate decisions.[6] Interpretation usually gives way to action, both on the eve of the FOMC meetings, with more pronounced fluctuations in the exchange rates and stock trends, and, surprisingly, even immediately after the meetings, with speculation over what will happen at the next one.

This attitude is probably influenced by the awareness that, for about a year now, the US unemployment rate is at or slightly below the NAIRU, and that the growth rate compatible with price stability is similarly beyond its historical values. And yet US inflation remains stable, which – in the absence of an explanation that is convincing or at least generally accepted – keeps traders in a mode of alert nervousness. This is certainly not mitigated by Greenspan, who on Thursday, 18 July, while announcing the Fed's forecast of an economic slowdown in the second half of the year, reiterates that he is ready to raise interest rates if the available economic data indicate with some degree of reliability (in the words of the President of the Fed, "*the evidence persuasively suggests*") that there is an inflation risk (2324).

We have a manifest example of this general market sentiment in July, after the Fed leaves interest rates unchanged at the meeting of Wednesday, 3 July. The foreign exchange market does not show any reaction to this decision (surprising even commentators, 2262), so that in the days immediately following the event the Dollar fluctuates against the Deutschmark within narrow limits, while as of mid-June the Yen is still influenced by the news mentioned above.

Then, on Friday, 5 July the Dow Jones slides back, presumably because of fears of an interest rate increase (2270), even though two days earlier rates have been left unchanged and nothing has happened since.

This is the first inkling of a Wall Street crisis starting on Thursday, 11 July. The profit warning of a major IT group causes the loss of approximately 100 points in the Dow Jones, as well as the beginning of a significant devaluation of the Dollar that lasts for all of July, "costing" approximately 6 pfennings and 4 Yen. See Figure 2.4, upper panel.

The stock market plunge is almost immediately compounded by fears of future interest rate increases the following week.[7] The Dollar continues to weaken – because of the uncomfortable situation in the US financial markets – down to end-of-the-month lows, with an overshooting in the last two days, Tuesday and Wednesday, 30 and 31 July, when there is also an independent strengthening of the Deutschmark, caused by a inter-European portfolio reallocation (2357, 2360), and probably by a delayed reaction to the Bundesbank decision not to cut interest rates at its last meeting prior to the summer recess, on Thursday, 25 July (2343, 2346).

During the month of August the favorable US news of economic growth without inflation continues (2364, 2365, 2386, 2437, 2451), while in other respects the markets remain relatively calm during the summer recess month, which often records substantial fluctuations in the financial variables.

On Tuesday, 20 August the German M3 growth slows down relative to previous levels – a recognized signal for a German interest rate cut – and on Wednesday 21 the Munich IFO business climate index turns out to be surprisingly positive, a signal that goes in the opposite direction. All of this generates uncertainty regarding the Bundesbank's decisions at its first meeting after the summer recess, on Thursday 22, as shown by the fluctuations of the Deutschmark in those days. In the end Buba decides in favor of an unusual repo rate cut of 0.3 percentage points, much higher than that expected by the markets. See Figure 2.4, upper panel.

This interest rate cut seems to have only a temporary effect on the Deutschmark exchange rate, which is still below 1.50 against the Dollar and only 5 pfennings above the early 1996 level, recovering only to a slight degree the marked appreciation of 1995. Then the Bundesbank's "heavy artillery" is activated, with wisely administered and well-timed reports and announcements:

(a) On Friday, 30 August Tietmeyer states that the fundamentals of the US economy should imply a higher value for the Dollar (2455);
(b) On Monday, 9 September Tietmeyer states that a strong Dollar is in everybody's interests (2484);
(c) On Thursday, 12 September the Bundesbank hints at possible cuts in the German interest rates (2497).

At the end of this therapy the Deutschmark recovers approximately 3.5 pfennings.

On the other side of the Atlantic expectations of a rise in interest rates are still high despite the fact that the US economic cycle is producing non-

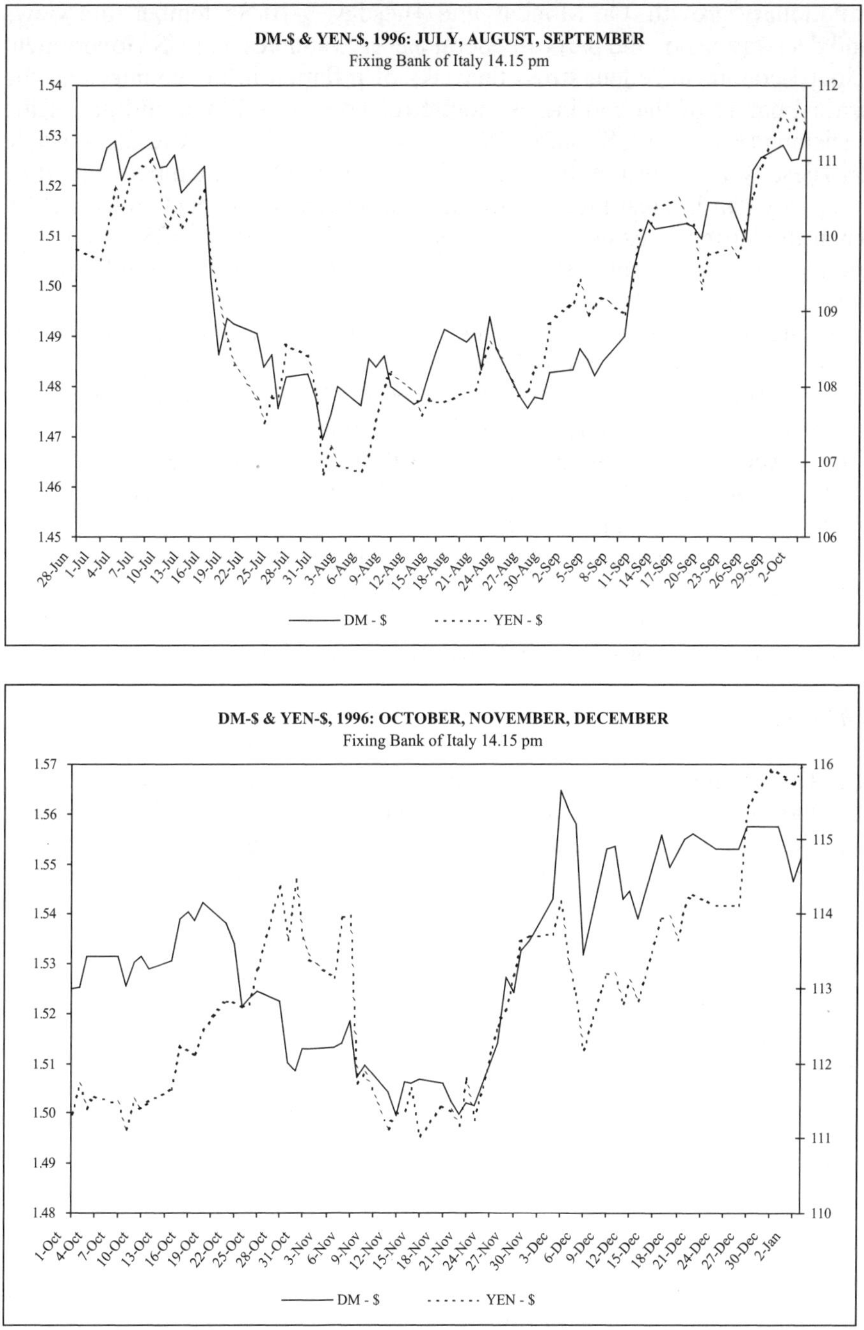

Figure 2.4 DM-$ & Yen-$, 1996: July, August, September – October, November, December

inflationary growth. On Monday and Tuesday, 9-10 September interviews and declarations on the part of Federal Reserve sources and US Government Chief Economist Yellen, stress the risks of inflation in the country and the critical nature of the coming economic releases on inflation, in light of the decisions regarding US interest rates (2483, 2486, 2487). A Reuters article on Tuesday 17 reporting that eight of the twelve FOMC members would be in favor of an interest rate rise further reinforces such expectations (2509). Then the strong housing starts of Thursday, 19 September (2521) confirm the likelihood of an interest rate rise at the FOMC meeting of the following week.

At the end of the Tuesday 24 meeting the interest rates are left unchanged (2537), surprising the US bond and stock markets (2538, 2546), which react very favorably on the 25-26 September (2544, 2553), thus giving new impetus to the Dollar. Lastly, a decisive support of the US currency comes the weekend of 28-29 September, in the form of pro-Dollar announcements by G7 Ministers of Finance gathered in Washington for the International Monetary Fund's autumn meeting (2566).

In these days at the end of the summer, from late August till the end of September, the simultaneous – but not necessarily co-ordinated – actions of the Bundesbank and of major US policy-makers allow a recovery of the Deutschmark of approximately 6 pfennings. See Figure 2.4, upper panel.

The Fourth Quarter

The Dollar remains at the same high levels of late September, partly due to the good performance of the US financial markets between Wednesday, 2 October and Monday 14, as Wall Street shoots through the 6,000 ceiling. The Dollar reaches its maximum level since the end of May on Friday, 18 October, in the wake of the financial markets' reaction to Yeltzin's removal of General Lebed from his important office as national security advisor to the Russian President (2640). See Figure 2.4, lower panel.

As already observed in June 1995 with Yeltzin's hospitalization, Russian events are followed very closely by financial markets and exert a considerable influence over the Deutschmark – perhaps an excessive influence, considering the values at stake. The markets view this news unfavorably, given Lebed's prestige domestically and in the United States, particularly since the close collaboration with the Russian President had led them to hope for a succession to power that would have been viewed as favorable to the international equilibrium. Hence the depressing effect of the news on the Deutschmark.

The Deutschmark strengthens from its October peak in three stages. The first one occurs on Tuesday-Wednesday, 22-23 October, resulting from profit-taking on the German currency, following the significant strengthening of the previous month (2661), from capitals flowing to the Deutschmark (for the acquisition of the first *tranche* of the stock issued in the privatisation of Deutsche Telekom (2667)), and probably from Issing's announcements regarding German interest rates (2666).

The second stage is produced by the publication, on Tuesday, 29 October, of the forecasts run by the six major German economic research instates, which double the previous estimates of economic growth for 1996 (2691) warning at the same time that the country will not reach the magic 3% deficit-GDP ratio in 1997 (2686).

The third stage originates in Japan: between Thursday, 7 November and Monday 11 the Japanese Ministry of Finance lets it be known, through announcements made by one of its Director-Generals – the famous "Mr Yen" Eisuke Sakakibara – and through agency news, that it no longer intends to favor a weak Yen (2732, 2742). The significant strengthening of the Yen caused by this verbal intervention – from 114 to 111 approximately – drags the Deutschmark with it (2733, 2735, 2741). See Figure 2.4, lower panel.

It is interesting to note that the Bundesbank tries to intervene with its "heavy artillery" also in this probably undesired instance of a strengthening Deutschmark. The first attempt is made on Friday, 25 October, without success and with a curiously contradictory result, when Issing, Welteke and Sievert (2677) foreshadow the possibility of further cuts in German interest rates, with immediate denials from Tietmeyer (2678), who on the contrary believes that the rates are at their proper level. The second attempt is made on Tuesday, Wednesday and Thursday, 12-13-14 November, with greater success, when Bundesbank officials release pro-Dollar declarations through Tietmeyer (2746 and 2759), and declarations in favor of an interest rate cut through Zeitler (2749).

This time, however, the Bundesbank's intervention yields barely a pfennings, nowhere near the over 3.5 pfennings of September (compare upper and lower panels in Figure 2.4).

Thus a new bearish trend takes shape – beyond the German borders – both because of the obvious limitations of a purely verbal support of the sole Bundesbank, and because the value of the Deutschmark, leading currency of the European economy, may still seem too high against the Dollar – even after so many attempts to weaken it for more than a year – with EMU so imminent. Be it as it may, in an interview on Wednesday, 20 November, French ex-President Valéry Giscard-d'Estaing declares that the French Franc is "*trop fort*", although he is ambiguous enough not to reveal against which currency the Franc should be devalued: whether unilaterally against the German Deutschmark or simultaneously against the Deutschmark and the Dollar (2776).

This initiative is somewhat disconcerting (2782, 2783, 2807) and does not seem to have any noticeable effect on the Franc, also because of the ambiguity already mentioned. Giscard returns to the subject on Wednesday, 27 November clarifying that the proposed devaluation of the Franc should be read against the Dollar, and therefore at the same time against the Deutschmark (2806). This idea finds ample support and a favorable resonance also within the Bank of France, so that – in a "German-like" procedure highly unusual in the French institutional context – two members of the Bank's Monetary Council, Marchelli on Tuesday, 26 November (2801) and Gérard on Thursday 28 (2813), publicly declare their support in favor of a simultaneous devaluation of the two main European currencies against the Dollar.

Evidently these two declarations, operating within the much wider European area, are much more effective than Germany's stand-alone initiatives, generating a slide of the Deutschmark of 6 pfennings in five working days, which not even a resentful expression of dissent by Bank of France Governor Trichet on Friday 29 can contain. On the other side of the Rhine this French hyperactivism is viewed coolly at first – statements by Kohl (2807) and Tietmeyer (2862) – giving way later, from the beginning of 1997, to a series of interventions targeted at weakening the Deutschmark. See Figure 2.4, lower panel, and Figure 2.5, upper panel.

This episode of hetero-directed weakening of the Deutschmark takes place in the same period that the Lira returns into the EMS and shortly before EU countries agree in Dublin to a stability pact, much desired by the Germans and which reinforces EMU's credibility.

This series of French statements, not contradicted by equally decisive interventions on the part of German officials, together with the US interest in strengthening its own currency – originally expressed in strong terms by Greenspan on 26 March, 1996 (1933), and later confirmed on several occasions by Rubin because of the obviously anti-inflationary benefits of a strong Dollar – is at the base of a long devaluation period for the Deutschmark, from about 1.50 against the Dollar on 20 November, to almost 1.90 on 6 August, 1997.

The Dollar descends slightly from its peak of over 1.56 reached on Monday, 2 December with Greenspan's declarations before Congress on Thursday, 5 December, when he attacks the excessive activity of the US stock markets coining the famous expression of the "irrational exuberance" of American savers and their advisers (1244), whereupon Wall Street collapses (2856, 2857) – with the consequent weakening of the Dollar. See Figure 2.4, lower panel.

Because of what has been said above, however, the weakening of the American currency is only temporary and it changes direction on Monday, 16 December, immediately after the weekend during which EU Finance Ministers agree on a "Stability Pact" for EMU. The markets (2910) believe the pact makes it more likely that EMU will take place, but that it will probably start with a weak Euro.

The year 1996 closes with good news for the Dollar, on Thursday, 19 December (2935), when an unexpected improvement in the US trade deficit seems to give the green light to a revaluation of the US currency, which will indeed take place in 1997.

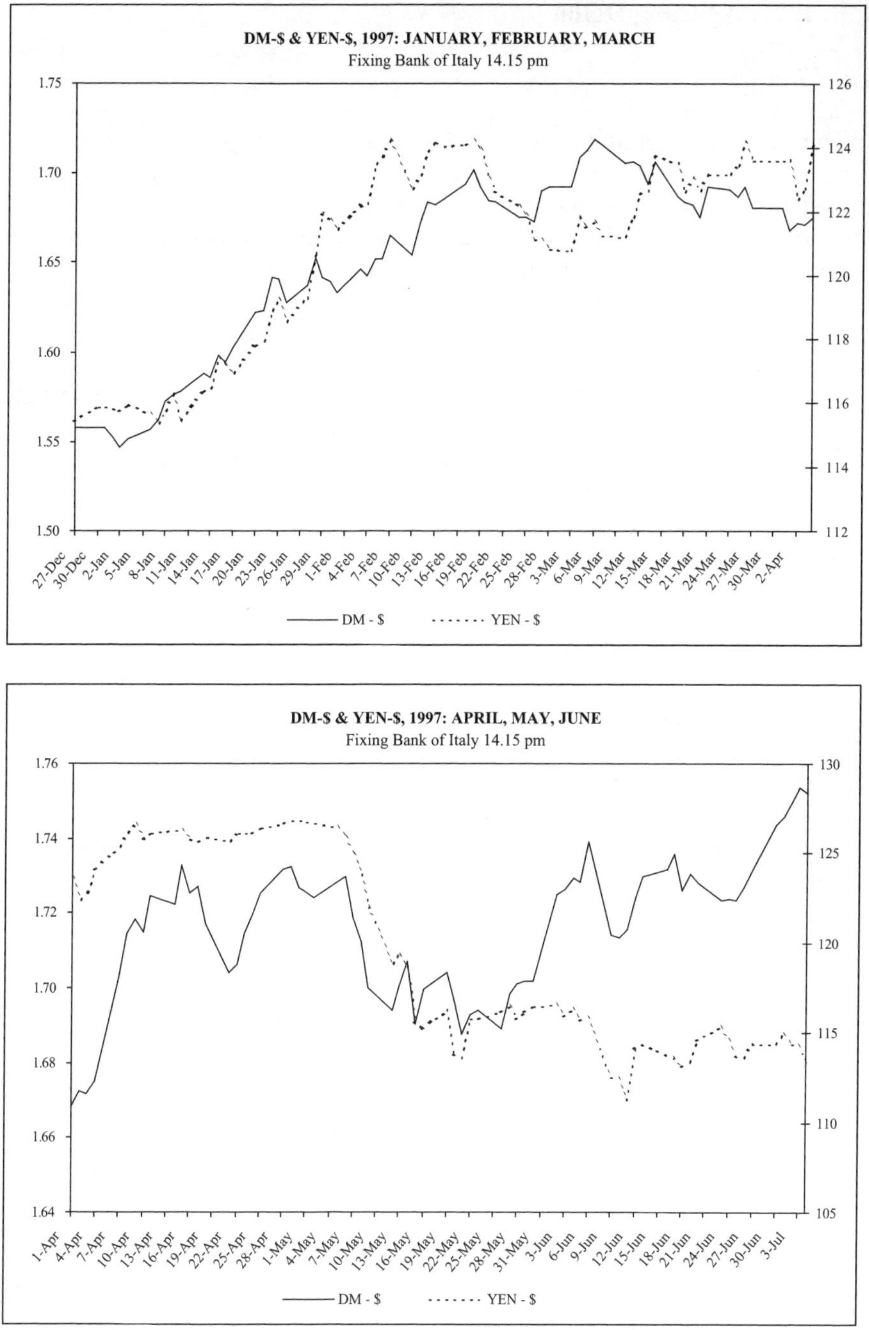

Figure 2.5 DM-$ & Yen-$, 1997: January, February, March – April, May, June

2.3 1997: A Strong Dollar

The First Quarter

In an article commenting on 1996 and making forecasts for 1997 (*Financial Times*, 6 July, 1997), American National Bureau of Economic Research President Martin Feldstein expresses his surprise at the simultaneous drop in unemployment and inflation in the United States, forecasting a moderate economic growth for 1997 primarily because of the probable monetary restrictions of the Fed. These restrictions will be almost inevitable given the probable increase in inflation generated by the excessive reduction in unemployment under NAIRU and the continuing growth of the US economy beyond the levels compatible with inflation stability. The financial markets seem to share this view (see 1997, news 2966 and 2967).

This view is also supported by Fed President Greenspan who, in his regular presentation on monetary policy to the Senate on Tuesday, 21 July, regrets the excessive pressure of the economy on labour market resources – with an unusual employment of retired workers and extension of working hours – possible harbinger of future wage increases beyond productivity increases, and therefore of inflation (3049, 3057 and *Financial Times*, 22 July and 3 February).

In Europe the economic cycle is much weaker, with widespread unemployment and expectations of further significant reductions of public deficit-driven growth in 1997, in the final rush to get into EMU. Evidently, this depressed state of affairs exerts a devaluing pressure on the Deutschmark, which indeed suffers from the unemployment and growth results released on Thursday, 9 January (2986, 2987), with effects that carry over into Friday 10 (2999) and then again the following 13 (3005). See Figure 2.5, upper panel.

The Deutschmark is already being pushed towards depreciation by the economic fundamentals, when the Bundesbank comes into play, between Monday, 13 January and Wednesday 22, communicating through Tietmeyer (3006), Hesse (3014), Sievert (3015), Krupp (3032), Zeitler (3042) and Welteke (3058), that there will be an interest rate cut and that the Deutschmark will weaken. This clearly obtains the expected effect, or perhaps more than expected, given that on Wednesday 29 Tietmeyer (3092) feels the need to preannounce that the downward correction of the German currency will soon level out and that in any case the Bundesbank's policy remains that of a strong Deutschmark. Meanwhile, the Deutschmark clearly does as it is told. See Figure 2.5, upper panel.

On the EMU front, France (on 12 February, 3149) and Germany (on 15 July, 3022) find that in 1996 they have exceeded the established budget limits, and on three occasions – on 7 January (2979), 2 February (3102) and 9-10 March (3266, 3271) – German research institutions express their doubts regarding Germany's ability to meet the Maastricht criteria. These episodes – together with others taking place in 1996 – give way to several primarily German requests to postpone EMU, which will be the prevailing *leit motif* for the best part of the year.[8]

In early February there is the shocking announcement, on Thursday 6, of an increase in Germany's jobless by 500,000 in the month of January alone (3125). Other negative announcements occur on Wednesday 5 and Tuesday 11 (3122, 3145). Thus the Deutschmark continues to devalue with some regularity. See Figure 2.5, upper panel.

This by now spontaneous trend of the Deutschmark to devalue based on the growth fundamentals between the German and the US economies triggers a new intervention of the Bundesbank's "heavy artillery", which tries to halt or at least slow down the devaluation of the Deutschmark, with only temporary success. On Thursday 13, Wednesday 19 and Thursday, 20 February, Gaddum (3159), the Bundesbank's Economic Bulletin (3178) and finally Tietmeyer (3185) in turn, state that the Deutschmark devaluation "has gone on beyond what is reasonable".

The Bundesbank intervenes again in March, after limited episodes of slight weakness of the Deutschmark (Figure 2.5, upper panel), with Welteke, on Monday, 3 March and Friday 7, and with Tietmeyer, on Wednesday 12, restating the proposition that the Deutschmark is now sufficiently weak (3225, 3261, 3282).

These three interventions by Bundesbank Monetary Council members – which will occur again to guide the Deutschmark in the desired direction for the remainder of 1997 – punctuate two interventions by Greenspan on the US economy and above all on the US stock market.

The first intervention is effected in two stages, the first one on Wednesday, 26 February when the President of the Fed, in the first part of his testimony before Congress, expresses his concern regarding a creeping inflation growth originating primarily in the labour market, thus also dealing a blow to Wall Street, always guilty of excessive optimism (3214, 3215 and *Financial Times* of 27 February).

The Dollar weakens slightly, but not for long, as traders' optimism prevails in the face of the American economy's brilliant performance – particularly relative to Germany and Japan – as evidenced by strong economic results on Monday, 3 March (NAPM, disposable income and consumer spending, 3231, 3232, 3233, 3234).

The second stage of the intervention, on Wednesday, 5 March, moves along the same lines, also causing a slight retreat of the Dollar given that – as mentioned earlier – it is often the financial markets that move the currency (3253).

The President of the Fed intervenes later, on Thursday, 20 March at the Congress' Joint Economic Committee, stating that the labour market is still under pressure, that the economy is strong and that therefore the Fed is ready to increase interest rates (3321 and *Financial Times* of 21 March), which indeed occurs a few days later at the FOMC meeting on Tuesday, 25 March

(3339, 3342). Here we can observe that the Dollar strengthens temporarily after the two events – announcement and effective interest rate increase – as expected, but then weakens against the Deutschmark due to the downward pressure on the US financial markets of the increased interest rates: from Thursday, 27 March to Wednesday, 2 April Wall Street falls and the Dollar slides with it (3358, 3362, 3363, 3368, 3372, 3379).

The Second Quarter

The Deutschmark devalues by approximately 6 pfennings in the first half of April, between Friday 4 and Tuesday 15, escaping the fluctuation range – between 1.68 and 1.72 against the Dollar – within which the German Monetary Authorities had been able to contain it. These results are determined by two joint events taking place on both sides of the Atlantic. (Figure 2.5, lower panel)

In Europe the declarations of Minister Weigel on Sunday 6 at the ECOFIN summit of Ministers of Finance in Noordwijk regarding the possibility of softening the 3% Maastricht criterion (3402), causes the feeling – as of the following Monday 7 – that German priorities are moving away from the previous stance of rigour at all costs on the Maastricht criteria towards the respect of the agreed timeline to introduce the Euro. Hence possibly the belief that the Euro cannot be as solid as the Deutschmark (3406, 3408, 3409, 3423, 3438, 3449). This feeling accompanies the weakening of the Deutschmark until Tuesday, 15 April. The underlying reasoning is self-evident: if the Euro will be implemented and it will be weak, then the value of the Deutschmark against the Dollar may fall to reflect the lower value of the Euro against the Dollar.

In the United States a sharp increase in the hourly earnings, communicated to the markets on Friday, 4 April, together with the usual employment statistics (3397, 3398, 3399, 3401), convince the markets that Greenspan's repeated warnings regarding labour market pressures are coming true (recently on 26 February, 3214, 3215 and *Financial Times* of 27 February). In the following days, until Monday 14, market comments continue to indicate bullish expectations regarding interest rates (3396, 3406, 3423, 3437, 3444, 3447). Unlike at least two previous episodes, in July 1996 and in March 1997, these expectations are matched by a stronger Dollar, since the US stock and bond markets do not show any signs of nervousness, perhaps because the next FOMC meeting is still distant.

It does not appear possible to attribute a single cause for the Deutschmark-Dollar exchange rate dynamics in the first half of April. Attributing such a strengthening of the Dollar to the optimism regarding EMU is a novelty in the market comments, and in order to be really convincing it should be accompanied by a general belief that a timely EMU will imply a weaker Euro relative to the Deutschmark. Also, to attribute the strengthening of the Dollar to the expectations of rising interest rates, after the hourly earnings communicated on 4 April, is also in contrast with previous experiences in the US, when the fear of increases in interest rates has depressed the financial markets and weakened the American currency.[9]

The rally of the Dollar cannot go unnoticed by the Bundesbank, which at this point does not appear to welcome further devaluations of the Deutschmark. President Tietmeyer intervenes on Thursday, 17 April and on Monday 21 (3476, 3498), with an encouraging result at minus two pfennings. However, the Dollar continues to rise due to local market dynamics together with some external events (3577, 3525, 3530, 3538, 3539). See Figure 2.5, lower panel.

This time the breaks on the rising Dollar are applied by a joint announcement of the G7, at the end of their meeting over the weekend of 26-27 April, according to which the US currency has strengthened enough against the Yen, and that a closer collaboration of G7 policy-makers is needed to stabilise the US exchange rate (3541, *Financial Times*, 28 April).

This action, however, does not work immediately, since G7 announcements are usually expressed in highly diplomatic terms, subsequently needing a "true interpretation" from those who actually move the markets. This interpretation is provided on Tuesday, 6 May by Bundesbanker Welteke (3596) and on Thursday 8 by "Mr Yen" Sakakibara (3608), confirming Germany's and Japan's determination to weaken the Dollar, or at least this seems to be the markets' conclusion (3598, 3608, 3609, 3613).

In the evening of Thursday 8 Governor Greenspan comments on the possible slow down of the American economy towards the end of 1997, which renders improbable any increase in interest rates (3615). The Dollar weakens as a consequence (3616, 3617).

The US currency then devalues unilaterally against the Deutschmark and the Yen until Monday 12, fluctuating thereafter in expectation of subsequent events. See Figure 2.5, lower panel.

Two episodes determine the exchange rate dynamics and the market sentiment in June: the "Bundesbank gold" and the victory of the Left in the French elections.

On Thursday, 15 May German Minister of Finance Weigel (3654) proposes the revaluation of the Bundesbank's gold reserves at market prices, with the objective of transferring the proceeds to the Federal budget and thus solve the German problems relative to the Maastricht criteria. The Deutschmark does not appear to react to this proposal (3662, 3669, 3664) but the effect on German public opinion and on the major international analysts and commentators is quite strong (3661, 3665). The Bundesbank rejects this plan (3718) on Wednesday, 28 May – this time causing a weakening of the Deutschmark – and then Weigel tries to impose his point of view (3733), among the generalized confusion of analysts and markets (3726, 3727, 3734, 3743). The proposal is finally withdrawn (3751) on Tuesday, 3 June.

On Sunday, 25 May, at the first round (3704), and Sunday, 1 June (3740), at the second round, the Left wins the political elections in France, imprudently called for by President Chirac in the hope of consolidating his majority in Parliament. Immediately after the first round, Prime Minister Juppé resigns (3705).

As seen above, Weigel's plan regarding the Buba gold does not appear to have strong consequences for the Deutschmark-Dollar exchange rate, but it certainly determines a strong consolidation of the expectations of a weak Euro (3664, 3665, 3726, 3727). The victory of the Left in France on Monday, 2 June, and the relative coolness shown by electoral winner Jospin towards EMU in his first statements immediately after the victory (3741), together with his reiterated intention of including the French communists in his government (3752), confirm that the rigorous position regarding the European budget is moving towards a softer stance (3753).

This situation therefore determines a renewed weakening of the Deutschmark, observed from Friday, 13 June to Tuesday 17, at the same time as the summit of European heads of state that closes the Dutch semester of EU presidency in Amsterdam (Figure 2.5, lower panel). In this period a lively argument develops between the French and the Germans regarding the weight to be attributed within EMU to unemployment and the need to employ European funds to intervene on this serious continent-wide problem (3803, 3809, 3810, 3811, 3814, 3818, 3819, 3823, 3826, 3827).

The month of June closes with a further weakening of the Deutschmark, determined again by a long series of German statements regarding EMU (3903, 3904, 3910, 3911, 3912) and by the markets' doubts – in part caused by such statements – regarding the strength of the Euro (3918). They no longer seem to believe German speeches on rigour; they do not believe Weigel when on Friday, 27 June he states in a Bundestag interview that the Euro will not be soft (3906), nor Kohl when on Monday 30 he reiterates that the EMU selection criteria will not be watered down (3918). The declarations of French Minister of Finance Strauss-Kahn, on Thursday, 3 July, to the effect that the French public deficit is likely to be higher than 3% of GDP in 1997 (3936), further confirm the markets' feeling and the Deutschmark weakens again (3947). See Figure 2.5, lower panel.

But the level of the Deutschmark in these days is still 10 pfennings below the level it will reach against the Dollar only a month and a half later, in the first ten days of August, and as we will see the effects of the changing mood over the Euro determined by the European events of May and June will still be felt in July and August.

Third Quarter

Following the episodes recounted above, the international financial markets consolidate two fundamental beliefs regarding EMU:

(A) that it will take place as scheduled (3423, 3438, 3449, 3665); and
(B) that the Euro will be weaker than the Deutschmark (3664, 3665).

Consistently with these beliefs, every time the news confirms belief (A) the Deutschmark devalues, because according to belief (B) it will be substituted by a weaker currency, and on the contrary when the news directly or indirectly implies a delay in EMU the Deutschmark strengthens, because according to belief (B) it is stronger than the Euro.

For instance, the appreciation of the Deutschmark the morning of Monday, 7 July, on fears of a delay in the implementation of EMU, is particularly noticeable (3956) and it requires the joint intervention of Weigel and Strauss-Kahn (3959). This strengthening is only temporary as the markets' belief that the Euro will be weak consolidate further: this is the reason for the weakening of the Deutschmark from Tuesday, 8 July to Monday 14 (3962, 3970). See Figure 2.6, upper panel.

The depreciating trend of the Deutschmark related to the optimism over EMU implementation might have been strengthened by the international reallocation – or interruption of reallocation – of portfolios towards currencies with much higher interest rates than the German ones: if the EMU goes forward there is the possibility of fund outflows from the Deutschmark towards the Lira or the Peseta, as already happened in the autumn of 1996, since they have much higher interest rates than the Deutschmark, and vice versa (see 3449, 3392, 3648, relative to a drop in long-term Italian Treasury Bond yields the day of the announcement of the plan for the Bundesbank gold).

The phase of rapid depreciation of the Deutschmark begun at the end of May naturally attracts some verbal attempts at containment. But in this instance the chorus is not unanimous: on Thursday, 17 July Tietmeyer tries to slow down the Deutschmark devaluation (4008), but on Friday 18 Kohl does not consider the devaluation "earth-shaking" (4015) and even within the Bundesbank there is a more doveish opinion, with Welteke – in apparent disagreement with President Tietmeyer – stating on Monday, 21 July his belief that the German interest rates will remain unchanged (4029). In any case the Deutschmark's depreciation does slow down in those days.

However, it resumes with renewed intensity on Tuesday, 22 July when Greenspan presents the Fed's revised forecast, which contain more growth and less inflation than the previous version (4032, 4033, 4038). The following day Greenspan reiterates in Congress that it is not his intention to increase interest rates given the no-inflation growth of the US economy (4039). The US stock market obviously benefits from the scenario outlined by the US Governor and the Dollar climbs by another four pfennings (4042). See Figure 2.6, upper panel.

The last and decisive surge of the Deutschmark takes place on Wednesday, 6 August, once again on expectations that a "strong" Deutschmark will be substituted with a "weak" Euro (4063), and following the publication on Friday, 1 August of the NAPM price figures and of highly positive results for the US unemployment figures (4084, 4085, 4089, 4090,

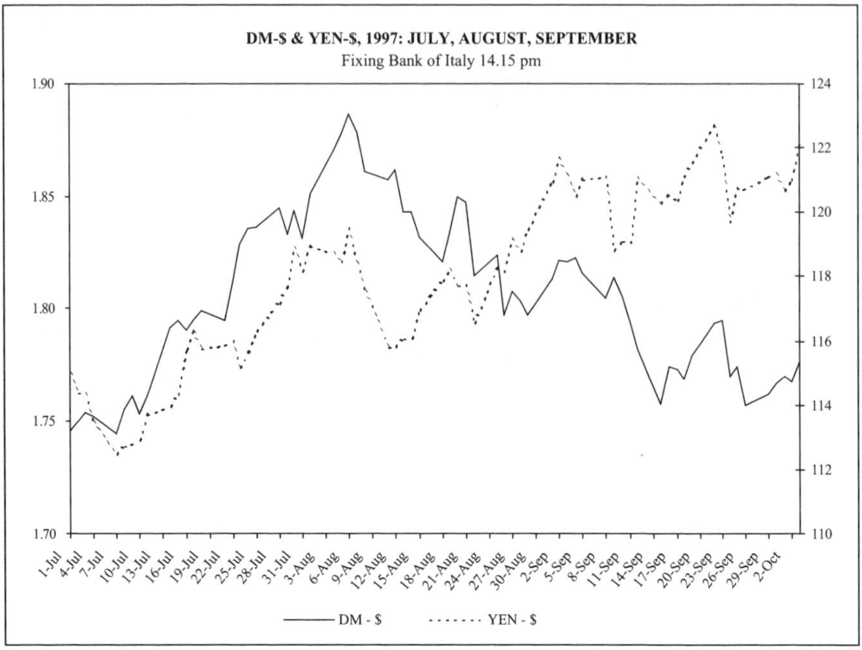

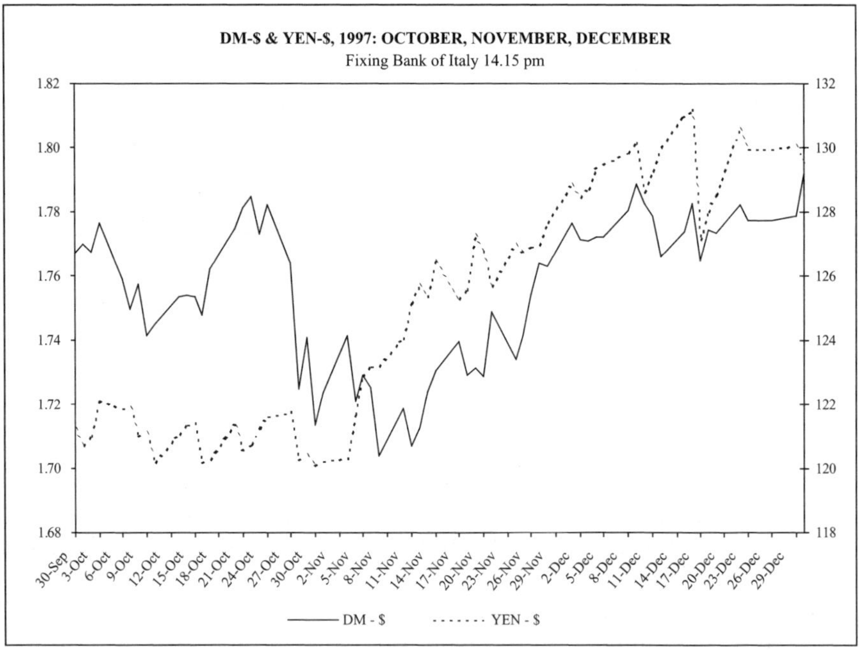

Figure 2.6 DM-$ & Yen-$, 1997: July, August, September – October, November, December

4091), compared to the German unemployment record announced on Wednesday 6 (4110, 4112).

In the meantime, on Thursday, 24 July the Bundesbank interrupted its regular twice-weekly meetings; the Deutschmark is protected only by the repo rate and the statements of those Council members who are active during recess. Indeed Jochimsen and Zeitler speak on Friday, 25 July, in order to generate some doubts as to the direction of the German exchange rate (4053, 4054).

As mentioned earlier, the Dollar flexes after 6 August. See Figure 2.5, lower panel.

The recovery of the Deutschmark may have been influenced both by the summer recess and by the vigilance and fears of Bundesbank interventions, which leaves rates unchanged when it fixes the repo on Tuesday, 12 (4130) and Tuesday, 19 August (4159). At its first post-recess meeting on Thursday, 21 August the German Central Bank hints that interest rates could go up (4178, 4179), also because the weakening of the Deutschmark in the first half of 1997 has created renewed inflation, with a record increase for July (4131). The fear of a new inflation wave in Germany seems a convincing argument in favor of a revaluation of the Deutschmark.

The Deutschmark may also have been influenced by the primarily domestic political debate in Germany regarding the future of EMU and the strong stance on the part of several Christian Democrat representatives regarding the need to avoid launching a weak Euro (for instance Stoiber on 14 August, 4142), invariably opposed by Chancellor Kohl (for instance on 17 August, 4153).

In this period there is also a strange call for a government reshuffle coming from Minister of Finance Weigel, on Thursday, 14 August (4145), repeated on Sunday, 24 August (4190), strongly opposed by Kohl (Monday 25, 4191) and then abandoned (on 31 August, 4242) to give way to a much publicized reconciliation between the two (Friday, 5 September, 4279). The political mini-crisis between Kohl and Weigel does not, however, appear as the specific cause for the recovery of the Deutschmark.

At the beginning of September the German economy shows contradicting signs, of recovery in industrial production (Wednesday, 3 September, 4269) and GDP (Wednesday, 10 September, 4303), and of stagnation in the job market (Tuesday, 9 September, 4299). But the markets polarize their attention on the wholesale price index results, announced on Monday, 15 September (4340), which, at 3.3% on an annual basis, are 0.6 percentage points higher than expected. Between these two dates the Deutschmark recovers approximately 5 pfennings, on fears that the Bundesbank, forced by renewed domestic inflation, may increase interest rates (4304, 4312, 4326). See Figure 2.6, upper panel.

The topic of renewed inflation is quite hot in Germany from the middle of August, when the highest consumer price increase since 1995 is announced (4131). In addition, it is hard to implement monetary restrictions, given the still high unemployment levels in Germany as well as the Maastricht constraints that do not allow any fiscal policy relief.

It therefore comes as no surprise that, in the first three weeks of September, several contradicting statements are forthcoming from some ten Bundesbank members: Sievert starts on Tuesday, 2 September (4259, against an interest rate increase), followed by Tietmeyer (4265, in favor), Welteke (4297, against), Jochimsen (4298, against), Zeitler (4308, in favor), Issing (4315, in favor), Krupp (4316, against), Koebnick (4327, against), Tietmeyer (4342 and 4343, in favor) and lastly Welteke (4370, in favor) on Wednesday, 17 September. With what result? Utmost uncertainty: five members in favor and five members against. The net result, in any case, is a strengthening of the Deutschmark, probably because of the underlying macroeconomic fundamentals, including the US'.

There is a brief strengthening of the Dollar, caused by the announcements of four members of the Bundesbank Monetary Council regarding a possible stability in the German interest rates, on Monday, 22 September (Koebnick, Kuehbacher, Issing and Meister, 4401, 4402), as well as the contents of the official communiqué of the G7 meeting in Hong Kong over the weekend of 20-21 September, which does not mention any limits to the revaluation of the US currency (4393, 4400). Thus on Wednesday, 24 September, Tietmeyer and Sakakibara decide to intervene in order to stop a new "take off" of the Dollar (4419, 4420). Figure 2.6, upper panel.

The Fourth Quarter

Towards the end of September the first symptoms of an unexpected political crisis in Italy begin to appear. On this opportunity, as on preceding ones, the Deutschmark appreciates partly as a result of the weaker Lira. The strengthening of the Deutschmark is also caused by market concerns regarding the final launch of EMU. The probability of Italy's inclusion have increased significantly during the course of 1997, because of the spectacular improvement in the country's public accounts, the clumsy German attempt at "fixing" its own public accounts – with the revaluation of the Bundesbank's gold reserves – and the victory of the Left in the French elections.

Unlike previous occasions, this time the strengthening of the Deutschmark is modest and short-lived, ending on Thursday, 9 October with a German Central Bank increase of the repo of 0.30 percentage points, as a reaction to the increasing domestic inflationary pressures, created in turn by the by now considerable weakening of the Deutschmark since November 1996 (4531). The following day the Italian crisis is resolved (4537) and the markets move towards the view that the recent Bundesbank repo rate increase is the last one for some time to come (4542), given Germany's domestic economic situation and in particular the critical conditions of the job market (see the most recent news: 4502, 4509, 4511). Thus the Deutschmark weakens again against the Dollar (Figure 2.6, lower panel).

This weakening accelerates significantly from Friday, 17 October when strong US economic figures are published (4598, 4600). This time the depreciation of the Deutschmark is "helped" the same day by statements from Tietmeyer ("the Dollar is a strong currency", 4601) and from Kuehbacher ("interest rates will not rise", 4602). In this phase the peak point occurs on Wednesday 22, after a significant reduction in the German money supply on Tuesday, 21 October (4618, 4619), underscored by a favorable comment by Tietmeyer (4620).

The Asian crisis begun in early July with speculative attacks on the Thai baht, spreads – both in geographic terms and in the intensity of the speculative moves of the following two months – reaching even Hong Kong. Here, after a few weeks of fluctuation, the stock exchange plunges 10% on Thursday, 23 October (4636) transmitting turmoil to the foreign currency markets and to all the other securities markets (4639). Although Hong Kong rebounds the following day (4642), American traders consolidate their concerns regarding the impact of a Far Eastern recession on the US semi-conductors computers sector (4645), leading to a 554-point drop in Wall Street on Monday, 27 October (4654, 4655, 4656, 4657). The US stock exchange then gains back 337 points the following day, reducing the fluctuation range, helped by Greenspan's reassuring intervention on Wednesday, 29 October (4673, 4684, 4685, 4686). But this is the beginning of a turbulent period for the international stock exchanges that causes a strong drop in the Dollar and marked fluctuations perfectly in tune with the stock exchange news, until approximately Friday, 7 November. See Figure 2.6, lower panel.

After appreciating by approximately 8 pfennings, following the turmoil in the international stock exchanges, the Deutschmark – which is now some twenty pfennings below the year's high – seems to be in an ideal position to stimulate the intervention of Buba's "heavy artillery", always ready for action when the German currency experiences a long period of appreciation or depreciation. From Thursday 13 to Thursday, 27 November Kuehbacher (4818), Tietmeyer (4829), Issing (4869), Koebnick (4856), Zeitler (4882), Palm (4938) and Meister (4953) periodically communicate to the markets that the German interest rates will remain stable, thus favoring the Dollar. In this particular international economic situation, moreover, the markets have welcomed the message of interest rate stability, and consequently there is a slight depreciation of the Deutschmark.

The year 1997 closes with a renewed period of turmoil originating in Asia, in the first half of December, particularly because of the Korean events (see various entries in the database) and the good news on the German inflation on Monday 22, determined by the decrease in raw material prices which softens the impact of the Deutschmark's depreciation (5116, 5119). The good performance of Wall Street in the period from Christmas to the end of the year, together with Tietmeyer's optimistic statements regarding the German interest rates on Wednesday 31 (5165), determines a year-end rally for the American currency. See Figure 2.6, lower panel.

2.4 The Lira During the Berlusconi Government: March-December 1994

The Second Quarter

The elections of Sunday, 28 March, 1994 are the first ones under a new electoral law that, unlike the previous one, tends to reward electoral rather than parliamentary coalitions, with a view to creating a two-party political dynamics. The parties' leaders thus find themselves working within a new framework.

The period under study therefore lends itself to an analysis of the impact of political rumours on the financial market dynamics since, on the one hand, the relationship between the Government and Parliament is still on new ground, and on the other hand the financial markets' interpretation of political events is still uncertain and in evolution.

In the days immediately following the electoral consultation the Lira shows a predictably positive reaction to the electoral victory of the Polo (1, 3, 10, 14): between Monday, 29 March and Friday, 1 April it gains approximately 17 points on the Deutschmark, with a basically stable Dollar, and it ignores two adverse news items regarding public finances (9, 15), which will later have a significant impact on the exchange rate. See Figure 2.7, upper panel.

Monday, 4 April confirms the first indications – perceived the previous week – of a cooling in the negotiations within the Polo, in preparation for the meeting with Scalfaro to form the Government, with the first clash between Bossi and Berlusconi (23, 25, 28). The Lira remains stable for a few days – but weakening relative to the Deutschmark-Dollar trend – and then continues its revaluation process when the negotiations climate improves after Gianfranco Fini's intervention, between Thursday 7 and Friday 8 (29, 31).

On Saturday, 16 April the presidents of the two houses of Parliament are elected – Irene Pivetti (Lega) for the Lower House and Carlo Scognamiglio (Forza Italia) for the Senate. This takes place amid some tension, since the simultaneous election of two members of the same coalition to the presidencies of the Lower House and the Senate goes against a deeply-rooted parliamentary tradition, not specified in the constitution but observed in practice, of conceding one presidency to the opposition (34, 37, 16).

This is fundamentally a positive period for the Lira, which goes from 980.92 to 955.88 against the Deutschmark, after reaching a minimum of 948.85, for a total appreciation of 3.84%. In the same period the Dollar appreciates against the Deutschmark by 2.94%. This ratio indicates that, on

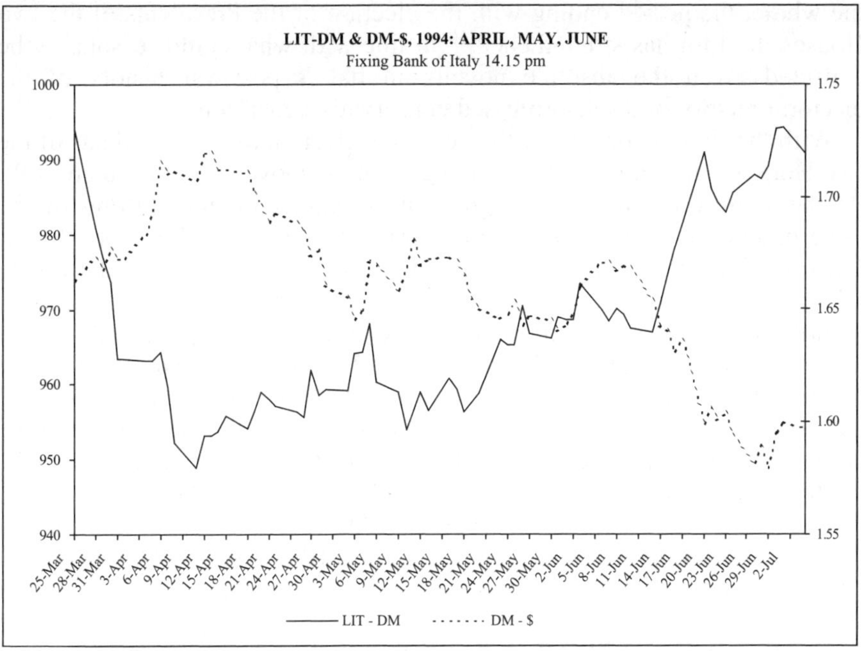

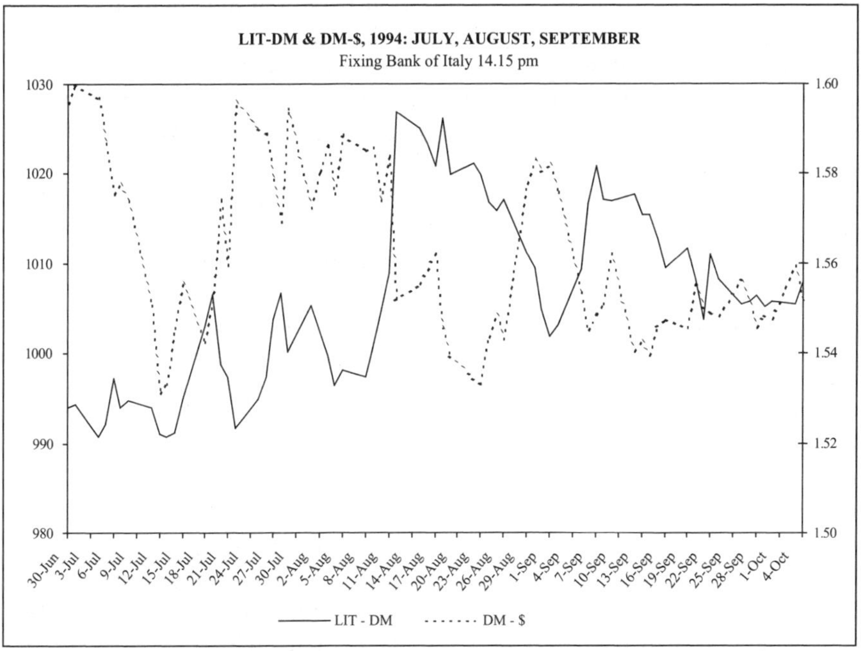

Figure 2.7 LIT-DM & DM-$, 1994: April, May, June – July, August, September

the whole, the period ending with the election of the Presidents of the two Houses the Lira has strengthened,[10] in line with what could reasonably be expected given the absolute novelty in Italy's post-war history of the electoral victory of a self-professed conservative coalition.

With the first victory under the belt – the election of the Presidents of the two Houses – the Polo continues to develop the Government program (49). At the same time there are ongoing negotiations for the staffing of the government, after the important ceremony charging the Hon. Silvio Berlusconi with forming the government on Thursday, 28 April (68), to which the markets react favorably, even though it cannot be considered at all an unexpected event (i.e. a news item). See Figure 2.7, upper panel.

This negotiation phase abounds in conflict between Lega Nord leader Bossi and Polo leader Berlusconi, as was to be expected (55, 70, 80, 83, 85, 89). The markets do not seem unduly concerned since the devaluation of the Dollar does not produce a parallel devaluation of the Lira, which on the contrary appreciates slightly between 16 April and the birth of the Berlusconi Government, on Tuesday, 10 May (91), (-2.51% compared to -0.19%), assisted by positive inflation figures (the final ISTAT report of 3 May, 78) and by a favorable announcement regarding the public finances, on 29 April (71). See Figure 2.7, upper panel.

On Wednesday, 11 May (94), the Bank of Italy cuts the discount rate as a result of the good situation on the inflation front and the creation of a new government that promises political stability in the new Italian electoral context. The first doubts regarding this scenario of stability begin to arise in this period, as evidenced by the increased relative weakness – between 10 May and 3 June – of the Lira (2.04%) relative to that of the Dollar (-0.50%) against the Deutschmark.

The most salient events in this period are the slender majority in the vote of confidence in the Senate on Wednesday, 18 May (102) – where four PPI dissidents and the senators for life play a key role – and the heavy defeat of the Polo coalition in the vote for the presidencies of the Senate commissions between Wednesday, 1 June and Friday, 3 (127, 130). During this period the Lira devalues heavily, as the major financial commentators, internally but especially internationally, see at close range how precarious the Polo's parliamentary majority is.

On Friday, 10 June (147) there is the first news on an expected but punishing sentence of the Court on pension payments that were due but had not been paid by the Treasury. The sentence contemplates the reimbursement on the part of INPS (Istituto Nazionale della Previdenza Sociale – or Social Security) to some of its registered members of an amount between 7,000 and 30,000 billion Lire, according to the various calculations of the Court itself and of the Ministry of Labour (149, 155). The markets clearly do not appreciate the news and penalize Italian assets (152, 158). The reaction to the Polo's victory in the European elections on Sunday, 12 June, on the other hand, is highly positive (150). See Figure 2.7, upper panel.

Spurred by the INPS episode, the Government announces a corrective measure (163, 165, 169) that is favorably received by the markets but is later abandoned (171, 174). The Dollar continues its downward trend, losing 2.57% in a week, between Monday, 20 June and Friday 24, while the Lira remains strong enough, at +0.40%, in the same period.

From Thursday, 30 June to Friday, 1 July (187, 193, 212) the first episode of institutional conflict – captured by *Newsmetrics* – between the Premier and the President of the Republic occurs, with a relative weakening of the Lira when Scalfaro imposes some modifications to the order of the executive to dissolve the RAI's Board of Directors.

The Third Quarter

On Monday, 4 July, the drop of inflation to its lowest levels in the last twenty-five years and the positive conclusion of the metal workers' labour contract (196, 197, 204), in line with the scheduled inflation and without strikes, cause a strong rebound of the Lira. See Figure 2.7, lower panel.

On Tuesday, 5 July Minister Biondi proposes to the cabinet (198, 226), among disagreements also within Forza Italia, radical reforms of the criminal law, in the form of a simple ministerial decree. His presentation generates an avalanche of criticisms, producing the resignations of some leading judges of the Mani Pulite Investigative team on Thursday, 14 July, 222 (presented but not confirmed) and of Lega Minister of the Interior Maroni (threatened but not presented) on Saturday, 16 July (228). The decree is later passed, with substantial changes, on Tuesday, 19 July (233).

This is the first political-institutional episode that has the effect of an earthquake in the financial markets, because of the rupture within the majority and the additional animosity in the accompanying political debate. The Lira experiences a substantial depreciation, corresponding to a revaluation of the Dollar, contrary to the empirical regularity of this period. See Figure 2.7, lower panel.

The launch of the Decreto di Programmazione Economica e Finanziaria (or DPEF – Economic and Financial Planning Document) for 1995, while favorably received by the markets on Thursday, 21 July (238), gives way to particularly animated and controversial episodes in the period immediately preceding the August recess: those related to the bribes to the Guardia di Finanza (Tax-Police), involving also Paolo Berlusconi, brother to the Premier (between Tuesday, 26 July and Thursday 28, 249, 254); those regarding television publicity spots illustrating the measures taken by the Government in flattering tones; those related to the Fininvest proposal to resolve the issue of Premier Berlusconi's conflict of interests (256, 258, 263, 265), between Saturday, 30 July and Wednesday 3. All of this leads to a series of accusations and insults among the major leaders of the Polo (between Monday, 8 August and Wednesday 10, 274, 275, 279, 286) that generates serious repercussions in the financial markets, causing the Bank of

Italy to intervene with a raise in the discount rate on Thursday, 11 August (278). For its part, the Dollar weakens against the Deutschmark by -1.41%, but the Lira doubles in the same direction, +2.80%.

After such a convulsive period, nothing remarkable happens during the traditional summer recess. In this period, the Dollar strengthens by 1.83% against the Deutschmark and the Lira does the same more than proportionately, by -2.14%.

Then, from Saturday, 3 September to Wednesday 7 (321,324, 325, 326) a scuffle erupts between Minister Biondi and the Mani Pulite investigative team following the unexpected participation of Assistant Public Prosecutor Di Pietro to the traditional catch-all seminar of Studio Ambrosetti in early September, with statements that, objectively, look quite harmless. The Lira records two instances of weaknesses on 6 and 7 September for reasons that may be traced back to the currency traders, uncomfortable with the events relating to the administration of justice, which, while not having a direct impact on the financial markets, are a manifestation of a lingering uncomfortable political-institutional situation, harbinger of political instability, with the consequent increase in interest rates in a country with a substantial public debt.

The Di Pietro-Biondi episode is followed by the period of greatest activity for the preparation of the Budget, during which the Lira strengthens: in the face of a stable Dollar, the Lira strengthens against the Deutschmark by 1.47%.

Remarkable events in this period include: (a) a parliamentary debate in Commission on RAI, which witnesses the creation of a Lega-PDS axis against the new RAI Board of Directors appointed by the government, foreshadowing the future governmental alliance after the year-end government overturn (337, 369), and (b) the first confrontation between the government and the unions regarding the pensions reform to be included in the Budget, greatly opposed by trade unions (343, 350, 353, 355). With the opening of the RAI debate, the Lira weakens against the Deutschmark in relative terms, as was to be expected, especially because of the emergence of a new parliamentary (albeit in Commission) majority, frequently feared in the previous months, while on the contrary it strengthens – always in relative terms and always in accordance to the psychology of the markets – when there are news of a fracture between the Government and the unions on pensions. See Figure 2.7, lower panel.

The presentation of the Budget brings the third quarter to a close, offering a new opportunity for friction between Premier Berlusconi and President Scalfaro. On Saturday, 1 October (361, 370) the latter asks that the pensions reform be eliminated from the Budget because it refers to a structural reform that transcends the financial scope of the Budget. The Lira weakens as a consequence.

The Fourth Quarter

The month of October begins with bitter conflict following an interview to Mani Pulite Chief Prosecutor Borrelli, on Wednesday, 5 October (368), on the problems of the judicial system, with an implicit criticism to Minister of Justice Biondi (in his past role as criminal lawyer). As a protest, Minister Biondi presents his resignation the next day. The episode causes a weakening of the Lira between Wednesday 5 and Monday, 10 October, when the situation is somehow patched up (374, 379). See Figure 2.8.

On Monday, 17 October (388), Biondi orders a ministerial inspection to the Milan Attorney's Office. This, unlike the previous episode, does not appear to have any consequences for the Lira even though it is the opening scene of the incredible "judiciary soap" of the Mancuso case in the spring of 1995.

In this period of parliamentary approval of the Budget, there is an intensification of the institutional problems related to the Government's political action and its interpretation of the boundaries between discretionary administrative action and the limitations provided by the Constitution and by law.

Such institutional problems are manifest in the long and troubled course – at least relative to previous experiences – that between Wednesday, 19 October and Friday, 4 November (394, 397, 418) leads to the government's ratification of the Bank of Italy's appointment of Dr. Vincenzo Desario as Director General of the Institute, viewed with a certain apprehension by the markets, as indicated by the anomalous weakness of the Lira on 19 October, Monday 31 and 4 November.[11] See Figure 2.8.

The case leading to the appointment of two Italian Commissioners to the EEC (Mario Monti and Emma Bonino) is probably of a similar nature. The appointment is not the joint expression of the will of the majority and the opposition, but the direct designation by the Premier's party, in disagreement with Lega Nord, on Friday, 28 October (407). The markets are troubled by this episode, primarily because of the deep fracture created within the majority, which will eventually result in the Lega's withdrawing of its support from the Berlusconi Government.

As mentioned above, it is well known that the coalition supporting the Berlusconi Government was elected with a different electoral procedure compared to previous republican legislatures, the so-called majority system. This new situation induces the Premier and authoritative representatives of both the Government and the majority to repeatedly vindicate the right to take charge of all the political and administrative aspects of public management.

A first shining example of this institutional interpretation is given by the April election of persons indicated by the governing coalition to the presidencies of both Parliamentary houses, against the usual practice of conceding one to the opposition parties; a second example is given by the appointment of a new Board of Directors and a new President for RAI; a third, equally remarkable example is given by the role of the Executive in the appointment of the Directors of the Bank of Italy – a body that in the Italian institutional context and in most industrialised countries is independent from the government – when Director General Lamberto Dini, new Minister of the Treasury since May 1994, must be replaced.

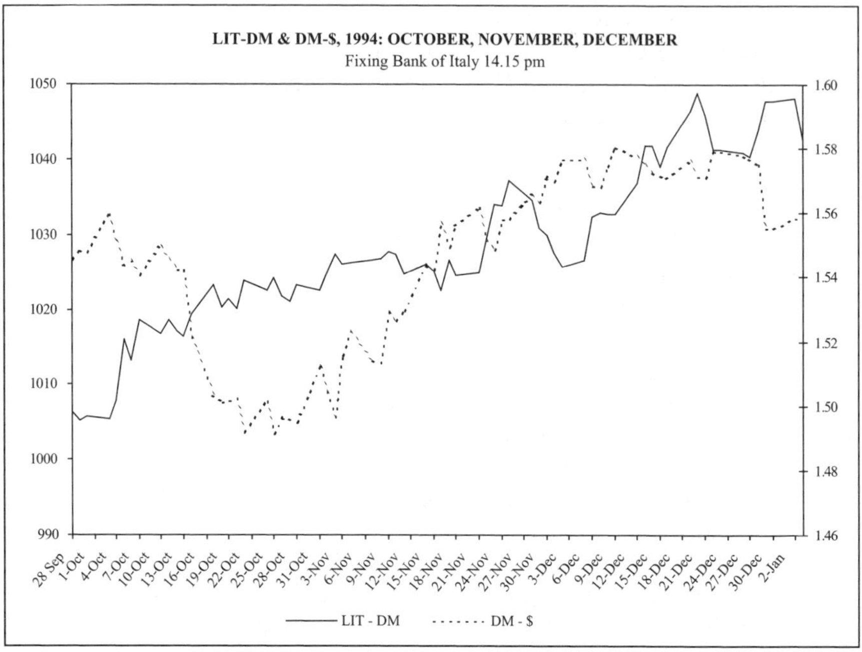

Figure 2.8 LIT-DM & DM-$, 1994: October, November, December

It is therefore not surprising that at the end of so many convulsions the Lira devalues proportionately more than the Dollar: 2.02% compared to -1.60% between 3 October and 4 November.

The disastrous floods in the north (423, 424, 425) weaken the Lira, as is to be expected given the fragility of the public accounts, especially on Wednesday, 9 November.

The municipal elections of 20 November (443) indicate an advancement for AN in the North at the expense of Lega and Forza Italia, causing a significant weakening of the Lira, not least because these are the first hints of possible crumbling of political alliances, as it will indeed happen a few weeks later. However, the great "bomb" in this period is the writ of summons to Berlusconi, the first one to a Premier in office in the history of the republic, to which the Lira responds with a drastic weakening on Wednesday and Thursday, 23-24 November (448, 452). On Friday 25 the Constitutional Court emits a sentence considering the concentration of three television channels in the hands of a single owner excessive (456). This too weakens the Lira. See Figure 2.8.

December sees an acceleration of the process leading to the fall of the Berlusconi Government. On Tuesday, 13 December the Premier is questioned by the Court (485). Then, from Wednesday 14 to Friday 16 (488, 491, 495), there follows a series of intense consultations and negotiations among PDS, PPI and Lega culminating on Saturday 17 with the drafting of three motions of no confidence (498, 499), which in turn lead – after the approval of the 1995 Budget on Wednesday 21 (501) – to Berlusconi's resignation on Thursday, 22 December (504). See Figure 2.8.

2.5 The Lira During the Dini Government in 1995

The First Quarter

The Berlusconi Government crisis begins on Friday, 23 December, 1994, followed by the traditional consultation period of the Head of State, matched by a foreseeable hyper-turmoil of the Lira. On the afternoon of Friday, 13 July (560) – after the exchange rates used in this analysis are recorded by the Bank of Italy – President Scalfaro asks Dr. Dini to form a technical government. New York Bankers Trust data, taken at 9 p.m. Italian time, shows a strong revaluation of the Lira.

On Monday, 16 July the Lira revalues by 1.3% relative to the previous Friday, amidst euphoria in the financial markets. Although the appointment of Dr. Dini as President of the Council is done with the approval of the Polo delle Libertà, and although the new Government includes members approved by the Polo, the Berlusconi coalition maintains a wavering attitude both during the casting of the vote of confidence in Parliament and particularly during the approval of the traditional second mid-year public accounts corrective measure. The support of PPI, PDS and Lega is more compact. The vote of confidence is finally passed on Wednesday, 1 February (618).

From the beginning the Dini government has the mandate to implement a precise program, with the commitment to resign as soon as it is completed. Its main task is to implement three main measures: the immediate launch of a public accounts adjustment measure, the so called "second corrective measure" of public finance; the reform of the pension system, to be approved during the summer; and the preparation of the 1996 Budget, to be completed within the timeframe established by law.

The vote of confidence on Wednesday, 1 February, is preceded by a sharp confrontation – between Wednesday, 25 July and Monday 30 – between Polo and Scalfaro over a supposed commitment of the President to call for

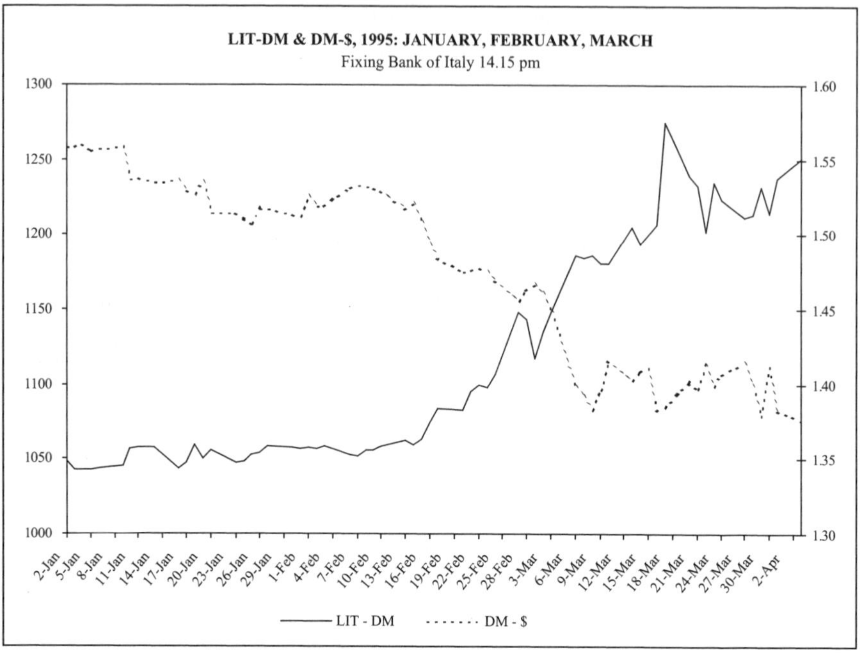

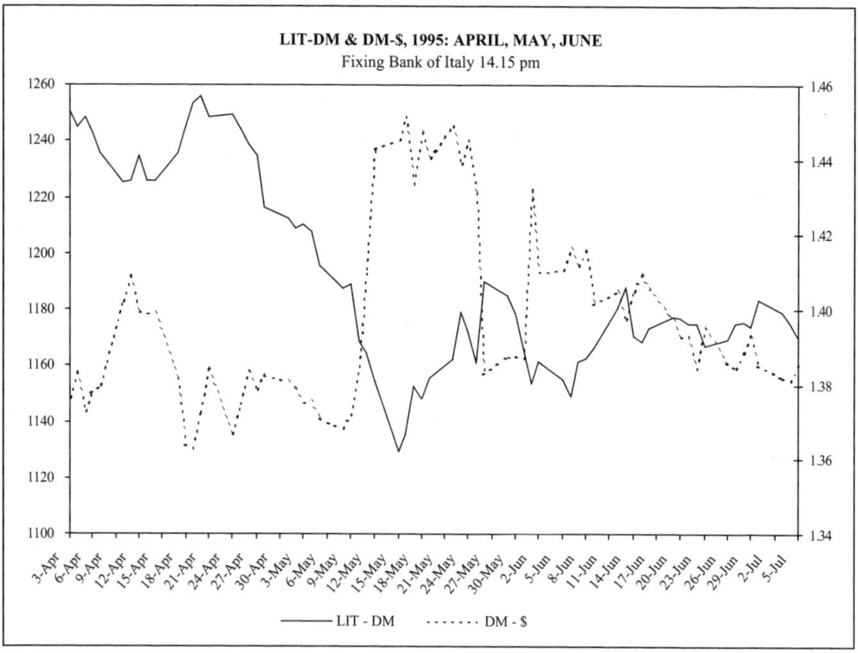

Figure 2.9 LIT-DM & DM-$, 1995: January, February, March – April, May, June

elections even before Dini completes the three main tasks assigned to him, and therefore quite soon (595, 601, 610). As the vote of confidence for the Dini government has not yet been cast, the financial markets react to this conflict with great nervousness (688), Figure 2.9, upper panel.

In early February the Dollar begins to collapse, dragging the Lira down with it. Thus the Lira becomes the target of both international and domestic turmoil (656, 660). See also Figure 2.1. But worse is still to come.

Immediately after the vote of confidence and until the beginning of the discussion of public finances measures in Parliament on Wednesday, 22 February, the Government prepares – taking longer than expected by the markets – the anticipated "second corrective measure", rendered necessary by the unexpected increase in interest rates in the second half of 1994, caused in turn by the political agitation developed within the Berlusconi Government, especially after the beginning of August. The Polo rejects the proposal (673) but indicates a propensity for abstention (678), which will be withdrawn later causing wild fluctuations in the exchange rate.

On Friday, 17 February there is a significant exchange over the second corrective measure among Hon. Gasparri (AN) and Hon. Visco (PDS, 661), which coincides with the first sharp slide of the Lira (Figure 2.9, upper panel), which fully reveals the psychological and political consequences for the Polo of the sudden passage of the government to the opposition and market fears regarding a still precarious political scenario. Gasparri says "The corrective measure? Good luck to those who vote it", given the toughness and unpopularity of its measures to contain the public accounts. Visco replies he does not believe the PDS should be made responsible for the unpopularity of measures that were made necessary by the political turmoil of the Berlusconi Government (*Il Sole XXIV Ore*, Saturday, 18 February).

The Dollar drops further as of the second half of February, as we have seen in the reconstruction of international events. During the period of the preparation of the corrective measure the Lira devalues far more than the Dollar, but still not as much as during the episodes of political and financial turmoil characterising the next phases of parliamentary approval for the second corrective measure. On Tuesday, 21 February, consumer prices in the sample cities reveal a strong and unexpected inflationary growth for the month of February (670). Immediately thereafter the Bank of Italy increases the discount rate (669), and the markets react with a downward pressure on the Lira. See Figure 2.9, upper panel.

As we have already seen, an increase in the discount market rates can exert a double effect on the exchange rate. This can be observed immediately if the markets value primarily the central bank's anti-inflationary inclination, and the trend can continue if at that time the exchange is governed by a Mundell-Fleming logic. Alternatively, in a situation of heavy public indebtedness such as Italy's, the markets translate the interest rate increase into a greater interest burden on the public debt and fear for the country's financial stability. Hence a sale of Lira-based activities and a weakening of the exchange.

On Monday, 27 February the increase in the basic prices by 5.4% on an annual basis for the month of December 1994 (691, 693) confirms the effects of the weakening Lira in 1994, foreshadowing a persistence of the phenomenon also in 1995. In this period there is a division within the Partito Popolare Italiano (629, 685, 720, 738, 744, 759) – one of the parties supporting the Dini government – and there are continuing differences, between Friday, 24 February and Tuesday 28 (686, 689, 694, 698), between the Presidency and Polo members, which in the past had already been responsible for instances of weakening of the Lira: all these events continue to depress the Lira. See Figure 2.9, upper panel.

Having announced its abstention on the second corrective measure on Thursday, 23 February (678), and having confirmed its willingness to support the corrective measure, at least indirectly, on Wednesday, 1 March (695, 698), the Polo changes its attitude between Thursday 2 and Friday, 3 March (709) with a cumulative loss on the Lira for the two days of approximately 2.70%, while the Dollar devalues by only 1.18%. The Senate – where the Dini Government is more self-sufficient – then approves the corrective measure on Tuesday, 7 March (716).

At the same time the Dollar is undergoing a crisis of its own, despite central bank interventions on 2, 3 and 8 March (707, 713, 722) and supporting verbal interventions on both sides of the Atlantic on 8 and 9 March (723, 724, 727, 728), thus dragging down the Lira, which between end of February and beginning of March devalues much more than the Dollar. See Figure 2.9, upper panel.

After two defeats in the Lower House on the second corrective measure, the Government is forced to call for a vote of confidence, with the concomitant collapse of the Lira, on Wednesday, 15 March (745). The vote of confidence and the approval for the corrective measure obtained the following Thursday 16 (754) "by the skin of its teeth", do not resolve the situation with the financial markets: on Friday 17 the Lira devalues against the Deutschmark, for no apparent reason, by 5.6% in a few hours while the Dollar remains fairly stable (761). The corrective measure is then definitively approved by the Senate where it returns for a second vote on Tuesday 21 (765). Here the Government can count on a solid majority and therefore the Lira recovers, on Monday 20 (762, 764) and on Tuesday 21 (765), the absurd devaluation of Friday 17. See Figure 2.9, upper panel.

The Second Quarter

The period from the end of March to the end of April is fairly calm, with the Lira fluctuating at high levels – never under 1200 Lira against the Deutschmark – and devaluing slightly. On Thursday, 23 March the meetings over the pension system reform between the Government and the social parts (777, and references in 780, 820) and the campaign for regional elections begin, without undue disturbances.

The elections are held on Sunday, 23 April (879), resulting in a defeat for the Polo, to which the markets react favorably taking it as an indication that the Dini Government will now be able to implement the corrective measures entrusted to it by the President of the Republic and the Parliament, and that Polo pressures for new elections will now cease. See Figure 2.9, lower panel.

The proceedings – or rather the negotiations – on pensions enter their final phase on Thursday, 27 April (895) with meeting upon meeting (899, 907, 910, 913, 917, 923, 925), accompanied by the markets with positive jolts on the Lira, especially on Friday, 28 April and Friday, 5 May. Between 23 April and 8 May, during the initial phase of the negotiations, the Lira appreciates against the Deutschmark much more than the Dollar.

In this period – between Tuesday 9 and Monday, 15 May – we observe the first instances of the muffled conflict between Minister of Justice Mancuso and the Mani Pulite investigative team (926, 937, 946, 951), the latter supported by the Dini Government majority, which includes Minister Mancuso in its folds. Consequently, this person's actions generate an understandable discomfort within the majority. The problems of the administration of justice have already created serious ruptures and much uncertainty in the markets during the Berlusconi Government. The disagreements caused by Minister Mancuso and by several related episodes of small-scale market turmoil will continue sporadically (1021, 1026, 1076, 1082, 1087, 1091, 1105), until the final expulsion of the Minister on Friday, 20 October at the end of a violent showdown between the majority and the opposition. The rally of the Lira ends on 15 May, and may probably be traced back to the markets' uneasiness with this renewed judicial unrest, considered the preface to political turmoil.

From Tuesday, 16 May – end of the negotiations on pension reform and handing in of the bill to Parliament (953, 958) – to June – the day of the referendum on the televisions – there are intense negotiations in Italy to avoid the referendum on the concentrated ownership of several television channels in the hands of a single person (Berlusconi in this case) and on the limitations to ownership in the communication sector, with committed participation of the political forces (962, 967, 969). The markets react negatively to the victory of the Polo, reading it as a further push towards a fracture in the already fragile parliamentary balances, and the Lira devalues. The ill feelings generated by Minister Mancuso's initiatives persist, with some episodes on Wednesday, 7 June (1021, 1026). On Friday, 26 May (985) the Bank of Italy raises the discount rate again, in response to ever more alarming inflation figures (971, 973). See Figure 2.9, lower panel.

A remarkably successful appearance in Wall Street of Premier Dini among American traders on Monday, 19 June (1050) stabilises the exchange rate over the following days, Figure 2.17. The next day, Tuesday, 20 June, marks the beginning of a period of contact and negotiation among the political forces of the majority and the opposition over the so-called playing rules ("*il tavolo delle regole*") that leads to some visible result as early as Friday, 30 June and then again between Tuesday 4 and Thursday, 6 July (1056, 1091, 1095, 1101, 1113). Also this event allows the Lira to remain stable. See Figure 2.9, lower panel.

The Third Quarter

Between Monday 26 and Thursday, 29 June (1076, 1078, 1082, 1087) and then again between Tuesday 4 and Thursday, 6 July there is a return to the agitation over judiciary matters tied to Mancuso, with the proposal of a no-confidence motion towards him initiated by the PDS on 29 June (1087). The Polo for its part vigorously defends the Minister's actions, creating confusion in the markets. The no-confidence vote is put on hold on Thursday, 6 (1105) by Dini and D'Alema so as not to disturb the approval of the pensions reform (1086, 1092, 1094, 1100, 1104).

The end of June to the beginning of August is a period of definite recovery for the Lira, which appreciates against the Deutschmark despite the stability of the latter relative to the Dollar. This period is primarily characterised by the long marathon towards pension reform, after the initial skirmishes (1086, 1092, 1094, 1100, 1104). It starts on Tuesday, 11 July (1124), it obtains a first approval in the Lower House with a comprehensive reform proposal on Friday 14 (1129, 1136) and is then finally approved in the second round by the same House on Thursday, 3 August (1149, 1160, 1165, 1178, 1182, 1200). The parliamentary course of pension reform is supported by a continuing series of good news on the public accounts (1127, 1155, 1209) and by inflation figures in the sample cities that are much more contained than the markets expected (1161, 1163, 1164). We thus have a long period of revaluation of the Lira, of almost 100 Lire per Deutschmark, from the beginning of July to the end of August, assisted towards the end of the period also by the Dollar. See Figure 2.10, upper panel.

The revaluation continues between 7 and 24 August, albeit with less intensity, due perhaps to a certain prudence on the part of traders after the upheaval of the recent past and in anticipation of the fight over the Budget during the fall, while the Dollar sets out on a path of strong revaluation caused by the G3 Central Banks (see paragraph 2.1). The series of political-journalistic initiatives (with their summery flavor, 1225, 1231, 1233, 1239, 1245), regarding the current and future political position of Premier Dini, whose popularity with the public opinion is on the ascent, certainly do not encourage the markets to launch initiatives on the Lira.

There is another moment of uncertainty for the Lira, between Saturday 26 and Tuesday 29, following a statement realised by D'Alema in an interview regarding the limits of the PDS's support to the Budget (1266, 1267, 1272). As in the earlier similar situation, between those two days the Lira devalues, while it should have moved in the opposite direction given the performance of the Deutschmark. See Figure 2.10, upper panel.

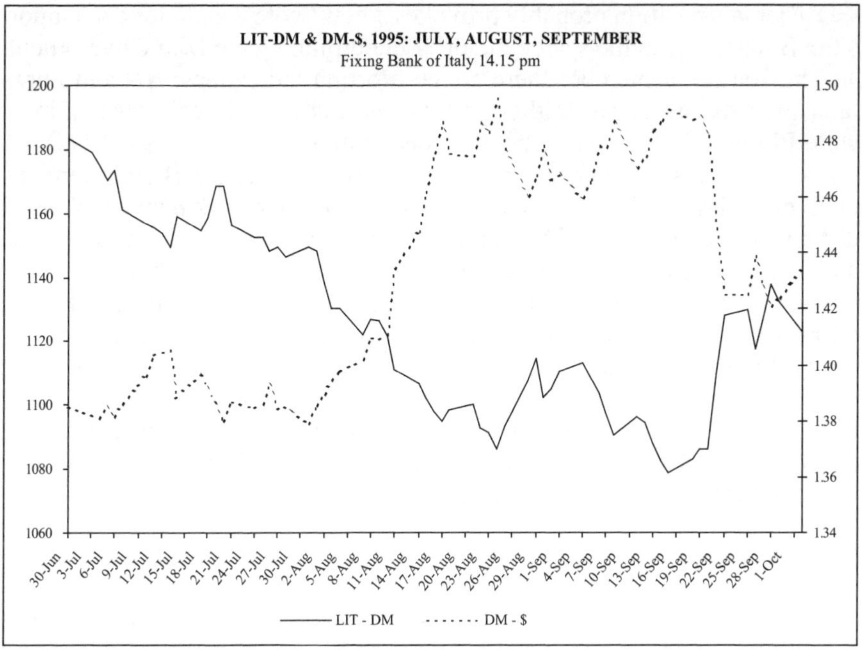

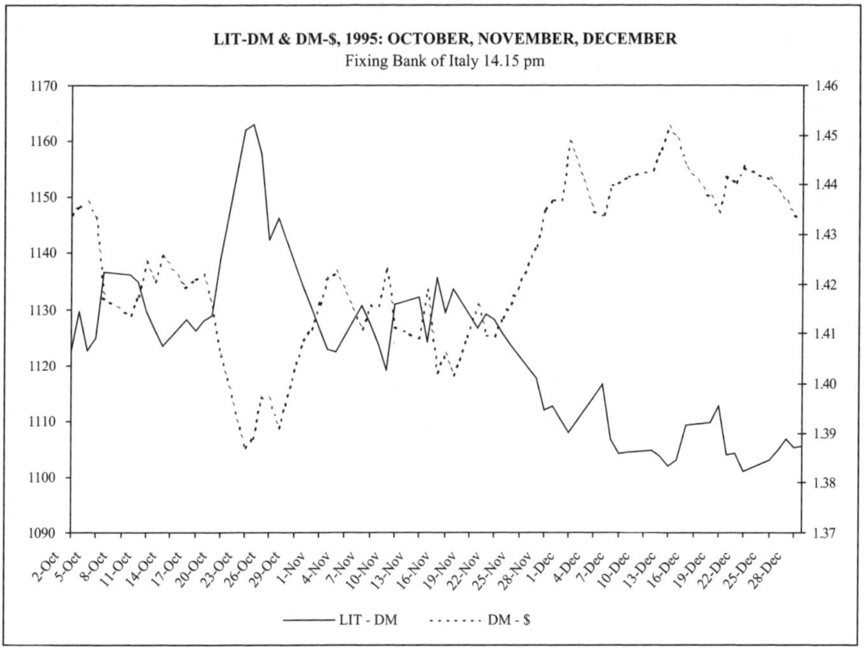

Figure 2.10 LIT-DM & DM-$, 1995: July, August, September – October, November, December

D'Alema's position probably provokes a new "vote count" for the support to the Budget, given the scarce majority underpinning the Dini Government. On Thursday, 7 September there are comforting indications: AN and Forza Italia give the go ahead, although they request a "political clarification", while PPI and PDS release a positive declaration of intent (1294, 1295).

Like the previous year, the period of preparation of the Budget remains relatively calm: the Lira devalues against the Deutschmark between the end of August and the end of September, in line with the devaluation of the Dollar. The obsessive debate over early elections resumes in this period, but as usual the markets do not pay much attention to it.[12] The period ends with the presentation of the Budget on Thursday, 28 September, which is not received with particular enthusiasm by the markets, causing a downturn in the exchange rate of one per cent in one day (1360). We have already discussed in the international section the devastating impact on the Lira of Minister Weigel's famous declarations of Thursday, 21 September (1332, see paragraph 2.1). See Figure 2.10, upper panel.

The Fourth Quarter

Between Wednesday, 18 October and Thursday 26 we can see the last act of the progressive distancing of the forces supporting the Dini Government from the measures of Minister of Justice Mancuso. As mentioned earlier, a first no-confidence motion towards Mancuso had been presented by the PDS in early July, and then put on hold on 6 July (1105) in order to allow a rapid approval of the pensions reform. The motion – on hold since then – is presented again and the discussion thereof is scheduled for Friday, 20 October. After a sharp confrontation between the majority and the opposition on Wednesday, 18 (1410), and on the same day scheduled for the discussion of the no-confidence motion (which is later approved, 1424), the Polo presents a no-confidence motion against Dini – who also seems to attract the interest of Rifondazione Comunista (1427). The markets obviously go crazy, as all of this takes place in the middle of the discussion of the Budget. Then, after the discussion on Tuesday and Wednesday 24-25 (1431, 1436), the no-confidence motion is rejected on Thursday 26 with the help of Rifondazione Comunista, which changes its mind at the end of a widely publicised meeting between Dini and Bertinotti (1442). Thus the Lira returns to the values where it was after the presentation of the Budget. See Figure 2.10, lower panel.

After the Mancuso crisis, the revaluation of the Lira resumes between the end of October and the end of November (-1.16% against a revaluation of the US currency of 0.90%), partly because of the positive effect of the successful conclusion of the first parliamentary review of the Budget, which takes place on Tuesday, 21 November (1504) in the Senate, with the decisive support of the Polo, made necessary by the sudden withdrawal of the senators of the Lega as a protest against the softness on the immigration decree, a decree this party had extorted a few days earlier with the threat of sabotaging the passing of the national budget act (1493).

The last part of 1995 is devoted to the final approval of the Budget in the Lower House, where the majority supporting the Dini Government is more uncertain, as demonstrated by two rejections in Commission on Wednesday, 29 November (1524). This situation forces the Government to continuously resort to the vote of confidence (1549, 1554, 1556, 1565). Two confidence motions pass, somewhat theatrically, on Monday, 18 December (1568). By the third time Dini gives up; the measures presented in the legislative text being challenged are then appropriated by the Lower House's Budget Commission (1574) and submitted to the assembly in its own name, and they are finally approved on Friday, 22 December (1587, 1590).

The final steps of the approval go against tradition and the markets are understandably nervous. The final approval of the withholding tax on government securities for non-residents, which occurred on Wednesday and Thursday, 6-7 December (1537, 1541), had resulted in a good rally of the Lira which had returned to a level of 1100 Lira against the Deutschmark, after having departed from it towards the end of September following Weigel's comments (1332) and the markets' uncertain reception of the Budget. The uncertainty generated by the process of approval of the Budget in the Lower House had further weakened the Lira. The relief at the end of the 1996 Budget odyssey is such that in December the Lira revalues against the Deutschmark by -2,08%, while the Dollar shows +1.68 against the same currency. See Figure 2.10, lower panel.

2.6 The Lira in 1996: Crisis of the Dini Government, beginning of the Prodi Government, re-entry into the ERM

The First Quarter

Having completed the government programme entrusted to him by President Scalfaro at the beginning of 1995 (i.e. additional corrective measures to the 1995 Budget, pensions reform and 1996 Budget), Dini offers his resignation on Friday, 29 December, 1995, confirming it on Friday, 12 January, 1996 (1654). In the intervening ten days an intense debate develops (1604, 1612, 1637, 1640) around the benefit of guaranteeing an incumbent and possibly stable government during the semester of the Italian presidency of the EU, but which substantially responds to more banal domestic political needs: early political elections and constitutional reforms, especially where the direct election of the Head of State and the powers attributed to it are concerned.

After confirming his resignation, Dini remains available to succeed himself, so that on Thursday, 18 July the press speaks of an almost certain reappointment (1675) – duly celebrated by the markets – but the candidacy

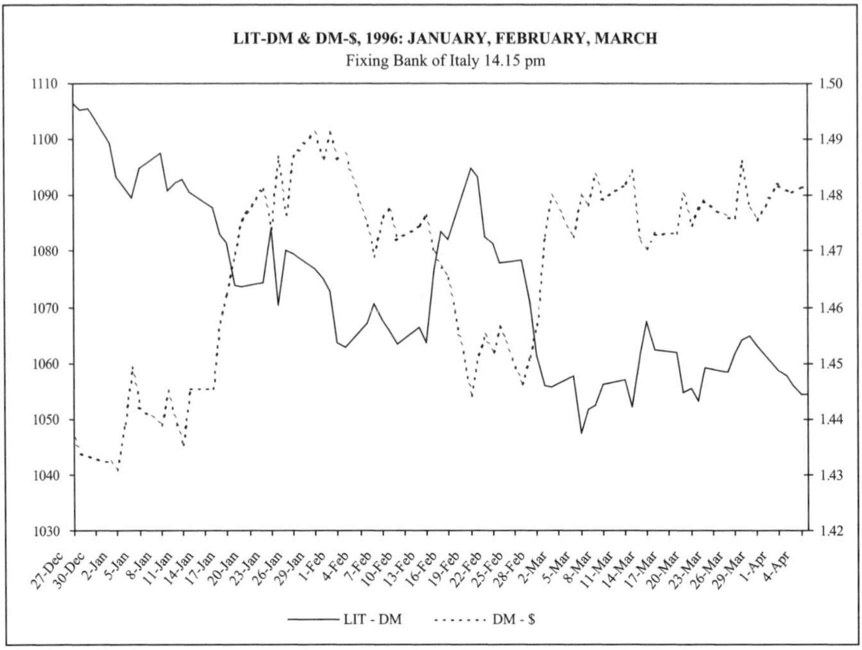

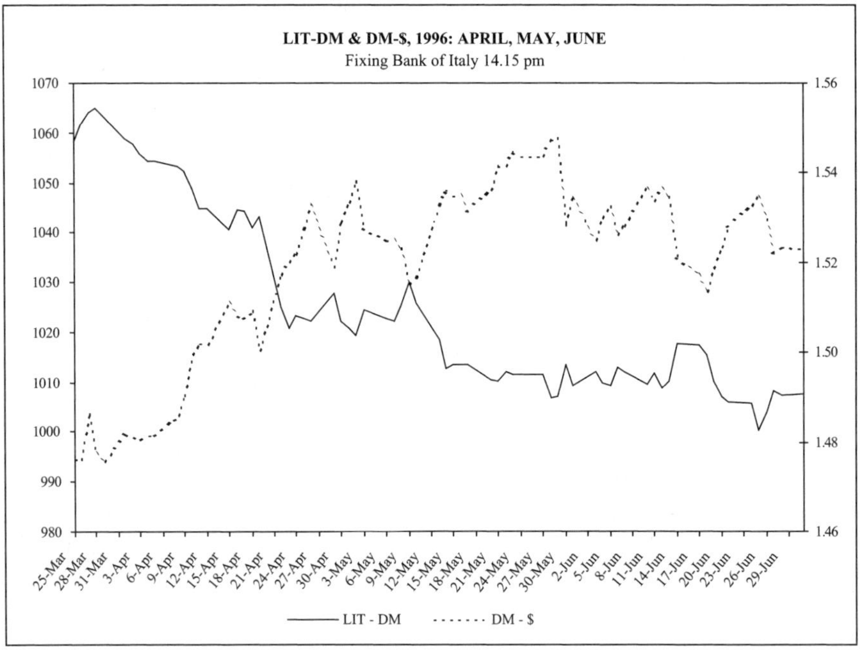

Figure 2.11 LIT-DM & DM-$, 1996: January, February, March – April, May, June

wanes on Saturday 20 and the following days due to the hostility of Alleanza Nazionale Secretary Fini, who in the end successfully imposes his point of view (1687, 1689). The Lira devalues significantly on the following Tuesday 23. See Figure 2.11, upper panel.

From the debate that follows (1712, 1723, 1736) a consensus emerges on the advantages of entrusting the Hon. Maccanico with an explorative mandate to form a new Government, with the primary objective of implementing a presidential reform in the Italian institutional system. The explorative mandate is formally given on Thursday, 1 February (1753); elements of crisis appear already on Monday 12 (1789), and the final resignation occurs on Wednesday 14 (1795, 1796). On Friday 16 (1803) Parliament is dissolved and new elections are called for Sunday, 21 April. In the late afternoon of Friday, 23 February, with the markets already closed, the retiring Premier Dini announces his candidacy to the leadership of the Ulivo (1831). The markets react very favorably to this news on the following Monday 26.

The Second Quarter

The Ulivo victory in the elections of Sunday, 21 April is welcomed by the markets on the following Monday 22. It should also be noted that the Dollar had been in a strengthening phase for some time, and therefore the revaluation of the Lira may be a result of this to some extent. Indeed, in the following days until approximately Tuesday, 7 May, the Lira remains basically stable, while the Dollar continues to appreciate. Probably after a more careful reading of the electoral result the markets realise that the Ulivo has not achieved a self-sufficient majority, requiring the votes of Rifondazione Comunista in the Lower House. See Figure 2.11, lower panel.

And this, as we shall see, will turn out to be a powerful constraint.

It should thus come as no surprise if, on the first instance of conflict between the majority and the opposition, with cross-vetoes on the presidencies of the Lower House and the Senate, the Lira weakens, on Tuesday and Wednesday, 7-8 May (2060, 2062, 2067). See Figure 2.11, lower panel.

After the cross-vetoes event, the Lira appreciates for a few days, primarily as the result of the Dollar's positive performance and then, to a lesser extent, because of the possible immediate launch of new corrective measures for the public accounts, prepared by the previous Dini Government (2075, 2079). Designated Premier Prodi, moreover, decides to adopt his own corrective measure on 15 May (2085).

On Thursday, 16 May, Prodi receives the official mandate to form the Government (2090). The following day he communicates the list of Ministers (2094). On Wednesday 22 he presents his programme and his cabinet to the Senate (2112, 2120) and, later, to the Lower House, which casts the final vote of confidence on Friday 31 (2141). From Figure 2.11 we can see that from mid-May to mid-June the performance of the Lira mirrors that of the Deutschmark against the Dollar, but now the fluctuations of the Lira seem more modest relative to those of the Dollar. This may indicate interest and confidence on the part of the financial markets. In the second half of June the appreciation of the Lira appears more than proportional relative to the weakening of the Deutschmark.

The Prodi Government gets down to work straight away, primarily focusing on the mid-year public accounts corrective measure, which has now become a familiar event in the Italian public finance landscape (2146, 2165, 2179, 2182). In the meantime Minister of Finance Visco is working on a tax reform for financial income, which creates some concern in the financial markets (2174). All these events, however, leave no observable trace in the performance of the Lira exchange rate of 31 May to 17 June. See Figure 2.11, lower panel.

On this last day Minister Ciampi presents the budget corrective measure, which is about thirty per cent heavier than the one prepared by the Dini Government and described above (2191). The favorable reaction of the markets, supported also by rumours of an upgrade in Moody's ratings, results in a further strengthening of the Lira on Tuesday 18 (2197).

The quarter closes on a positive note with the results for production inflation, the lowest since 1992 (2201), the better-than-expected results for consumer inflation in the sample cities on Wednesday and Thursday, 20-21 June (2206, 2216), and with a cut in Treasury Bill interest rates on Tuesday 25 (2223).

The Third Quarter

The compliance, the statements, the indiscretions relative to the creation of EMU and the conditions for Italy's entry, begin to attract the attention of the markets in 1996. As far as Italy is concerned, although there was a clear intention to participate from the very beginning, as indirectly confirmed by Weigel's cutting comment on 21 September, 1995 (1332), it is with the Prodi Government that this ambition becomes the driving force behind every decision related to budget policy (2165).

Thus the Lira is first shaken by an international item of gossip on Friday, 14 June, according to which the British Chancellor of the Exchequer Lawson had spoken at an interview of some hostility on the part of the Bundesbank to Italy's entry into EMU (2186).[13] The Lira then depreciates on Monday, 8 July on a negative comment by the EU's technical organisms regarding the consistency of Italy's budgetary policies, which in any case is in good company with Germany and France (2276, 2277). Then the flow of news and the comments on EMU increase in intensity, often involving Italy even if indirectly. In autumn the frequency of interventions regarding the desirability of Italy's participation to EMU will increase noticeably in the preparatory phase of the Lira's return to the European Exchange-Rate

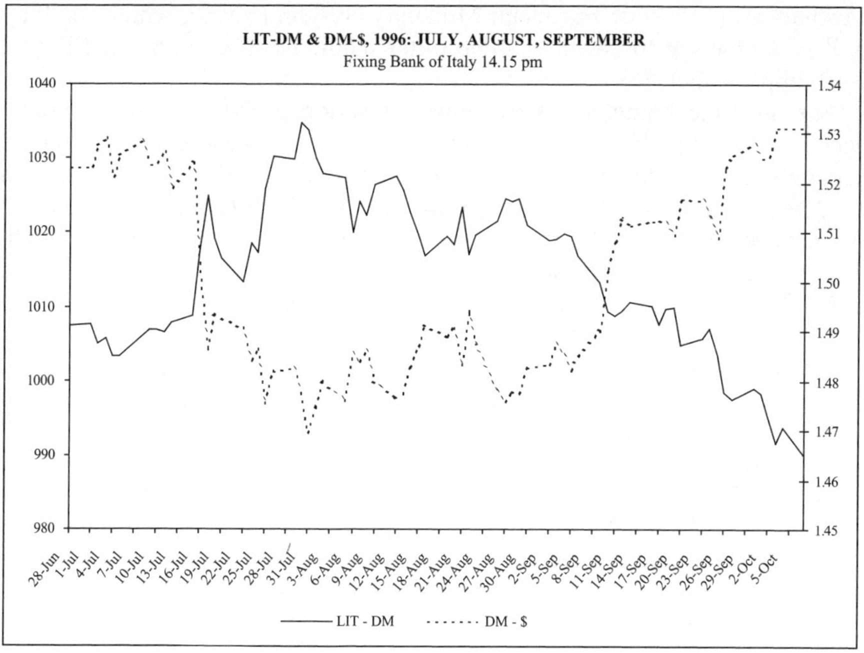

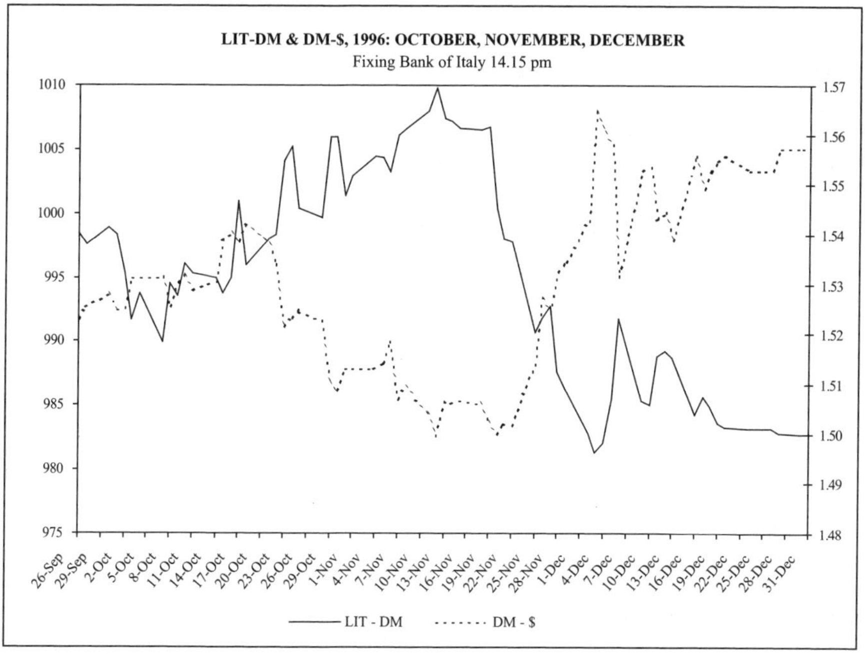

Figure 2.12 LIT-DM & DM-$, 1996: July, August, September – October, November, December

Mechanism (ERM) or European Monetary System (EMS), which for Italy will mean having to swallow some bitter medicine (see 2166). See Figure 2.12, upper panel.

For the time being, the Government's action is focused on the public accounts, on two fronts: (a) the mini-adjustment measure for the public accounts of the current year, 1996, presented by Minister Ciampi on Wednesday, 19 June (2203) and (b) the DPEF, which should constitute the framework for the 1997 Budget, the year of reference for the Maastricht Treaty criteria. The mini-measure seems to have a less difficult path (2213, 2261, 2358) than the DPEF, which after being approved by the Government on 27 June (2239), immediately meets with an unfavorable vote from Rifondazione, which votes with the Polo in the Lower House Commission, on Tuesday, 9 July (2278), causing a slide in the Lira in the following days (2302). The conflict between Rifondazione and the Government is later resolved with the approval of the DPEF on Tuesday 16 (2311).

A few days later, on Wednesday, 24 July, the Bank of Italy cuts the discount rate (2339), but the Lira does not benefit from it, primarily because of the turmoil in the international picture in those days, following the Bundesbank decision to go into recess without having cut the interest rates (2346), as had been expected (2336).

However, with the vote of confidence in the Lower House on Wednesday, 31 July (2358, 2361) the Lira regains the ground lost after the approval of the "mini-measure" of public accounts adjustment.

This leads into the "Mediterranean August", a month which in Italy is generally not rich in economic and political events. The only event worth mentioning, not so much for the markets' reaction but because it foreshadows future turmoil, is Bertinotti's threat to unleash a crisis over the privatisation of STET, expressed on Monday, 19 August (2410, 2411). On Thursday 22 there inflation figures from the sample cities are good (2427).

As if responding to some unexpressed international command, the beginning of September witnesses an inflow of funds towards Italian and Spanish fixed-income securities (2523, 2525). The underlying reason is clearly the expectation of a convergence of Italian and Spanish long-term interest rates towards the German ones, under the EMU hypothesis. Both countries are gaining credibility with budget corrective measures that may enable them to meet the Maastricth criteria in 1997, even if there is surliness among overseers in Europe – for instance the Bundesbank President, who on Thursday, 12 September reminds that the Maastricht criteria must be interpreted in the strictest sense (2498).

Among the yuppies of international finance, Italy, Spain and Portugal are collectively called the "Club Med". Aware of this definition, in mid September, before completing the budget for 1997, Premier Prodi goes to Spain to learn of Prime Minister Aznar's plans, discovering that Spain is determined to present its 1997 public accounts in order and is not willing to join Italy in an attempt to pressure the EU to "water down" the EMU criteria

(2550 and Financial Times of 27 September, p. 2, which contains our news in detail, summarising many Italian press articles on this subject).

Upon his return, the Prodi Government forces a strong acceleration on the magnitude of the adjustment – also contemplating a one-off (una tantum) Eurotax – in order to enable Italy to fully meet the 3% deficit-GDP ratio. The Lira exchange rate immediately reflects this change in gears. On Thursday, 26 September the Government officially announces that it will propose a 1997 Budget of 50,000 billion, and this takes place without prompting Rifondazione Comunista's veto (2549, 2555). See Figure 2.12, upper panel.

The Fourth Quarter

The Italian Government's sudden acceleration of pace to join EMU is accompanied by a more pressing offensive on the diplomatic and financial fronts in order to accelerate the return of the Lira to EMS, which as we know represents one of the prerequisites to participate in the single currency.

On Monday, 30 September the international press reports excerpts of an intervention on Sunday by French President Chirac at a French industrial meeting, during which he apparently defined the Lira's return to EMS as "dangerous" (2563). The Lira weakens as a result, obviously, but then recovers the next day when Chirac repeats the concept in a softer way and apologizes immediately afterwards (2574, 2577). See Figure 2.12, lower panel. The following Saturday, 5 October, after one of the periodic Italo-French meetings, the two countries arrive at an agreement in principle to initiate the technical negotiations – clearly centred around the exchange rate level for the Lira relative to the other European currencies – with a view to a quick return of the Lira to the EMS (2587, 2593).

The Lira then weakens again slightly under the attack of the Bundesbank's "heavy artillery", with a first round of interventions: Tietmeyer on Monday 7 (2595, 2596), Zeitler and Kuehbacher on Tuesday 8 (2600, 2601), and again Tietmeyer on Friday 11 (2614). Although with different emphases and arguments, they all reiterate the dangers of accounting "face lifts" carried out to gain entrance into EMU, and the attendant risks of higher interest rates. These arguments find an attentive audience in Paris, where Minister of Finance Arhuis repeats similar concepts on Monday 14 (2618, 2622).

All of this persuades the Italian Government to strongly reiterate its own determination to re-enter the EMS, which Premier Prodi does in person visiting German Chancellor Kohl in Bonn on Wednesday 16 (2632).

The second round of Bundesbankers' interventions against the re-entry of the Lira into the ERM starts on the same day, lasting until Monday 21: Tietmeyer and Koebnick on Wednesday 16 (2635, 2636), again Tietmeyer on Thursday 17 (2641), and lastly Kuehbacher on Monday 21 (2656). Then they finally turn their attention to their own interest rates.

In this cauldron of initiatives the Lira loses approximately 15 Lire, from the meeting in Naples on Saturday, 5 October, to the eve of the French definite "yes" to the Lira's re-entry into the EMS, on Thursday, 14 November (2750). See Figure 2.12, lower panel.

Shortly after the final go ahead from France, the Lira revalues again towards parity at 990 Lire against the Deutschmark, which had been indicated by commentators as the most realistic level and which indeed later becomes the official rate.

The Lira re-enters the EMS at precisely this level during the weekend of 23-24 November (2785, 2787, 2790, 2791), appreciating by a further ten Lire the following week.

Some international commentators[14] have observed that, from Italy's declaration of its intent to re-enter the EMS until the beginning of October, the Bank of Italy had tried to first weaken and the maintain the Lira in order to enable a re-entry at a more "convenient" exchange rate. Our reconstruction clearly indicates that the causes of the October weakening of the Lira can be found more probably in the Bundesbank's press releases.

After re-entry in the EMS, the Lira-Deutschmark exchange rate continues to maintain – for the remainder of 1996 and then often in 1997 – an indirect relation with the Deutschmark-Dollar exchange rate, a constant in the Lira's free-floating period after the autumn of 1992. The logic governing EMU membership clearly requires a joint fluctuation of the Lira with the Deutschmark until both currencies disappear. This will finally take place in 1998.

In the meantime the 50,000 billion Budget continues its uphill road, with deep disagreement from the opposition and with some bickering within the Ulivo over the Eurotax, between Wednesday 27 and Friday, 29 November (2803, 2811, 2815), but without leaving any traces on the Lira exchange rate, still surrounded by euphoria after re-entry in the EMS.

The last episodes of 1996 relate to the important agreement over the Stability Pact among Ecofin Ministers, on Thursday and Friday, 12-13 December (2880, 2890, 2899), right before the Dublin summit, with a weakening of the Deutschmark that – in our decodification of this type of events – translates into an increased probability of completing EMU within the scheduled time. The Lira strengthens following the usual empirical rule. See Figure 2.12 , lower panel.

The final rush on the 1997 Budget (the Euro Budget) is implemented and completed between Monday 16 (2904) and Monday 23 (2951). The Lira barely budges.

2.7 The Lira in 1997: The Prodi Government and the Debate on the European Monetary Union

Re-entry into EMS represents a deep change of regime for the Lira. Even if the fluctuation ranges are still wide enough in the current version of the

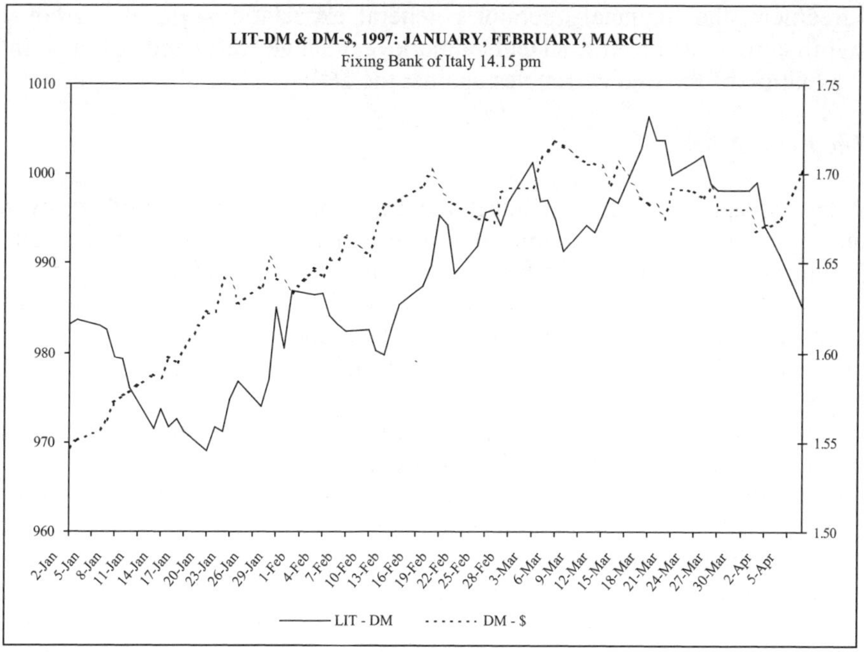

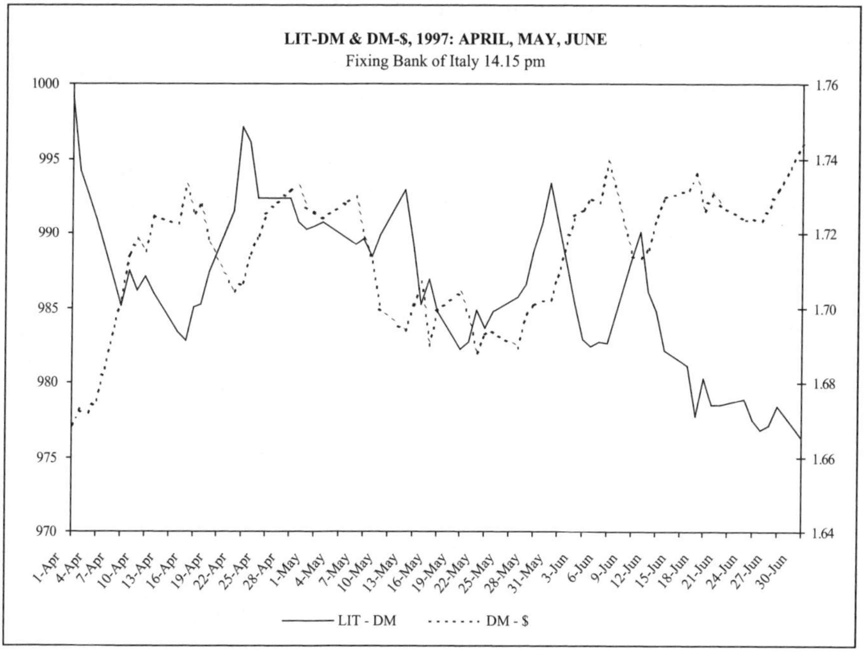

Figure 2.13 LIT-DM & DM-$, 1997: January, February, March – April, May, June

agreement, the financial operator's general expectations are of a gradual stabilisation of the Lira-Deutschmark exchange rate and of a joint fluctuation of the two currencies against the Dollar.

The First Quarter

After the approval of the Budget the Lira continues to strengthen, even during a period of dynamic dialogue between the Government and Rifondazione, between Wednesday, 15 July and Tuesday 21, over the privatisation of STET (3018, 3027, 3047). In this same period, however, the Deutschmark is weakening rapidly, after the Franco-German decision to this effect towards the end of 1996 (see paragraphs 2.2 and 2.3). See Figure 2.13, upper panel.

After Monday 20 the Lira-Deutschmark exchange rate matches the same trend as that of the Deutschmark-Dollar exchange rate for little over a week. On Tuesday 21 the Bank of Italy cuts the discount rate (3045), and in the following days the Lira continues to weaken following the Deutschmark-Dollar exchange rate.

With respect to the minimum level of just under 970 of 20 July, the Lira depreciates, generally following the Deutschmark until it reaches the level of 1,000 towards the end of February. The factors determining its dynamics are tied to the international debate regarding the progress of EMU. Thus the Lira weakens between Tuesday, 4 February and Friday 7, between Wednesday 12 and Tuesday, 18 February and then again between Monday 24 and Friday 28. See Figure 2.13, upper panel.

In the first instance a Financial Times article reveals a Franco-German agreement whereby Italy would be offered the possibility of an honorable withdrawal from EMU (3115); Prodi immediately speaks directly with Chancellor Kohl who denies the existence of any such agreement (3130, 3131).

The two other instances are determined, respectively, by supposed difficulties for France and Germany to meet the Maastricth criteria on the public debt (3146, 3149, 3155, 3160, 3166, 3169), and by news from the European bond markets that seem to indicate an interruption of convergence trading in expectations of EMU (3200, 3222, 3225, 3226).

After a maximum relative level around 1,000 Lire against the Deutschmark, on 28 February, at the end of the previous phase of EMU-related fears, the Lira shows again an inverse relation with the Deutschmark-Dollar exchange rate until approximately the middle of May (Figure 2.13). From Monday 3 to Wednesday, 19 March there is still a brawling period between Ulivo and Rifondazione Comunista representatives of the Government majority (3246, 3248, 3254, 3260, 3267, 3278, 3285, 3296, 3298, 3300, 3305, 3311). The real object of contention is the usual second corrective measure to "balance" the public accounts (3161, 3174, 3199,

3223, 3228), with Rifondazione attempting to gain something in exchange for its support in terms of the privatisation of STET and interventions on labour issues.

On Wednesday 5, Rifondazione obstructs the privatization of STET (3246); on Friday 7 an agreement is found regarding the magnitude of the measure, which will be limited to 8,000 billion (3260); on Monday 10 negotiations over employment measures begin (3267); on Thursday 13 an agreement is found, with 100,000 jobs agreed for the South (316); on Wednesday 19 the so-called "Treu Package" is finalized (3311).

At the end of this labour, on Thursday, 27 March an agreement is ratified for the public accounts corrective measure, which at 15,000 billion Lire has almost doubled, probably because of the interventions in the South (3357).

The Second Quarter

The Lira appreciates after the launch of the second corrective measure until it encounters the next obstacle: the parliamentary vote regarding intervention in Albania (3412). Here too Rifondazione plays a decisive role. On Tuesday, 8 April the Senate approves the "peace mission" in Albania with the critical vote of the Polo, which demands a political exchange for the vote in the Lower House (3411, 3412). On Wednesday 9 the Lower House approves the mission but Prodi is forced to call for a vote of confidence in Parliament over the Government's overall action (3418, 3419, 3420). This is discussed in the Senate on Thursday 10 (452) and in the Lower House on Saturday 12 (3442, 3443). It is worth noting that in this crisis the Lira weakens only on Tuesday 8, and then, thanks to the Deutschmark's favorable trend, it continues its process of revaluation. See Figure 2.13, lower panel.

The next hurdles come from Brussels – from indiscretions of Thursday, 17 April, it appears that EU forecasts for 1997-98 estimate the Italian deficit-GDP ratio at 3.2% (496) – and from the Italian Parliament, with the defeat of the second corrective measure on Friday 18 (3483). In the same day, according to the *Financial Times*, there are rumours of a secret Franco-German agreement to exclude Italy from the initial group of EMU countries (3488). Enough to presuppose a weakening of the Italian currency, which loses "only" a dozen Lire in three days, with the usual help from Tietmeyer who, making the most of a favorable moment, on Tuesday 22 speaks of EMU being for a select few – the implications are obvious (3510). Figure 2.13 , lower panel.

In the meantime the EU forecasts take on the proportions of a diplomatic incident, with interventions by the Italian Commissioners (3497) immediately after the first indiscretions (3470), and with heavy complaints by Scalfaro (who speaks of "an accountant's approach") and Prodi ("incomprehensible forecasts") when the figures are actually published on Wednesday, 23 April (3515, 3516).

Once the storm is over the Lira revalues again, with some breaks, after the definitive approval – through a vote of confidence – of the second corrective measure in the Lower House on Tuesday, 6 May (3592), until the next two crises: one domestic and one international.

The first crisis develops from Monday 19 to Friday, 30 May, with a strong impact on the exchange rate in the last day (3720, 3736), Figure 2.13, and is related to the usual political exchange between the Ulivo and the Government, in this case over the launch of the 1998 DPEF (for the preliminary phases of this document see: 3604, 3646, 3658, 3684), and between Ulivo and Rifondazione Comunista, which wants something in exchange for its support and intends to defend its position of principle on employment and welfare (for the preceding phases see: 3611, 3628, 3639, 3660). This time the rumpus flares up over pensions and, more generally, over welfare (3667, 3674, 3690, 3700, 3706, 3729). The concluding phases of the definition of the DPEF take place from Tuesday, 27 May (3713) to Friday 30 (3735).

The international crisis is far more extensive and relates to two events that will influence the entire road to EMU, until its final approval at the beginning of May 1998. The crisis concerns the revaluation of the Bundesbank's gold reserves and the victory of the Left in the French elections, both described earlier (par. 2.3). Minister Weigel's proposal is made on Thursday, 15 May (3654), the victory of the French Left in the first electoral round occurs on Sunday 25 (3704), and Juppé's resignation takes place on Monday (3705). The second round takes place on Sunday, 1 June confirming the overall results of the first round (3740).

The Lira depreciates with the domestic events, but does not react to the international events. There probably was a private, celebratory reaction among the most prominent leaders of Italian economic policy. Undoubtedly one of the effects of the clumsy Bundesbank story is to silence the anti-Italian comments of its leaders. Indeed, *Newsmetrics* does not present any further judgements, observations, opinions or advice related to Italy from any of these gentlemen. The only exception are Tietmeyer's (4213) and Koebnick's (4214) comments at the end of August, at the time of Bertinotti's push on pensions (4212), which would then lead to the mini-crisis of October.

After these events and a few other starts, the Lira appreciates until the end of the month by approximately fifteen Lire against the Deutschmark, returning below the central parity of 900. The tensions in the Bicameral Commission, after the surprise vote on semi-presidentialism of Wednesday, 4 June (3755), do not alter the profile of the exchange rate, which on the contrary draws even more enthusiasm from the Euro-optimism following the Amsterdam summit over the weekend of 14-15 June (3817), the final approval of the 1998 DPEF on Tuesday 24 (3873), the inflation drop announced on Friday 20 (3853), and the discount rate cut of Friday 27 (3902). See Figure 2.13, lower panel.

The Third and the Fourth Quarters

The last two quarters of 1997 are treated together because by now the Lira fluctuates within narrow margins. The highest values are recorded in the first three weeks of October, with the government mini-crisis caused by Rifondazione Comunista.

In the third quarter the Lira fluctuates between only 971 and 978 Lire per Deutschmark. The impact of news is by now quite limited by the belief that the Lira is constrained by an exchange rate agreement. The fluctuations against the Deutschmark are therefore minimal while those against the US currency, which we do not study directly, have the same range as the Deutschmark-Dollar exchange rate. For instance, the Deutschmark depreciates against the Dollar from mid-July to a maximum of approximately 7.5% on 6 August; the Lira, on the contrary, depreciates against the Deutschmark by about 0.8%. See Figure 2.14.

The August weakening is sympathetic with the Deutschmark's. This is preceded by a much more marked instance of depreciation after Wednesday, 2 July, coinciding with a sentence of the Constitutional Court concerning pension rights which seems to give renewed energy to litigation that is quite damaging for the Italian public accounts (3928, 3945).

The Lira weakens again, always imperceptibly relative to past values, when negotiations over welfare resume on Wednesday, 27 August, with the usual cohort of combative statements (4212), and after the comments by Tietmeyer and Koebnick mentioned above, doubting Italy's participation in the first phase of EMU (4213, 4214).

Finally, after lengthy negotiations among the social parts, Rifondazione Comunista, Ulivo and the Government, on pensions, welfare and the reduction of working hours to 35 hours a week, in view of the coming approval of the Budget,[15] and after almost daily declarations of opposition to any intervention on pensions and threats of crisis on the part of Rifondazione Comunista – for instance on Tuesday, 9 September (4293), Monday 15 (4336), Tuesday 16 (4350) and Monday 22 (4399) – the conflict is resolved.

The Government passes the bill of law for the 1998 Budget on Saturday 27 (4439). On Monday 29 (4441) Bertinotti votes against the bill and on Wednesday, 1 October (4463) he has his vote ratified by his party's parliamentary group. There follows a period of deliberation (4464), a period for negotiations (4475) and some positive international Italo-French meetings resulting in the possibility of an agreement between the two countries over the 35-hour week, which may also be used as an exchange coin with Bertinotti (4474, 4485).

On Monday and Tuesday, 6-7 October there are frantic negotiations between Rifondazione and the Government (4493, 4504). On Thursday 9 the Government resigns (4515, 4526), between Friday 10 and Monday 13 Bertinotti reverses his position in exchange for a guaranteed 35-hour week

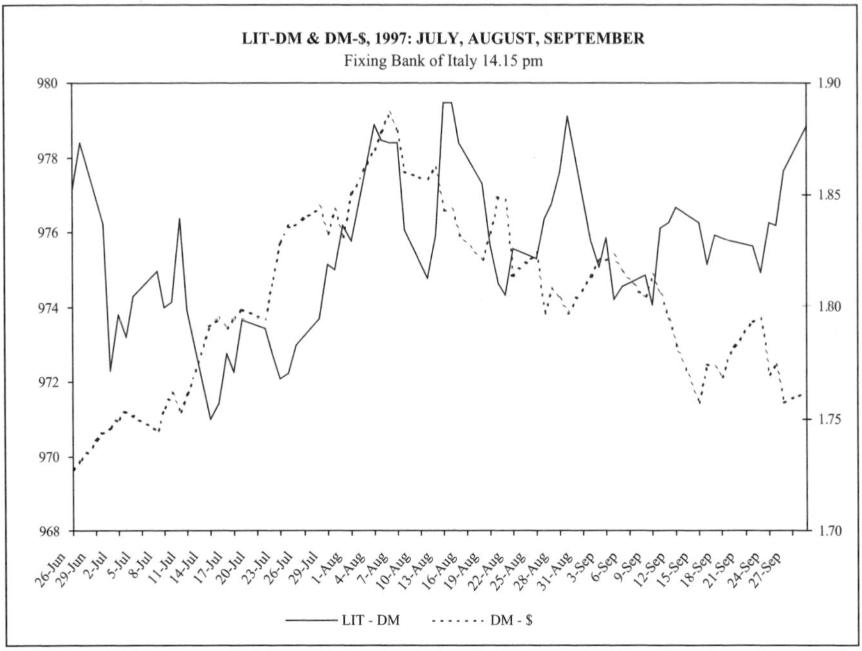

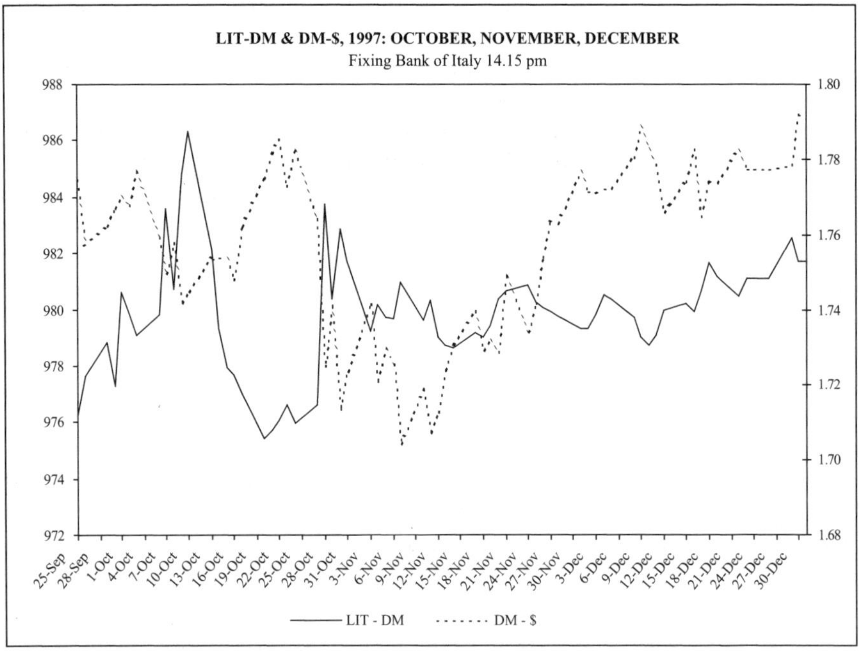

Figure 2.14 LIT-DM & DM-$, 1997: July, August, September – October, November, December

(4537, 4553), and on Thursday 16 Prodi obtains the vote of confidence in the Lower House and in the Senate (4586).

After Friday 10 the Lira already gains back the ten points lost since 22 September. As a matter of fact, the financial markets had never been fully persuaded of Rifondazione Comunista's determination to push the political crisis to the its bitter end, with two exceptions where the overall scenario was more complex: 4452, 4466, 4486, 4494, 4507, 4519, 4527, 4538, 4554. See Figure 2.14, lower panel.

The October mini-crisis is the last big trauma of the Italian currency in *Newsmetrics*. Thereafter the Lira weakens again by eight points around Monday, 27 October, but because of international factors: the Wall Street tumble due to fears surrounding the Asian crisis (4654, 4655, 4656, 4659, 4660). The Lira then settles for the remainder of 1997 at around 980 Lire.

Notes

1 The numerical references indicated in parenthesis refer to the news of the years covered in this paragraph, as recorded in the events database of this research. For indications on how to access it, please see page xxi. The text narrative is complemented in this chapter by 14 figures showing the daily trends of the Deutschmark and the Yen against the Dollar and of the Lira against the Deutschmark, and by a series of bracketed numbers containing references to the most relevant news or market phases.

2 In traditional economic theory, the effect on the exchange rates of relative interest rate variations can be observed in the short-term sectors of the financial markets (see, for example, HALLWOOD-MACDONALD [1995], Chapters 3 and 11). With the progressive acceleration of the international financial integration, the quota of medium- and short-term financial flows has expanded substantially, especially through institutional investor activity. It is therefore natural that variations in interest rates may have divergent effects on the short- and long-term sectors of the financial market, with contrasting consequences for the currency market.

3 Other circumstances that weaken the Deutschmark are rumours of intervention on the foreign exchange markets (1842) and a statement by Scharping on the seriousness of the unemployment situation in Germany (1848).

4 See the considerations regarding policy-maker interventions mentioned in paragraph 6.4.

5 The Japanese Monetary Authorities will admit it openly at the end of August/beginning of September 1997. See 1997 news 4257.

6 This attitude is particularly evident in the tone of *Financial Times* and *Wall Street Journal* articles of this period, more than in the entries in *Newsmetrics*.

7 This interpretation is more visible in the writings of the major international economic newspapers than in our bank.

8 In market comments (3270, 3275, 3302) and policy statements (see Kuehbacher (3307) and Dini (3335), in the first quarter of 1997). Doubts concerning the benefits of introducing EMU within the established deadline will appear often later: Donges, one of the German Government's three "wise men" (3534), Stoiber (3911, 3951, 4142), and again Dini (4256).

9 This episode can be compared to a similar event in July 1996, when the American stock exchange and the Dollar weakened immediately after the Fed left the interest rates unvaried, in anticipation of what could happen at the subsequent meeting of the FOMC.

10 In our sample period the Lira-DM exchange rate is tied to the DM-$ exchange rate by a strong inverse relationship. The econometric results of Chapter 7 confirm the results in TIVEGNA[1996].

11 It is not surprising that the Lira should have weakened the day in which Dr. Desario's appointment was confirmed, since the markets do not perceive the immediate positive consequence of improved operations of the Central Bank – guaranteed by the internal procedures that were made necessary by the long *vacatio* – but rather the negative consequences associated to a diminished independence of the institute's top levels.

12 It is precisely for this reason that *Newsmetrics* does not report many news regarding this subject: see 1284, 1314, 1341.

13 Before this date there are several events and comments relative to EMU that will be illustrated in greater detail in Chapter 5. With the exception of Weigel's famous comment mentioned earlier, the events captured by *Newsmetrics* before the period that concerns us do not have particularly significant effects on the Lira.

14 Indirectly also by the *Financial Times* of Monday, 25 November, 1996.

15 See: 4212, 4221, 4234, 4245, 4248, 4254, 4262, 4263, 4272, 4273, 4293, 4301, 4336, 4350, 4362, 4363, 4372, 4399, 4413, 4422, 4434.

Chapter 3

The Italian News

3.1 Introduction

This chapter describes the news relating to Italy, as well as the selection criteria used and a running history to clarify the choice of events included in the database and their classification. For Italy, as for the other countries, we have qualitative and quantitative events (see last paragraph of section 1.2).

The Italian quantitative macroeconomic news has been gathered following the indications provided by the economic literature[1] and, where relevant, traders' opinions as expressed in the specialized press and in direct interviews.

Gathering and organising the qualitative news (news of a political and institutional nature) has been more complicated due to the absence of similar experiences. They have been collected on the basis of their operating and statistical relevance, as described in a note to section 7.3.1. The Italian news has been further tested in TIVEGNA[1996] and FORNARI-MONTICELLI-PERICOLI-TIVEGNA [1999]. Thus we have chosen not to include in this database all the qualitative news that could potentially have an effect on the exchange rate, or more generally on the prices of the main financial activities. The news that has been included are derived from statistical procedures and from the studies mentioned above.

3.2 Quantitative News

The Italian quantitative news reviewed in this work relate to:

(1) rates of change in consumer prices, on a monthly and yearly basis, both in the monthly readings taken in the sample cities around the twentieth of each month, and in the official announcements made monthly in the first days of the month following the month of reference[2] (code INFCONS in *Newsmetrics*);
(2) rates of change in production costs (INFPROD), on a monthly and yearly basis, observed every month;[3]
(3) rates of change in ISTAT's official industrial production indices (PRINDUF), on a yearly basis, observed every month;
(4) rates of change in the industrial production forecast by a panel of firms and collected in the quick survey of the Centro Studi Confindustria

(PRDCONF), on a monthly and yearly basis, observed every month;
(5) rates of change in the industrial contractual hourly earnings (RETROR), on a monthly and yearly basis, observed every month;
(6) currency balance (BILVAL), announced every month by the Ufficio Italiano dei Cambi (UIC – the Italian Financial Intelligence Unit equivalent);[4]
(7) interest rates of the Banca d'Italia spot-forward operations in Lire (PCTOPER), with an irregular occurrence;
(8) 3-month BOT interest rates at auction, with the amounts bid and offered, observed every fifteen days;[5]
(9) 7-year CCT interest rates at auction (CCTASTA), with the amounts bid and offered, and with the values of the opening auction (CCTRIAP), observed every 15 days or less;
(10) long-term BTP interest rates at auction (BTPASTA), limited to 10-year bonds, with the amounts bid and offered, and with the values for the opening auction (BTPRIAP), observed every 15 days or less.

The observations relative to auctions, auction yields and amounts bid and offered for CCT and BTP and the respective openings were interrupted as of 2 November, 1995.

3.3 Qualitative News

The Italian qualitative news refer to events of economic policy and of politics in general. They have had a significant impact on the exchange rate in the period covered by *Newsmetrics* (see TIVEGNA [1996] and FORNARI-MONTICELLI-PERICOLI-TIVEGNA [1999]).

The economic policy news refer to variations in official rates, announcements regarding the trends of public accounts released by the official institutions that collect statistical data, and the budget policy guidelines, both in terms of the preparation of the Budget and the DPEF (Economic and Financial Planning Document) and of the analysis and debate related to the preparation of corrective measures in the years covered by *Newsmetrics*. Interest rate news is collected at the same time as public accounts news since, in this period, the markets immediately connect variations in interest rates with variations in the interest burden on the public debt.

Political events refer to different types of events that have had a significant impact on the Lira exchange rate dynamics. The period under consideration has been quite a troubled one for Italian politics. It has seen the first experiences of the so-called Second Republic, the primary novelty of which was a political dynamics characterised by a bi-polar regime, the result of a 1993 electoral law reform. Despite its promises of a greater political stability, bi-polarism has seen the rapid succession of three governments: Berlusconi, Dini and Prodi.

The type of political events gathered is quite specific to the three governments mentioned above. In the description of the news categories we have used to classify the political events occurring in the sample period, we will refer – with few exceptions – to these three governments. The economic events are more generic and will therefore be treated in isolation.

3.3.1 The News of the Berlusconi Government

As the first government of the Second Republic, the government led by the Hon. Berlusconi feels the impact of the novelty the most. This period is characterized by political controversy, involving the Premier as an ex-businessman, and manifests itself in a constant re-examination of the country's institutional order in terms of the administration of justice and the relationship between the various constitutional organs: the President of the Republic, the Parliament and the Government. This situation is compounded by the debate within the March 1994 elections winning coalition, primarily because of the Lega Nord's "deviation" from the coalition on many political topics. As we know, such "deviation" will eventually lead to the crisis of the Berlusconi Government after the famous "government overturn" ("*ribaltone*").

The following is the classification we therefore thought best suited for the events of this period, comprised between the electoral victory of the Polo delle Libertà on 27 March, 1994 and the mandate to form the Government given to Doctor Dini on 13 January, 1995, after the Hon. Berlusconi's resignation on 22 December, 1994.

Conflict within the Polo delle Libertà (CONPOLO). The Polo is the coalition that wins the March 1994 elections and forms the Government majority in office until 22 December, 1994, fallen after the Lega's defection. This family of events consists of events of political contrast over Government offices and the Government programme preceding the formation of the Berlusconi Government, and of those events that have subsequently characterized the difficult coexistence between the Lega and the other parties of the coalition, until the Lega leaves the majority with the consequent Government crisis. This code also gathers episodes of the Government crisis following Premier Berlusconi's resignation on 22 December, 1994: the double round of consultations between the President of the Republic and the political forces and the mandate to Dr. Lamberto Dini to form a technical government. This category includes the judiciary events directly involving the Prime Minister and his brother Paolo, i.e. those relating to the court appearance summons to Paolo Berlusconi for his involvement in the real estate events of June 1994, and those relating to Berlusconi himself, in November of the same year, over the Fininvest bribes to the Guardia di Finanza (Tax Police).

Institutional conflict (CONISTI) between leading members of the Polo delle Libertà and of the Berlusconi Government and the President of the Republic, Scalfaro. The financial markets react negatively to the conflict and the strong disagreements over key issues in the public life of this period (for instance the direction of RAI, the possible conflict of interests between the office of Prime Minister held by Berlusconi and his role as main shareholder of Fininvest). This category includes also the long confirmation process for the appointment of a Director General for Banca d'Italia to substitute Dr. Dini, the first post-war attempt at explicit interference in the appointment of Banca d'Italia's top management on the part of the Executive.

Political and judiciary events (CONGIUD), consisting of contrasts among members of the Berlusconi Government, including the Prime Minister himself as well as officers of Forza Italia and judges of the Mani Pulite investigative team: the Biondi decree and the internal and external conflicts it produced, the frequent skirmishes conducted through the press, the despatch of inspections, etc. – naturally until the fall of the Berlusconi Government.

3.3.2 The News of the Dini Government

The Dini Government is formed a few days after the mandate is assigned by President of the Republic Scalfaro. As mentioned earlier, this government is conceived as a "technical" government, with a limited mandate both in terms of content and time. In terms of content, the Dini Government is meant to effect only urgent interventions on (a) the public accounts, with the preparation of a corrective measure that became necessary after the Berlusconi Government, by then in full crisis, launched a 1995 National Budget that was insufficient, and (b) pensions expense restraint. Once these two tasks are completed in 1995, President Dini is also assigned the task to prepare and monitor the parliamentary process of the 1996 National Budget. Having completed also this task, the Head of the Government announces his intention to present his resignation on 29 December, 1995, later accepted.

Also the Dini Government operates in a climate of heightened political and financial turmoil, the latter partly induced by the strong devaluation of the Dollar in the first half of the year. We have gathered the political events of this period under three categories: (1) action of the Dini Government, with three clearly recognizable phases (approval of the second corrective measure, negotiations with the unions over pensions reform, and preparation of the 1996 Budget); (2) controversies over the administration of justice and the actions of Minister of Justice Mancuso; (3) the schism within the Partito Popolare Italiano (PPI – Italian Popular Party).

Let us look at the categories of news for the period between 16 January,

1995 and 29 December, 1995. As we know, the Dini Government remains in office even after the initial resignation, until the Prodi Government is sworn in. The episodes occurring between 29 December, 1995 and 17 May, 1996 are gathered in a category of events described in the following section.

Action of the Dini Government (GOVDINI). This heading collects various events, not necessarily all of a kind. They include, in brief: (a) all the stages of the presentation of the Government to both Houses, from the reactions to the mandate to the reactions at each parliamentary phase of the vote of confidence; (b) events connected with the initial proceedings, the preliminary discussion and the parliamentary approval of the Dini Government's three main tasks: the second corrective measure, approved in March; the pensions reform, agreed with the unions at the beginning of May and approved by Parliament in August; and the 1996 Budget. This heading also includes the events relating to the failed vote of no confidence against the Dini Government in October 1995, subsequent to the "removal from office" of Minister of Justice Mancuso.

Action of Minister of Justice Mancuso (MANCUSO): comments and inspections ordered by Minister Mancuso, negative reactions to both on the part of the forces supporting the Dini Government, approval of the Polo delle Libertà parties now in the opposition. The events take place from 9 May, 1995 to the traumatic epilogue of 19 October, 1995.

Crisis within the PPI (PPI). This category refers to a few episodes beginning in February 1995 relative to the split of the PPI into two components, the one following Professor Buttiglione –which will later generate the small CDU (United Christian Democrats) grouping within the Polo delle Libertà – and the component that chooses the Hon. Gerardo Bianco as party Secretary and will join the Ulivo, maintaining the name of "Partito Popolare Italiano". The reason for *Newsmetrics*' particular attention to these events is the importance of the PPI support of the Dini Government.

3.3.3 End of the Dini Government. The Maccanico Attempt. The Elections

The Dini Government completes its mandate at the end of 1995. At this point a comprehensive debate develops over the benefits of extending the life of this Government until the end of the Italian European Union presidency in the first half of 1996. The events related to this debate, and to the seesawing fortunes of one thesis or another (extension of the Dini Government vs. elections, with accompanying pendulum of the Lira), to the Hon. Maccanico's attempt to form a government, to the dissolution of Parliament following the failure of the latter, and to Dr. Dini's decision to candidate himself to the leadership of the Ulivo and to participate in the electoral campaign, were gathered under the following two codes.

Political events between 1 January and 26 February, 1996 (POL96). This code collects the debate among political forces over the benefits of extending the Dini Government and the conditions thereof; it includes the agreements, the quarrels and the role played by the main leaders – Dini, D'Alema, Berlusconi – in the course of the events.

Mandate to form a government to the Hon. Maccanico (MACCAN). These are the few – but not at all indifferent in terms of the impact on the Lira – events that relate to the Hon. Maccanico's short-lived attempt to form a government around an important constitutional reform: the direct election of the Head of Government, strongly favored by Alleanza Nazionale.

The period to which these two codes refer ends with the dissolution of Parliament (16 February) and with Dr. Dini's decision to candidate himself for the Ulivo leadership (26 February). After this *Newsmetrics* does not record any more events until the electoral victory of the Ulivo, on Sunday, 21 April, because linking exchange rate variations to political events of dubious interpretation such as those traditionally related to electoral competitions, is too arbitrary a decision. It is also difficult to attribute the strengthening of the Lira in the days immediately preceding the elections to the electoral surveys assigning the victory to the Ulivo – with very narrow margins – since it could equally have been induced by movements of the Dollar at the time (see Figure 2.11, lower panel).

3.3.4 The News of the Prodi Government

At the end of the spring 1996 electoral campaign the Ulivo wins the elections and a new "season" of political news begins, in which the strong Italian commitment to the European Monetary Union (EMU) is combined with a difficult relationship with Rifondazione Comunista, whose votes are needed in the Lower House to achieve the majority, and a lively interaction with the opposition of the Polo.

The two codes for the political news after the Ulivo victory at the 21 April, 1996 elections[6] follow below.

Action of the Prodi Government (GOVPRODI). After the victory in the political elections, the government must define the traditional "Spring corrective measure" for the public accounts. Once this is completed, the preparation of the 1997 Budget begins, 1997 being a critical year for EMU. This commitment is over at the end of 1996, and from the beginning of 1997 increasingly frequent instances of mini-crises begin to appear: over the privatisation of STET, over welfare, over the DPEF, over the Albanian situation, culminating in April with a vote of confidence. In February 1997 the debate over the traditional Spring corrective measure for the public accounts resumes, and the measure is finally approved in March. From the end of August the symptoms of a crisis with Rifondazione Comunista become more pronounced, resulting later in the October mini-crisis of government. The parliamentary process of discussion of the 1998 Budget and its final approval in Christmas 1997 are the last accomplishments of the Prodi government recorded in *Newsmetrics*.

Political action of Rifondazione Comunista (RIFCOM). As we know, the Ulivo victory in the April 1996 political elections does not provide a self-sufficient majority in both houses of Parliament. This situation significantly increases the weight of Rifondazione Comunista within the majority supporting the Prodi Government. The mainstays of Rifondazione's political actions are: (a) opposition to privatizations; (b) government use of direct interventions to support employment (for example the "battle" for the reduction of the working week to 35 hours); and (c) a determined stance against Italy's involvement in international actions consistent with its position in the North-Atlantic Alliance. All the episodes recorded in *Newsmetrics* and gathered under the code RIFCOM are affected, directly or indirectly, by these general principles. As mentioned earlier, the action of Rifondazione even leads to a government crisis, in October 1997.

3.3.5 Political News Common to All Three Governments

Some political events are common to the entire period under review. They relate to the markets' reactions to the electoral consultations and the numerous episodes of debate and contrast, at times even sharp, among the political forces. This last type of events does not cover those distinctly specific to each of the three Italian governments, such as for instance the Lega's political action within the Berlusconi Government (gathered under the code CONPOLO) or the political action of Rifondazione Comunista (RIFCOM).

Electoral results (VITTELE). This group includes the results of political, European, regional, municipal, provincial and referendum electoral consultations taking place in the period covered by *Newsmetrics*. The results of the electoral consultations have had different effects on the Lira exchange rate depending on the political situation at the time. During the Berlusconi Government the victories of the Polo (for instance in the June 1994 European elections) strengthen the exchange rate and vice versa the electoral defeats (for instance in the November 1994 municipal elections) weaken it. During the Dini Government, on the contrary, it is the defeats of the Polo, not its victories, that strengthen the exchange rate. This is evident after the Polo defeat in the regional elections at the end of April 1995, when the Lira consolidates the post-"Black Friday" rally initiated with the positive opening of the negotiations between the Dini Government and the unions over the pension reform. On the contrary, the victory of the Polo's position in the June 1995 "television" referendum produces a weakening of the Lira.

Relationship among political forces and dynamics within their ranks (SCHIAR). This heading gathers all the episodes that refer to the relationships among parties (Forza Italia, PDS, Alleanza Nazionale, etc.) and between the coalitions, Polo delle Libertà and Ulivo, and to their internal events. This type of episode counts very few instances in 1995, mostly the ups and downs in the definition of the "rules of the game". They become much more numerous in the 1996-1997 two-year period, most prominent among them those linked to the work of the Bicameral Commission, presided by the Hon. D'Alema.

3.3.6 The Economic News

The qualitative news are supplemented by those that are primarily economic in nature. We start with a category of events that is half way between politics and economics, relating to several episodes regarding Italy's participation to EMU, which, as we have already seen, has been the main commitment of the Prodi Government.

Already from the beginning of 1996, with the Italian semester of European Union presidency, the international debate over the convergence criteria to meet the Maastricht Treaty parameters that are at the base of EMU flares up. Italy is obviously involved. During all of 1996, until the re-entry into the ERM, the Lira exchange rate is strongly affected by this debate and by the many declarations of the European monetary establishment, with the Bundesbank Council members in leading position: this news is gathered under the code QUM.

Italy's participation to EMU (QUM). This code gathers multiple events directly or indirectly connected to Italy's participation to EMU. It therefore includes: (a) international events – also recorded under the code QUMIN – linked to the actual implementation of a monetary union; (b) events more directly traceable to the Italian Government's action to enter the EMU with the initial group of countries; and (c) the not infrequent statements by authoritative officials of the other European countries' governments and central banks – primarily Germany, France and the Netherlands – on the desirability of Italy's participation to the EMU from the outset and its real possibilities of doing so. The actions of the Italian Government towards EMU participation are obviously included in this category of events.

And, finally, we arrive at the classification of news that is expressed qualitatively but is of a strictly economic and quantitative nature.

News on public finances and interest rates (FINPUBL). This too constitutes a grouping of heterogeneous events. This type of news includes: (a) announcements relative to the results of public accounts, (b) the various phases of preparation, debate and parliamentary approval of public finance measures, and (c) increases or decreases in interest rates and the related events, in so far as they are directly relevant to the public accounts dynamics through the burden on the public debt.

Inflation announcements (ANNINFL). This category gathers headlines from *Il Sole XXIV Ore* that primarily communicate the various releases on consumer and production inflation, already collected in the database in their quantitative form under the codes INFCONS and INFPROD, and also provide indirect news on inflation, such as, for example, the rapid, no-strike conclusion of metalworkers' contract renewal in the spring of 1994.

News on the Italian short-term economic situation (ECON). This code gathers the various statistical announcements relative to the Italian short-term economic situation, which are collected in quantitative form under various codes, and several news ideas regarding the macro situation.

News on the Italian financial markets (QMFIT). This news refers to the Italian stock and bond markets, and generally provide information on the markets' reaction to the various events.

Notes

1 The literature mentioned in section 1.1. The quantitative news chosen for Italy reflect quite faithfully – with a few specific exceptions – those chosen for the USA which, as we have seen, conform the traditional empirical basis of the literature on the impact of news on the exchange rate.

2 In *Newsmetrics* the consumer inflation figure is usually accompanied by a qualitative news item, consisting of a re-elaboration of a *Il Sole XXIV Ore* column by the same title on this topic (ANNINFL). In addition, we have gathered some consensus estimates on the expected value of consumer price increases, published on *Il Sole XXIV Ore*. The importance of this value resides in the fact that this is the first flash estimate effected by a statistical centre. It is worth noting here that the procedure to release inflation estimates for sample cities has been modified by ISTAT since March 1996, following news leaks that troubled the financial markets in the hours immediately preceding the official publication. For more information on the new procedure see the article by Isabella Buffacchi in *Il Sole XXIV Ore* of 14 December 1995, as well as ISTAT's official publications.

3 Here too the code for the corresponding qualitative news is ANNINFL.

4 The codes for the qualitative news referred to in paragraphs (3), (4), (5) and (6) is

always ECON. With respect to paragraph (6), *Newsmetrics* contains also the capital movement balances for portfolio investments and the overall balances. These items are not mentioned in the text but are contained in the database.

5 The qualitative code generally used for BOT auctions is FINPUBL, to reflect the impact they have on the public accounts.

6 The relationship with the Polo, the Bicameral Commission episodes and other miscellaneous political events involving, directly or indirectly, the Government's stability and the overall political picture are gathered under the code SCHIAR, described later, which also contains similar news for the Dini Government period.

Chapter 4

Economic and Political News for Germany and the United States

4.1 Introduction

Qualitative and quantitative news was also gathered for Germany and the United States, with a prevalence of quantitative news for the United States. The *Newsmetrics* collection of political, economic and financial market news for Japan is less systematic than for the other countries in the database, which have a remarkable coverage of market news, under the code MJA (see the database).

The types of quantitative American and German news are described in sections 4.2 and 4.3 respectively, while section 4.4 describes the economic and monetary policy news for both countries (with emphasis on the official interest rate variations).

The quantitative economic indices collected in *Newsmetrics* have turned out to be the most significant ones from the point of view of the markets' reaction, especially in terms of the differences between actual and expected values. The United States is the country with the greater number of indicators. The data is collected primarily on a monthly basis (with the notable exception of the US initial claims, which are collected weekly) and is expressed in terms of percentage variations, balances, other values and interest rates. With sporadic exceptions, *Newsmetrics* includes both the official values announced by the institutions that prepare them and the values expected by traders.

The sources of the data vary according to the indices. American statistics are produced by various federal agencies and by a few private research institutes.[1] Prices and labour market statistics are prepared by the Bureau of Labor Statistics (BLS) of the Department of Labor (DL). Industrial production and capacity utilization statistics are provided by the central bank, the Board of Governors of the Federal Reserve System (Fed). Statistics relating to gross domestic product and its components, trade balance and income and savings composition are provided by the Department of Commerce (DoC), as are durable goods orders, retail sales and Leading Indicators, which recently have been calculated by the Conference Board (CB), a private organization. Also private is the National Association of Purchasing Managers (NAPM), which produces a popular leading indicator of production and industrial price dynamics, the NAPM Index. Finally, the consumer confidence index included in *Newsmetrics* is prepared by the Conference Board (CB). All these statistics have a precise announcement calendar, with day and hour of release, but they are often subject to substantial revision. The markets follow very carefully both the new data and the corrections to the previously announced data.

The German macroeconomic statistics included in *Newsmetrics* are prepared by the Bundesbank for variations on the M3 aggregate and by the Wiesbaden German Statistics Institute for consumer prices and unemployment, while the IFO business confidence index is prepared by the Munich research institute by the same name. It should be added that, with the exception of unemployment indices, the German authorities only provide the week of the official announcement of data, so that it is impossible to determine the precise day in which the economic indicators will be posted. In Chapter 7 we will see that this has consequences for the relation between exchange rates and news in Germany.

The weekly calendar published by *Il Sole XXIV Ore* and the *Financial Times* have been of great help, as they have enabled us to identify the precise day – or week in the German case – in which the quantitative news were to be announced. In addition, these weekly calendars also provide for each indicator the values expected by the markets. The expected values provided by *Il Sole XXIV Ore* have been collected, for the period of reference, by the consulting firm Mediolanum Consulenza Sim, while those of the *Financial Times* have been derived from a survey conducted by the firm Money Market Services (MMS).

4.2 American Quantitative News

The macroeconomic indicators followed for the United States are listed below:

1) **Consumer Price Index (USCPI)**: it indicates variations in the consumer price index. It is collected on a monthly basis by the BSL and it refers to the previous month. Our database includes the month-on-month variation in terms of both actual and expected values. The latter have been collected from the weekly calendars published by the *Financial Times*.[2]

2) **Producer Price Index (USPPI)**: this indicator shows variations in the industrial production price index. Again, it is collected on a monthly basis by the BLS with monthly and yearly variations. *Newsmetrics* includes the expected and the actual values of the percentage variations.

3) **Industrial Production (USINDPR)**: the industrial production index is collected on a monthly basis by the Fed, with monthly and yearly variations. The database includes expected and actual variations, both relating to the previous month.

4) **Initial Claims (USINCLM)**: this indicator shows the number of people who apply for unemployment benefits each week. It is announced by the DL every Thursday and it relates to the previous week. The difference between expected and actual values has a particular significance for economic operators. With the exception of a few missing data points, both values are included in our database.

5) **Civilian Unemployment Rate (USUNEMP)**: it indicates the unemployment rate in the previous month. It is prepared by the BLS on a monthly basis. The database provides both the expected and the actual values. In recent years this indicator, together with the next three, has been the most significant indicator for the financial markets.

6) **Non Farm Payrolls (USNOFARM)**: this indicator measures the variation in the number of pay statements – and therefore in the number of employees – in the various economic sectors except for farming. The BLS calculates this figure monthly, with reference to the previous month. The database includes the expected and the actual values.

7) **Hourly Earnings (USHEARN)**: this indicator shows the short-term variation in hourly earnings. It is calculated by the BLS on a monthly basis. The database includes the expected and the actual values.

The last three indicators relate to the labor market, and are announced on the same day, usually on the first Friday of the month.

8) **Consumer Confidence (USCCNF)**: this index, prepared by the Conference Board (CB) on the basis of a survey, records the combined effect of the consuming households' perception of the economy's overall situation, the availability of jobs and their own expected income at the time of the interview and in the following six months. Consumer optimism and pessimism are quantified with positive and negative variations of the index, which is set at 100 in 1985 and refers to the month preceding publication.

9) **Trade Balance (USTRBL)**: the DoC publishes the trade balance results on a monthly basis, expressed in billions of Dollars, with a two-month lag. The database includes the expected and the actual values.

10) **Retail Sales (USRET)**: this index measures the variations in the nominal value of retail sales. It is collected by the DoC on a monthly basis and it relates to the previous month. Also for this index the expected values are included in the database.

11) **Durable Goods Orders (USDURG)**: this index measures the percentage variation in consumer durable goods orders, on a monthly basis, with reference to the previous month. The expected value is published together with the actual value prepared by the DoC; both are included in the database.

12) **Personal Income (USPINC)**: this indicator, prepared on the basis of a sample survey, measures the personal income derived from direct employment, independent employment, investment in capital goods, public transfers of money, and foreign transfers. Estimates of this aggregate value are prepared by the DoC and are published monthly at the end of the month following the month of reference. Here too *Newsmetrics* includes the expected and actual values.

13) **Personal Consumer Expenditure (USPCE)**: this indicator, collected in the same sample survey above, measures the personal consumer expenditure; it is prepared in nominal terms by the DoC and is published at the same time as the Personal Income index. *Newsmetrics* includes the expected and actual values for this index.

14) **Leading Indicator (USLEAD)**: a cyclical indicator that predicts future movements of the aggregated economy for the quarter following the one in which it is expressed. For many years it was prepared by the DoC, but now it is prepared by the CB, with reference to the two months prior to publication. The database includes the expected value as well.

15) **NAPM Index (USNAPM)**: this indicator provides a concise forecast of various aspects of the manufacturing activity (new orders, production, employment, prices) in the form of a diffusion index; it has excellent predicting properties and is therefore carefully followed by the financial markets. The index is presented so that readings above 50 indicate an expansion, while readings below 50 indicate a contraction in manufacturing activity. The index is prepared and published by the NAPM in the first days of the month and refer to the previous month. The database includes an expected value.

4.3 German Quantitative News

The following are the macroeconomic indicators collected for Germany:

1) **IFO business climate (GEIFO)**: it indicates the level of business confidence. This index is prepared by the Munich IFO Institute for Economic Research, on a monthly basis and for various sectors of economic activity. The data are available from August 1996 and each

release relates to the previous month. Both the actual and the expected values have been collected in the database.

2) **Consumer Price Index (GECPI)**: it measures the variation in consumer prices both in the long and the short term. As in the Italian case, expected values are also released – although for the states of the German Federal Republic (the Länder) rather than for the cities as in the case of Italy. The database includes a preliminary estimate of the long-term variation in the index (for West Germany) in the last week of the month of reference, estimated by the Wiesbaden German Statistics Institute, as well as the values expected by the financial markets. In September 1995 the base year for calculation of the index and the variations was moved from 1985 to 1991.

3) **M3 (GEM3)**: the Bundesbank publishes the long- and short-term variations in this aggregate index. *Newsmetrics* includes the actual monthly variations announced by the Central Bank and the variations expected by traders. The base period for the calculation of the variations is modified every year in the month of February. The base is the fourth quarter of the previous year. The database also indicates the modifications to the base. The variations in the M3 aggregate refer to the previous month.

4) **Unemployment (GEUNEMP)**: the German Central Institute of Statistics announces the unemployment level for East and West Germany in the first ten days of each month. It announces the number of jobless, the overall figures, the long- and short-term relative variations and the unemployment rate. The database refers to the total number of jobless (in millions), adjusted for seasonality, in West Germany, which is considered more significant by economic operators. As usual, it includes both actual and expected values and they refer to the previous month.

4.4 American and German Qualitative News on the Economic Situation and on Monetary Policy

This category includes news with codes QUS, QGE, TUS and TGE. The first two relate primarily to news on the economic situation of the countries under consideration, and miscellaneous news only indirectly related to the economic situation or to the debate on the country's economic policy; the other two are directly and indirectly related to variations in official interest rates.

The news on the economic situation generally reproduce almost *verbatim* – with more details, since 1997, or in the simple form of journalistic headlines until then – the American and German quantitative news described in the two preceding sections. They often indicate an economic event that has not been explicitly considered in these paragraphs.

The American news, classified under the code QUS, generally refer to the macroeconomic variables described in section 4.2 with some additional detail, for instance the description of the short-term survey carried out monthly by the banks of the Federal Reserve System in the districts of their respective competence, the so-called "Beige Book". They also contain miscellaneous news relating to the US economic performance, for instance news on the sharp conflict between Congress and the President of the United States over the 1996 Federal Budget, between the end of 1995 and the beginning of 1996, which resulted in the closing of several Government offices in Washington and the consequent interruption of the preparation of the country's economic data.

The German news, classified under the code QGE, are also of a primarily short-term nature, with reference to a wider number of indicators than those considered in section 4.3. Among these the news relating to unemployment carry particular significance. In addition, news on this country's economic situation are enmeshed with news on the European convergence towards the Maastricht criteria and on the debate over the adequacy of monetary and fiscal policy in Germany and in the other major European countries. This last type of news will be described next in Chapter 5.

The news regarding monetary policy, classified under the codes TUS and TGF, refer to announcements of variations in official rates or, alternatively, news on the absence of variations. In addition, this category of events also contains market comments on exchange rate movements directly connected to variations, or the absence of variations, in the official interest rates.

The news regarding both the economic situation and monetary policy in the two countries which concern us here have numerous points in common with the frequent statements of principle and other declarations by the main players of economic policy, in particular those responsible for the monetary policy of the United States, Germany and Japan. The classification of news within this type of events was done according to the primary effect on official interest rates, exchange rates or other financial variables. This classification criterion, however, may lend itself to arbitrariness or error; in order to avoid these or similar defects in other parts of the database, the majority of the events described in *Newsmetrics* have more than one code.

Notes

1 See N. FRUMKIN [1994].

2 This applies to all the quantitative news that follow.

Chapter 5

The Events of the European Monetary Union

5.1 The Historical Timeline

The years covered by *Newsmetrics* see the final phases of the creation of the European Monetary Union (EMU). During 1994 and until September 1995 the attention of the international financial markets for this subject remains rather restrained and that of the Monetary Authorities of the main countries concerned quite limited. From 21 September, 1995 the Lira and the Deutschmark exchange rates against the Dollar begin to be increasingly affected by the events connected to the implementation of EMU. The starting point of this phase is marked by Weigel's statement about Italy's unlikely participation to EMU's first phase, widely publicised by the news agencies and the international press. This is the first EMU-related news in the database.[1]

This initial event effectively contains the topic that will dominate the interventions of the European monetary authorities in 1996, particularly the German authorities: the respect of the Maastricht convergence criteria. Side by side with these interventions, which become ever more pressing[2] during the course of the year, in 1996 the attention of commentators and the markets alike is focused on the domestic situation of Germany and France, the two countries that will supposedly constitute the foundation of the future EMU. The underlying reason is self-evident: as economic growth falls and unemployment rises, the achievement of a public administration deficit compatible with the values contemplated in the Maastricht Treaty becomes increasingly unlikely.

Already from January 1996 we see that these are the topics at the heart of the debate, when Duisenberg, the appointed president of the European Central Bank, denies that the EMU is a recession vehicle (1660). French ex-President Giscard d'Estaing is far from persuaded by this, and he pushes for a review of the EMU criteria (1705). At the end of the month unemployment in France tops three million (1744). In Germany, the first ten days of January are marked by a series of unfavorable economic and unemployment news (1606, 1634, 1648).

In the three following months German unemployment records an increase every time the relative statistics are published (1776, 1870, 1968), amid concerns over the effects that an ever increasing level of unemployment benefits can have on the German public administration current deficit. In this period there are already rumours of a possible postponement of EMU (1729, 1793, 1794) and severe warnings regarding the need to respect the Maastricht Treaty deadlines (1734, 1903).

Unemployment continues to worsen in France (2226, 2355, 2359, 2464, 2529, 2554, 2701) and Germany (2279, 2599, 2852) for the remainder of 1996, while the economic cycle also remains basically depressed (2010, 2026, 2087, 2108, 2464, 2779, 2820, 2840), even though there are occasionally some positive announcements, generally referring to fluctuations in the German industrial production. Against this background – which remains constant together with the repeated warnings regarding the need to respect the Maastricht criteria (see Tables 6.1 and 6.2) and with occasional indiscretions as to the countries to be included (in which Italy is never considered) or over possible postponements of EMU (1729, 1919, 1929, 2379, 2435) – the main events of the year are:

(A) the frequent controls during the year as to whether France and Germany will be able to reach the 3% of GDP deficit;
(B) Finland's entrance into the EMS, on 13 October (2615);
(C) the first agreement over the introduction of a stability pact into the public accounts dynamics once the EMU is implemented;
(D) the Lira's re-entry into the EMS;
(E) Italy's ability to produce a 1997 Budget that may enable the country to achieve the 3% GDP-deficit ratio;
(F) convergence trading on fixed income public securities in Italy and Spain, which determines a significant reduction in the long-term rates of these countries.

The first official criticisms over the inadequacy of the measures adopted to achieve the Maastricht criteria are voiced in July by the European Council of Finance Ministers (Ecofin) with respect to Austria, Germany, France and Italy (2272, 2276, 2277). The "Economic Outlook" of the OECD had already foreshadowed the possibility that France and Germany may miss the Maastricht 3% target (2210). Then the six main German economic research institutes consider the possibility that Germany may miss some of the key EMU criteria (2686). These are initial estimates that will become much more frequent during the course of 1997.

Faced with the "ferment of initiatives" displayed by the French and the Italians to meet the main Maastricht criterion on public deficit, during the course of 1996 the German Authorities consolidate the idea of containing the dynamics of this aggregate also in the period following the start of EMU. Tietmeyer and other members of the Bundesbank Council repeatedly assert[3] that the budget measures that France and Italy are preparing for 1997 may at most enable these countries to achieve the magic 3% figure in that year, without any guarantees of sustainability later. During the autumn of 1996 there are some negotiations (2494, 2526, 2633, 2716, 2821, 2839) and some positioning over the stability pact, which is later agreed to at the EU summit in Dublin, during 12-15 December, 1996 (2880, 2890, 2891, 2899, 2900).

The Maastricht Treaty requires EMU members to have participated in the EMS for at least two years prior to their entry in the Union. The spring of 1996 is therefore the period in which Italy should initiate the re-entry into the EMS. On 10 June, at one of the periodic Italo-French summits, the negotiations begin. France having repeatedly encouraged Italy to do so in order to put an end to the competitive advantage acquired with the 1995 devaluation (1899). On 30 September, immediately preceding an Italo-French summit, Chirac supposedly makes statements that are directly or indirectly adverse to the Lira's re-entry into the EMS (2563, 2577). Subsequently their differences are cleared up (2587, 2593), but immediately after there is a formidable volley of anti-Italian statements both from the French (2622) and, primarily, from the Germans (see section 2.6). The final phase begins on 14 November (2750) and re-entry takes place during the weekend of 23-24 November, at the end of very tense negotiations (2785, 2787, 2790, 2791).

The final phase of the Lira's re-entry into the EMS follows the approval of a substantial package of measures to reduce the 1997 deficit, which goes well beyond the measures outlined in the 1997 DPEF with a view to enabling Italy to participate in the EMU with the initial group of countries (2549, 2555). As we have seen in Chapter 2, this "change of programme" occurs after an Italo-Spanish summit in which Spain convincingly shows that it can meet all the EMU conditions, without resorting to any "allowances" (2550).

The real possibility that Spain and Italy may be part of the EMU from the outset generates in September a strong increase in the prices of Italian and Spanish fixed income securities (2523), as the yields on these instruments are much higher than those of the comparable German securities with which they will compete within EMU. This trend will continue vigorously for the entire autumn, substantially reducing the Italian and Spanish long-term rates and thus permitting a strong reduction in the interest burden on the public debt.

After a poor economic situation in 1996 and with still soaring unemployment levels in Germany, France and Italy, 1997 begins with a weakening of the European currencies against the Dollar, already started in November by a series of French verbal interventions (see section 2.2), which were certainly followed by a secret agreement between the German and the French governments to launch the Euro from a less punishing exchange level against the Dollar. Indeed, this first group of interventions is followed from the beginning of January 1997 by a series of interventions by Bundesbank members directed at weakening the Germany currency (see Table 6.1 and, for the Deutschmark, Figure 2.5).

The European growth remains fairly modest in 1997. German unemployment stays at high levels (3125, 3773, 3961, 4110, 4295, 4509). The consequences of this situation on the public deficit of the two major European countries fuels a series of negative comments (2979, 3155, 3266, 3271, 3307, 3456, 3534, 3535, 3640, 3936) regarding France's and Germany's ability to meet the Maastricht Treaty criteria. In May Germany is even forced to admit that it must raise its official unemployment estimates for 1997 (3620).

Within this depressed macroeconomic situation, the two most significant episodes in the year preceding the final official choice of the countries conforming the EMU in its initial phase – and which are determinant for this choice – are: (a) Minister Weigel's unfortunate proposal to revalue the Bundesbank's official reserves in order to "touch up" the German public accounts; and (b) the victory of the Left in the French elections, which shifts the political emphasis of EMU considerably, from a stance of fiscal discipline at all costs towards a model that takes into account the difficult unemployment situation in Europe.

These two more or less contemporary episodes, occurring on 15 May and 2 June respectively, mark an important turning point in the markets' direction and the tone of German statements, which are no longer aimed at a specific country – traditionally Italy and France – but now focus on the benefits of postponing the EMU. We see that – with very few exceptions, such as the last anti-Italian statements at the end of August, see section 2.7 – beginning in June there is a sudden interruption of the flow of statements regarding the need for discipline and the respect of the Maastricht parameters[4] and we see several instances of Germany adopting a strong position over the need to postpone EMU (Stoiber, 29 June, 3911; Stoiber, Schroder, 6 July, 3951; Stoiber, 14 July, 4142) – with an unusual contribution from Italian Minister Dini (4256).

But even this series of statements ceases completely after (a) a political clarification within the German Government coalition, made necessary by Minister Weigel's expressed intention to accept another office, in August-September (see section 2.3), and (b) an important Ecofin meeting on 14 and 15 September that fixes the criteria of parity with the Euro for the countries participating in the EMU during the transition period, until the substitution of the domestic currencies with the Euro (4332, 4233).

The final upheavals on the road to EMU occur in mid-November, with some measures to defer expenditures that Minister Weigel must adopt in order to meet the 3% target in 1997 (4796) and with the doubts put forward by the Government's council of economic advisers a technical consulting organism of the Government and by the social-democratic opposition regarding Germany's real chances of respecting all the Maastricht criteria (4831).

But now the die is cast and the greatest effect on the market climate and on future requirements is generated by comments and statements, generally by Bundesbank members, regarding the German interest rate levels and the difference between these rates and the European average before EMU (4342, 4557, 4605, 4647, 4728, 4729, 4730, 4731, 4749, 4818, 4829, 4856, 4882, 4952, 4953).

5.2 The Classification of Events

In terms of the currencies most affected by the events in the final phases of EMU, the corresponding news have been gathered in two groups, depending on the exchange rate most concerned: the Deutschmark-Dollar or the Lira-Deutschmark. The first group of events has been coded QUMIN, and the second QUM. Here too it is hard to define a clear dividing line between the news of the first and the second type. Thus we again employ the double code rule that typically brings together the two types of events, QUMIN and QUM. In any case there are numerous exceptions, the most significant one being the Italian public finances events of 1997 which, while primarily of domestic interest, have nonetheless been classified with the double code of FINPUBL and QUM because that was the year of reference for the evaluation of EMU candidate countries' achievement of the convergence criteria. These events were particularly numerous because this year concentrates on an extraordinary corrective measure for the public accounts between March and May, the usual DPEF process, and the preparation of the 1998 Budget, characterized by a lively debate over the pension reform, which even resulted in a short-lived government crisis in October 1997.

Notes

1 The EMU events and the reactions of the exchange rates are described in some detail also in Chapter 2. This section will therefore refer to the main events of EMU and to the main topics of the related economic and political debate.

2 Escalating from 8 events concentrated in the last quarter of 1995 to 31 events evenly distributed over 1996, see Tables 6.1 and 6.2.

3 See the declarations made to the Bundesbank officials in October and November: out of a total of 26 interventions, all of 14 refer to the unreliability of France's and Italy's budgetary measures.

4 We see that the great Eurocrats, Duisenberg (3775, 3905), Santer (3797) and Thibauld de Silguy (3872), react immediately to the new "climate".

Chapter 6

Statements by Monetary and Government Authorities in the United States, Germany and Japan

6.1 Introduction

Modern economic and financial communication has undergone deep methodological changes in the last 20 years, following the progressively increased use of mass communication media and the marked development of an integrated world economy and international financial markets. While after both wars communication was entrusted to official documents, press releases and technical papers in specialized publications (especially in the case of economic and monetary policy communications), today it is becoming increasingly frequent for policy-makers to communicate with electoral, business and financial communities directly.

The difference relative to the past is particularly glaring in the case of monetary and currency policy news management. Italian analysts and commentators still have fresh in their memories the shy, reserved attitude of the monetary authorities in the 1950s (Luigi Einaudi, Donato Menichella, Guido Carli). In the United States public communication has a more illustrious and open tradition, but here too the various McChesney-Martins, Burns, Volckers (in a double role as Treasury Under-secretary and Governor of the Fed) made their voices heard only on certain occasions – before Congress, in academic situations, at public events – basically just like Greenspan. But in the case of the United States it is the attention of the media that has grown significantly in recent years, despite the fact that the opportunities for public announcements of monetary and financial policy fundamental trends have remained relatively unchanged. In Germany and Japan too the communication model illustrated above has changed radically over time.

It is worth defining immediately what we intended for "statements" in our analysis. The definition includes: (a) an opinion expressed on current topics – related to the economic situation or to economic policy – considered particularly important by the person making the statement, or which requires an official opinion from the organization he or she represents; (b) information – raw or commented – regarding current events or in any case events that are relevant for the present and for the future. These statements are usually made: (a) at official speeches in various venues (Universities, conferences, meetings of economic authorities, etc.); (b) in an institutional framework, during official meetings, before parliamentary commissions or before international organizations; (c) directly to the media – formally, or more rarely, in a spontaneous manner – through newspaper, radio or television interviews. *Newsmetrics* classifies as statements also (d) stances taken by international bodies and monetary and economic policy authorities in written documents (press releases, documents, studies or official bulletins, such as those of the Bundesbank or the Bank of England).

Newsmetrics concerns itself primarily with events and statements directly or indirectly relevant to the movements in the Lit-DM, DM-$ and Yen-$ exchange rates. In that sense the statements recorded represent a subgroup of statements made by official bodies regarding economic and financial matters. Within this subgroup, the attention has been focused on the so-called "market-moving" events, i.e. those events considered most influential by financial market operators in the determination of the prices of financial activities.

Among the countries under review – Italy, Germany, the United States, Japan and to a smaller extent other countries such as France – Italy does not have specific entries under the "statements" category, because the Lira-Deutschmark exchange rate has long been the result of the Deutschmark-Dollar exchange rate while the upheavals of 1994 and 1995 have been determined primarily by political events.[1] Here communications and statements are clearly important, but – especially in 1995 – they have been regarded as events that have had repercussions on the Lira exchange rate,[2] rather than as statements. In addition, as already indicated in section 1.3, the tradition of economics and economic policy communication in Italy is somewhat idiosyncratic, and even if such communications have certainly had a long-term impact it is difficult to attribute an immediate market-moving effect to them.

This chapter examines the *statements* by the American, German and Japanese monetary and political authorities. They can be found in their full version in the database of this research, with the dates and the context in which they were made. A statistical summary is presented in Tables 6.1 to 6.6.

The graphs in Chapter 2 indicate the statements that have had the greatest impact on the exchange rate, or which alternatively have been able to move the market in a particular direction for a certain time.

Newsmetrics uses the following statement codes and the following type of statement-news:[3]

DGE: statements by Bundesbank members, German Ministers and the German Chancellor regarding the DM-$ exchange rate and the monetary and fiscal policies;

DJA: statements by Japanese monetary and economic policy authorities regarding the exchange rate and the monetary and fiscal policies;

DUS: statements on the DM-$ exchange rate and the monetary and fiscal policies by American and German Monetary and economic policy Authorities (with the exception of Governor Greenspan) made in the European afternoon; this code includes also US statements on the Yen-$ exchange rate and on Japanese policies;

GRE: statements by Governor Greenspan on the UD economy and monetary and fiscal policies.

Each of the database codes described above gathers different types of official statements. This chapter defines the various types and describes the dynamic exchange rate and market sentiment context in which they are made – and which contributes to shape them. The objective is to illustrate the complex motivations that are at the base of this considerable oratory production. We have seen earlier that statements are made essentially to inform and to influence. Here we see in what way these objectives are pursued.

The statements have been classified by the person making the statement (for instance Tietmeyer, Greenspan, Matsushita, Rubin, etc.), by subject and by expected positive (revaluation) or negative (devaluation) effect on the exchange rate. This last exercise is used later, in addition to the econometric analysis in Chapter 7, to build Tables 6.1 to 6.6, where the statements are summarised also on the basis of their probable effect on the exchange rate, or the effect desired by the statement issuer.

We have tried to collect the statements by subject. It must be noted here that (a) the *Newsmetrics* management software limits the length of all news to 250 characters and (b) they have been taken from the major economic newspapers rather than from the primary source. Under these conditions, inevitably some opportunity for analysis may be lost or the background of some statement may remain in the shadows – due to the possible "obscurity" of the statement (think of the "opacity" attributed to Greenspan) and the loss of nuances in the first interpretation of the agency source or in the passage from this to the newspaper and from the newspaper to our files. These circumstances may have produced some interpretative distortion, but we feel that the professionalism of the journalists whose articles we have used must have limited its extent. Having said this, the subjects of the statements have been collected under the following headings:

a) *Monetary policy and interest rates*. This category collects those statements that are typically the responsibility of the monetary authorities. In some statements the reference to the economic situation in relation to the prevailing monetary policy orientation is explicit and in others it is not, in some statements the underlying analytical framework is clear, in others it is less clear, in some statements there is an appreciable effort to be clear, whereas in others a deliberate ambiguity prevails.

b) *Dollar exchange rate in general and bilateral exchange rates against the Deutschmark and the Yen.* These statements are often veritable Monetary Authorities interventions in the currency markets, but without an associated reserves cost. As such they have acquired growing popularity in recent years and they have been used with such generosity as to prompt the specialized press to coin a new term: "talking the Dollar (or the DM or the Yen) up (or down)".

c) *Economic policy in general.* A small number of statements refers to economic policy in general. A classic example is given by the frequent criticisms of the German Monetary Authorities – in the first months of 1995, with the marked devaluation of the US currency – over the lack of fiscal policy discipline in that country and over the policy-makers' apparent indifference to the exchange rate level against the Dollar.

d) *European Monetary Union (EMU).* This subject is obviously of central importance in the period covered by *Newsmetrics*. The frequency of statements regarding EMU is low in 1995 but it increases in 1996, reaching a climax in 1997. The effect of these statements has worked in several directions. The Lira has often suffered, directly or indirectly, from the frequent German statements over the need to respect the Maastricht criteria "to the last decimal point". A statistical analysis of the effect of these statements on the Lira and on the BTP rates can also be found in FORNARI-MONTICELLI-PERICOLI-TIVEGNA [1999].

e) *United States-Japan bilateral trade.* This has been a fairly hot topic during the period of reference. The foreign exchange traders have often attributed the fluctuations in the Yen-Dollar exchange rate to the turbulent negotiations on this subject.

The interpretation of the positive or negative effect of these statements on the exchange rate is rather subjective, and the interpretation key used by the journalists reporting the statement (whether of a primary source or of the newspaper) becomes quite important. Our objective here is to perform a first descriptive analysis of the types of intervention and their impact on the exchange rate dynamics.[4]

Statistical summaries of the statements covered by subjects (a) to (e) above are gathered in six tables (6.1 to 6.6) – in chronological order, by month, and with reference to the main personalities making the statements, for the 1995-1997 three-year period. Tables 6.1, 6.2, 6.4 and 6.5 contain in chronological order the number of statements by Bundesbank members, by German Political Authorities, and by American and Japanese Monetary and Political Authorities, classified according to the four subjects selected above and according to their likely impact on the exchange rate.[5] The subjects regarding interest rates, exchange rates and the economic policy in general,

Table 6.1 Statements by members of the Bundesbank Council

	Interest Rates		Exchange Rates		EMU	Economic Policy			Tot +	Tot -	Total
	+	-	+	-		+	?	-			
1995											
January	1								1	0	1
February									0	0	0
March		1	5					1	5	2	7
April	2		2			1		2	5	2	7
May	5		2						7	0	7
June		2	1						1	2	3
July		1							0	1	1
August	1			1					1	1	2
September			2		1				2	0	3
October	1		1	1					2	1	3
November	1				1				1	0	2
December	2								2	0	2
Total	13	4	13	2	2	1	0	3	27	9	38
1996											
January	4		1		1				5	0	6
February		3	1		2				1	3	6
March	1								1	0	1
April			3			1			4	0	4
May	2	1	2		2			1	4	2	8
June		1	1	1					1	2	3
July		1	1	1	1				1	2	4
August	2	1		1	1				2	2	5
September	1	1	1	1	1				2	2	5
October	2	3		2	10				2	5	17
November	1		4		4				5	0	9
December		1	1		3				1	1	5
Total	13	12	15	6	25	1	0	1	29	19	73
1997											
January	1	2	2	2	1				3	4	8
February				5	2				0	5	7
March	1			3	3				1	3	7
April	2			2	4				2	2	8
May			1	1					1	1	2
June	1				2	1			2	0	4
July	1	2		4					1	6	7
August	5	4		3	2	1			6	7	15
September	9	5	3	3	2				12	8	22
October	9	10	2						11	10	21
November	10	4		1					10	5	15
December	2	2	2				2		4	2	8
Total	41	29	10	24	16	2	2	0	53	53	124

Table 6.2 Statements by German policy-makers

	Interest Rates		Exchange Rates		EMU	Economic Policy		Tot. +	Tot. -	Total
	+	-	+	-		+	-			
1995										
January								0	0	0
February								0	0	0
March								0	0	0
April							1	0	1	1
May								0	0	0
June								0	0	0
July								0	0	0
August			1					1	0	1
September					5			0	0	5
October								0	0	0
November					1			0	0	1
December								0	0	0
Total	0	0	1	0	6	0	1	1	1	8
1996										
January			2		1			2	0	3
February	1				1			1	0	2
March					2			0	0	2
April			1					1	0	1
May								0	0	0
June								0	0	0
July								0	0	0
August								0	0	0
September					1			0	0	1
October								0	0	0
November					1			0	0	1
December								0	0	0
Total	1	0	3	0	6	0	0	4	0	10
1997										
January					1			0	0	1
February				1	1			0	1	2
March					3			0	0	3
April				1	4			0	1	5
May								0	0	0
June					4			0	0	4
July			1		4			1	0	5
August		1		1	3			0	2	5
September								0	0	0
October								0	0	0
November	1							1	0	1
December					1			0	0	1
Total	1	1	1	3	21	0	0	2	4	27

Table 6.3 Statements by members of the Bundesbank Council and by German policy-makers (by name)

		Interest Rates		Exchange Rates		EMU	Economic Policy			Tot. +	Tot. -	Total
		+	-	+	-		+	?	-			
	1995	1		1						2		2
Bundesbank	1996	1			1	1			1	1	2	4
	1997	2	2	1	2			1		3	4	8
	1995	1	1	9	1	2			2	10	4	16
Tietmeyer	1996	3	6	10	2	14	1			14	8	36
	1997	7	5	1	13	9	2	1		10	18	38
	1995	1	1							1	1	2
Gaddum	1996		1								1	1
	1997	2	1		2					2	3	5
	1995											
Hesse	1996											
	1997		3		1	1					4	5
	1995	1	1	2	1		1		1	4	3	7
Issing	1996	2	4		1	2				2	5	9
	1997	4	4	1	2					5	6	11
	1995	2								2		2
Jochimsen	1996	2				2				2		4
	1997	1	2	2		3				3	2	8
	1995	2								2		2
Koebnick	1996	1	1		2	2				1	3	6
	1997	5	1			1				5	1	7
	1995	2								2		2
Krupp	1996											
	1997	3		1						4		4
	1995											
Keubacher	1996	1		1		2				2		4
	1997	3	1			1				3	1	5
	1995	1								1		1
Meister	1996	1								1		1
	1997	3	1	1						4	1	5
	1995											
Palm	1996											
	1997	2								2		2
	1995											
Schieber	1996											
	1997	1								1		1
	1995	1		1						2		2
Sievert	1996		1	1						1	1	2
	1997	2	1							2	1	3
	1995											
Welteke	1996	1		1		1				2		3
	1997	4	3	3	3	1				7	6	14
	1995	1	1							1	1	2
Zeitler	1996	1		2		1				3		4
	1997	2	4		1					2	5	7
Total		67	45	38	32	43	4	2	4	109	81	235

Table 6.3 (continued) Statements by members of the Bundesbank Council and by German policy-makers (by name)

		Interest Rates		Exchange Rates		EMU	Economic Policy			Tot. +	Tot. -	Total
		+	-	+	-		+	?	-			
	1995			1						1	0	1
Government	1996			2		1				2	0	3
Sources	1997									0	0	0
	1995								1	0	1	1
Kohl	1996					4				0	0	4
	1997			1		6				1	0	7
	1995									0	0	0
Rexrodt	1996			1						1	0	1
	1997									0	0	0
	1995									0	0	0
Stoiber	1996									0	0	0
	1997					3				0	0	3
	1995					6				0	0	6
Waigel	1996									0	0	0
	1997				2	7				0	2	9
	1995									0	0	0
Others	1996	1				1				1	0	2
	1997	1	1		1	5				1	2	8
Total		2	1	5	3	33	0	0	1	7	5	45

Table 6.4 Statements by US monetary authorities

	Interest Rates		Dollar		Yen		Trade		Tot. +	Tot. -	Total
	+	-	+	-	+	-	+	-			
1995											
January	1							2	1	2	3
February		1								1	1
March	1		3						4		4
April			2						2		2
May			2					1	2	1	3
June		2								2	2
July	1	1							1	1	2
August											
September	1		1						2		2
October			1						1		1
November	1								1		
December											
Total	5	4	9					3	14	7	21
1996											
January		1	1						1	1	2
February	1	1							1	1	2
March			1						1		1
April											
May			1						1		1
June				2						2	2
July	1		1						2		2
August											
September	4								4		4
October			1						1		1
November	1			1					1	1	2
December		1								1	1
Total	7	3	5	3					12	6	18
1997											
January	1		3						4		4
February	1			1				1	1	2	3
March	2			1				2	2	3	5
April	1		3			1		1	4	2	6
May		1	2						2	1	3
June			1		1			1	2	1	3
July	2			1					2	1	3
August			2					1	2	1	3
September	1		2		2	1		4	5	5	10
October	1	4						1	1	5	6
November			2					1	2	1	3
December					1	1			1	1	2
Total	9	5	15	3	4	3		12	28	23	51

Table 6.5 Statements by Japanese monetary authorities

	Interest Rates		Exchange Rates			Trade		Economic Policy			Tot. +	Tot. -	Total
	+	-	+	?	-	+	-	+	?	-			
1995													
January	1										1	0	1
February											0	0	0
March	1										1	0	1
April			5								5	0	5
May											0	0	0
June											0	0	0
July			2								2	0	2
August											0	0	0
September			4		1						4	1	5
October					1						0	1	1
November											0	0	0
December											0	0	0
Total	2	0	11	0	2	0	0	0	0	0	13	2	15
1996													
January											0	0	0
February		1	1								1	1	2
March											0	0	0
April		1		1							0	1	2
May			3								3	0	3
June			1								1	0	1
July											0	0	0
August			1								1	0	1
September	2										2	0	2
October	2	1									2	1	3
November					3						0	3	3
December		1			2						0	3	3
Total	4	4	6	1	5	0	0	0	0	0	10	9	20
1997													
January			2		4						2	4	6
February			1		2						1	2	3
March							1			1	0	2	2
April			2		7						2	7	9
May	1	2	2		3						3	5	8
June		1	2	1	1						2	2	5
July			2								2	0	2
August	1			1					1		1	0	3
September			1	1	2		1	2	1		3	3	8
October	1	2								1	1	3	4
November	2		1	1	3					2	3	5	9
December			1	1	9						1	9	11
Total	5	5	14	5	31	0	2	2	2	4	21	42	70

Table 6.6 Statements by monetary authorities of the United States and Japan (by name)

		Interest Rates		Exchange Rates			Trade		Economic Policy			Tot. +	Tot. -	Total
		+	-	+	-		+	?	-					
	1995											0	0	0
Fed Sources	1996	3										3	0	3
	1997	1				1						1	1	2
	1995	2	4	1								3	4	7
Greenspan	1996	2	1	1								3	1	4
	1997	7	4	1								8	4	12
	1995			6								6	0	6
Rubin	1996			3		1						3	1	4
	1997			15		4		9				15	13	28
	1995			2								2	0	2
Summers	1996					1						0	1	1
	1997			1		1		2				1	3	4
	1995	2						3				2	3	5
Others	1996	4	1	2		1						6	2	8
	1997	1	1			1		1				1	3	4
Total		22	11	32	0	10	0	15	0	0	0	54	36	90
	1995			1								1	0	1
Hashimoto	1996											0	0	0
	1997			2		1					1	2	2	4
	1995											0	0	0
Kubo	1996	1	1									1	1	2
	1997											0	0	0
	1995	1		1								2	0	2
Matsushita	1996	2	2	1		1						3	3	6
	1997	1	1		1	1			1			2	2	5
	1995											0	0	0
Mitsuzuka	1996											0	0	0
	1997	1		4	1	10		2		1		5	12	19
	1995			1		1						1	1	2
Sakakibara	1996			3	1	4						3	4	8
	1997		2	5	1	11				1		5	13	20
	1995	2		4		1						6	1	7
Takemura	1996											0	0	0
	1997											0	0	0
	1995			3								3	0	3
Others	1996	1	1	2								3	1	4
	1997	3	2	3	2	9			1		3	7	14	23
Total		12	9	30	6	39	0	2	2	2	4	44	54	106

when available, are common to all the tables. German statements touch also on EMU subjects, while American and Japanese statements refer also to problems in the bilateral trade between the two countries. Tables 6.3 and 6.6 collect, for the same subjects and likely effects on the exchange rate, some statistics for the main German, American and Japanese statement issuers, with reference to the three years during which the news has been collected – 1995, 1996, 1997.

Lastly, a word on the coverage of the entire universe of statements contained in *Newsmetrics*. The database contains only a sample, the primary inclusion filter being the presence of the statement in the daily Currency Market Report of the *Financial Times*. This is the main criterion. Many other statements have been taken from other sections of the *Financial Times*, from the *International Herald Tribune*, from the *Wall Street Journal* and from *Il Sole XXIV Ore*.

In the following sections we examine the statements by Bundesbank Council members, which constitute the largest group (section 6.2), then those by German government officials and by their most influential advisors (section 6.3). Then we move on to the less numerous but equally important statements by Fed Governor Greenspan and other representatives of the US Monetary Authorities and the US Government (section 6.4). The sample of European statements is completed by French representatives – whose weight is significant given the weakening of the Deutschmark from the end of November 1996 – and by representatives of other countries, intervening almost exclusively on EMU.[6] Even though the Lira and the Deutschmark are the most widely covered currencies in *Newsmetrics*, and the currencies on which the database has been centred, globalization in the currency markets is highly developed, so that a new term has been coined – "contagion" – and a new area of analysis has emerged to study the dissemination, often without apparent cause, of financial turmoil. On more than one occasion we have realised that the full understanding of the dynamics of the Lira against the Deutschmark required an in-depth analysis of the overall dynamics of the Dollar, which in turn is strongly influenced by events, policies and orientations of the Japanese economy and policy-makers. We have therefore gathered a fairly high number of events and statements relating to the Japanese economy and to the Yen, which are analysed and described in section 6.5.

6.2 The Bundesbank

As we have already seen in Chapter 2, the Bundesbank is by far the most "talkative" of the major international institutions, perhaps contrary to its monolithic and austere image as the guardian of monetary stability. Even the comments made on the same subject by members of the board of directors ("the council") of the German Central Bank are often in contrast with each other. The main reason is the composition of this Council, constituted by Governor Tietmeyer, who has the greatest authoritativeness in the matter of public statements, by the presidents of the central banks of the German länder, who are generally politically appointed, and by one staff member,

Chief Economist Otmar Issing (now member of the European Central Bank Board of Directors). Despite the not unusual differences of opinion, there are no public expressions of open disagreement on the monetary policy measures adopted by the Bank.

The statements by Bundesbank Council members are by far the most numerous in *Newsmetrics*: Table 6.3 shows that they are 235, out of a total of 476, i.e. nearly half. They can be commented from (a) the point of view of their timing relative to the cycle of the Deutschmark-Dollar exchange rate and their impact on the market, (b) from the nominal frequency of the interventions, and (c) from their consistency with the official position of the respective institution and with the contents of Governor Tietmeyer's statements. A similar reading will be given to the other categories of statement issuers, always bearing in mind the explorative nature of our analysis.

We now compare the contents of the chronological Table 6.1 with those of Figures 2.1. to 2.6 in Chapter 2, always bearing in mind that even then a lot of attention was devoted to Bundesbankers' interventions and their effects, from a more dynamic perspective.

The year 1995 is the year of the collapse of the Dollar, in the first quarter, and of the various reanimation attempts carried out by G3 monetary authorities in the following quarters. In 1995 these attempts take the form of real, often joint interventions of the central banks in the markets (see Chapter 2), but statements are used too.

Thus we see that in March, after the strong devaluation of the Dollar in February, Bundesbank officers intervene at least five times in one month trying to support the US currency (see section 2.1 and Figure 2.1). Following their support and that of the French authorities (at this stage the Japanese are still absent from the picture) the Dollar stabilises, albeit amid wide fluctuations in March and April. At the beginning of May there is a strange period of revaluation of the Dollar (Figure 2.1), in which Bundesbank members intervene with some Dollar-bullish statements, to push the US currency in the unanimously desired direction.

After the May "hump" the Dollar stabilizes again, following a temporarily positive intervention of the central banks on 31 May. A definite rally of the US currency – at least against the Yen – occurs in the beginning of August, after a series of highly positive events and some co-ordinated interventions, first by the Fed and the Bank of Japan, and then in mid-August also by the Bundesbank. In this episode there are no particular verbal interventions by the Bundesbank.

At the end of September, Weigel's famous statement on Italy marks the beginning of the EMU statements season, in which Tietmeyer plays a part too. As seen in Chapter 2, Germany pays for the German Authorities' militancy for rigour with all the weakening of the Deutschmark that had been achieved with the interventions of August, leaving the Deutschmark in a position of significant overvaluation for the whole of 1996.

The year 1996 is therefore still a year in which the statements by German central bank members lean heavily towards a weaker Deutschmark. We can see from Table 6.1 that out of a total of 73 interventions for the year, 29 are in favor of a weakening of the Deutschmark compared to 19 in the opposite direction.

The interventions in mid-January (Figure 2.3) and in April succeed in weakening the German currency. Tietmeyer's intervention on 10 June appears to be immediately positive but without a lasting effect in the desired direction, not least because there is no particular verbal commitment on the part of other Bundesbank Council members in this month or in July (see also Table 6.1). In July the Deutschmark apprcciates again due to US events (section 2.2 and Figure 2.4). In the remainder of 1996 – with the exception of November which we will discuss later – the verbal commitment is visible but does not go in a univocal direction: Table 6.1 indicates that many interventions go in the opposite direction.

In the first half of November 1996 we have a series of interventions by Bundesbank members aimed at weakening the Deutschmark (Table 6.1). Immediately afterwards, a climate favorable to the weakening of the French Franc and the Deutschmark against the Dollar develops. In the first half of November the Deutschmark still fluctuates around 1.50 against the Dollar, only 6 pfennings more relative to the beginning of the year. Following these verbal initiatives, the Deutschmark loses more than 6 pfennings in the last days of November (Figure 2.4) and, after a brief pause in December, it continues in the same direction in 1997, in January and February, when it reaches over 1.70 against the Dollar (Figure 2.5).

In January 1997 Bundesbank members continue to support the Dollar, but with less determination than in November. In February, however, they change their attitude and begin to "row" in the opposite direction, probably because the Deutschmark has devalued beyond their expectations (Figure 2.5 and Table 6.1), stabilising it around 1.67 – 1.70 also in March.

From mid-May the Deutschmark begins a long period of weakness culminating on 6 August with a value just under 1.90. From the collection of news and comments in our database, this phenomenon seems to be the result of a generalized perception that the Euro will be weak from the beginning, following the episode of the revaluation of the Bundesbank gold reserves and the victory of the Left in the French elections (section 2.3).

The devaluation experienced by the Deutschmark in the first half of 1997 causes an increase in the German domestic inflation already from July of the same year. From the second half of August – and for a few weeks – the Bundesbank tries to spread the expectation of an increase in the German interest rates, contributing to the recovery of the Deutschmark (see also section 2.3). In September several members of the Bundesbank Council openly oppose increases in interest rates – despite the renewed inflation – thus giving way to an internal strife that will continue for the entire autumn (see the last note of this section for the month of September and section 2.3 for the autumn), resulting only in a slight increase in the repo rate on 9 October.

The frequency of interventions by individual members of the Bundesbank Council is shown in Table 6.3. From this Table – which we leave to the reader's free interpretation – it is very clear that Governor Tietmeyer intervenes more often (90 times), followed at a distance by Issing (27), and then Welteke (17), Koebnick (15) and Jochimsen (14).

Bundesbank members' interventions are generally consistent, but there are a few episodes of clear dissonance. For instance, the sequence of statements by Issing, Welteke, and Sievert on 25 October, 1996 compels Tietmeyer's intervention on the same day to provide the markets with a "true interpretation" of the Bundesbank's orientation on interest rates (see 1066, 1067, 1068). In September and October 1997 the high levels of German inflation, a relatively depressed domestic economic cycle and record unemployment often produce discordant opinions regarding interest rates among "Bundesbankers".[7] As shown above, all of this results in only a slight reduction of the repo.

6.3 German Government Officials

The statements by German Government officials on matters directly or indirectly relevant to monetary policy and to Deutschmark exchange rate management are far less numerous than those of Bundesbank members. This situation is quite different from that prevailing in the United States or in Japan, where the interventions of the Political Authorities are more frequent than those of the Monetary Authorities.

Table 6.2 contains the type, the likely effect and the frequency of interventions over time, while Table 6.3 contains the summarised data. This table refers to the main statement issuers.[8] The number of interventions in this group is quite limited and is focused primarily on EMU. They are quite monothematic in content – the need to rigorously respect the EMU membership criteria – and perfectly in line with the interventions by Bundesbank members. The infrequent statements on the exchange rate are, in general, in line with those of the Bundesbank.

6.4 American Monetary and Political Authorities

The period analysed by *Newsmetrics* goes from a strong devaluation of the Dollar in early 1995, to a period of gradual recovery finally completed in 1997. After an initial weakness the American policy moves with increasing determination towards a strong Dollar objective. The only instrument actually used to achieve this target is the expression of a political will in that direction: the first statements by Treasury Minister Rubin date back to March 1995, after the collapse of the Dollar in February.

The most likely reason for this "strong Dollar" strategy is probably that in the three-year period analysed by *Newsmetrics* the American economy remains strongly expansionary – as it has been since the beginning of the 1990s – among the general astonishment of economists. It is even more surprising that an unemployment rate that is much lower than the NAIRU could coexist with stable prices, while the economy grows at a pace that is "econometrically inconsistent" with price stability.

This astonishing price stability allows the Federal Reserve to gradually reduce interest rates in the 1995-1997 period, after the initial increase on 1 February, 1995, albeit among frequent "threats" of increases. The combination of a growing economy, unemployment levels at their historical low, stable prices and therefore stable interest rates may cause, as indeed it does, a highly favorable stock market cycle. This feeds into the citizens' disposable income and the direct taxes they contribute, thus making it possible to achieve the balancing of the federal budget, a historical milestone, earlier than expected. The increase in disposable income results in a high growth rate, through consumption; the budget surplus may result in an objective impulse towards stability or in a reduction of interest rates. Both results fuel the mechanism of their success.

The main condition for the perpetuation of this growth mechanism is to be found in a strong Dollar that can maintain a low price for production inputs and for imported manufactured goods, which compete with those made in the USA, exerting a powerful calming effect on domestic prices. The database captures at least two instances in which Treasury Minister Rubin himself reiterates the details of this "virtuous" growth mechanism caused by a strong exchange rate – among the many instances in which he favors a strong Dollar: on 14 April, 1997 (3444) and on 1 August, 1997 (4088), this time in response to American car manufacturers complaining about the Dollar's excessive strength.

In the United States the division of tasks regarding communication to the public and to the financial markets seems to be quite precise: the Governor of the Fed, Greenspan, generally intervenes on monetary policy and interest rates. The Minister of the Treasury, Rubin, intervenes – in the statements collected by *Newsmetrics* – primarily on the exchange rate, directly or indirectly. The influential Treasury Under-secretary Summers (Treasury Minister since May 1999) generally intervenes on the Japanese economic policies. Table 6.4 presents the timeline and the subject of Greenspan's and the American Government Authorities' statements, Table 6.6 summarises with the same classification criteria the statements by Greenspan and by politicians –limited to Rubin and Summers.[9]

Table 6.6 shows the numerical dominance of Rubin's statements (38), followed by Greenspan (23) and by Larry Summers from a greater distance (7).

The impact of Greenspan's statements on the American financial markets is generally quite strong. *Newsmetrics* collects only the official interventions, which are the greater majority. The structure of such interventions is generally quite stable: starting from an analysis of recent events in the American economy, Greenspan focuses the main part of his intervention (especially in the official presentations to Congress) on the monetary policy adopted in the recent past, and he concludes with the possible future trends of the economy and the interest rates. The reports usually focus on this latter subject. However, on occasion the scenario conclusions are ambiguous and the markets then look for clarification in the descriptive part of the intervention, formulating their own interpretation of selective parts of it; this causes reactions in the asset prices that can be quite visible, even if at first sight the descriptive contents look harmless and contain no clear or even hidden indications of economic policy.

The effect of Greenspan's statements is generally seen first in the stock and bond markets (for instance 1150 and 1151 in 1995, 2855, 2857 and 2870 in 1996), and some times also directly in the exchange rate (for instance 1933 in 1996). But the effect of Greenspan's interventions on the Dollar is almost always seen through the financial markets. Thus, when he clearly indicates that the interest rates will remain stable or will move upwards – in a period when a decrease was expected – the Dollar should tend to appreciate. However, higher interest rates are adverse to the financial markets and a Wall Street drop can reduce the inflow of capitals towards the Dollar, weakening the exchange rate. There are therefore two contradicting effects which are generally hard to isolate with any degree of certainty.

With reference to the three-year period 1995-1997 – Figures 2.1 to 2.6 – and reasoning in approximate terms, the interventions of 1995 (675, 677, 723, 1058, 1059, 1150, 1151, 1157) seem to have a direct influence on the exchange rate. Greenspan's intervention of 22 February, 1995 (675, 677), in which he outlines an economic slowdown in the United States for the second half of the year, implying that the US interest rates could hardly increase, probably gives the Dollar – which had already depreciated substantially from the beginning of the month – its *coup de grâce*. The 1996 interventions seem to influence the exchange rate only indirectly, except for that just illustrated. For instance, the intervention of 18 July (2324) extends Wall Street's downward correction, begun a few days earlier, thus causing a strong devaluation of the Dollar, Figure 2.3. On 5 December, 1996 the famous intervention on the "irrational exuberance" of the US stock market (2855, 2856, 2857) causes a strong if temporary weakening of the Dollar, Figure 2.4. In 1997 the interventions of 20 March (2321, 2325) and 22 July (4032, 4038, 4039) seem to replicate the same indirect model of 1996, Figures 2.5 and 2.6.

American Treasury Minister Rubin's style is sharper and the effect of his statements on the markets is rarely ambiguous. Given the importance of a strong Dollar, discussed above, the leit motif of his statements is: "a strong Dollar is in the best interest of the United States".[10] The repetition of this credo is so much taken for granted by the markets when Rubin speaks on the

Dollar or on related issues, that the only time when he does not mention that America needs a strong Dollar (on 20 May, 1997, 3680) the Dollar weakens. Thus, unlike the Bundesbankers and the Japanese policy-makers, his interventions are characterized by a repetition of the American economic policy direction rather than by *ad hoc* interventions in circumstances that require "*talking the Dollar up or down*".

Particular attention is given, in some of Rubin's interventions, to bilateral trade issues between the United States and Japan, to Japan's trade balance surplus and domestic economic policy, and to the bilateral exchange rate between the two countries. The effects of these interventions are not widely visible, but they certainly have an impact on Japan's economic policy. A distribution of Rubin's interventions by subject is presented in Table 6.6.

Larry Summer's interventions focus on the trade disputes with Japan and the inadequacy of that country's expansionary measures, see Table 6.6.

Finally a word on the degree of "consistency" of US policy-makers' statements. The specific *de facto* division of tasks between Greenspan and Rubin obviously favors the harmony of statements. In the *Newsmetrics* sample there are no statements by Rubin on interest rates, while there is a "loud and clear" statement by Greenspan on the Dollar exchange rate (26 March, 1996; 1933). Having said this, the ambiguous mechanism of transmission of American interest rate variation effects on the Dollar exchange rate has certainly contributed – in practice – to reducing the visibility of possible differences in judgement over monetary policy and exchange rate management.

6.5 Japanese Monetary and Political Authorities

In Japan the Bank of Japan has jurisdiction over monetary policy, while exchange rate decisions are determined by the Ministry of Finance. This distribution of tasks is reflected both in the content of the statements and in the reaction of the currency markets to the interventions by officials of each institution.

Like their German counterparts, the Japanese Monetary Authorities, which in this case include the Governor and the directors of the Central Bank, the Minister of Finance and the General Directors of the Ministry of Finance – first among them the influential Eisuke "Mr. Yen" Sakakibara – are highly interventionist in their statements. Unlike their German counterparts, however, the number of people making statements is more limited: Governor Matsushita from the Bank of Japan (13 interventions, See Table 6.6), the Minister of Finance – Takemura (7) and Mitsuzuka (19) in the period under review – and General Director Sakakibara (30). The degree of consistency among the positions expressed by the various Japanese personalities is comparable to that present among the American Authorities and greater than that among Bundesbank members.

Following on from the previous section, Table 6.5 indicates a time distribution of the statements, together with the type of content and their likely effect, and Table 6.6 groups them by statement issuer, year of reference, content and possible effect.

Japan appears to be the country most affected by the Dollar devaluation because it coincides with the disastrous earthquake of 17 January, 1995 (567), which hit the country's most industrialized province and occurred concurrently with the first symptoms of a financial crisis that developed fully in the following years.

Thus in 1995 the time distribution of Japanese interventions sees a predominance[11] of interventions in favor of weakening the Japanese currency (Table 6.5), accompanied by a series of continuous interventions on the foreign currency markets (Figures 2.1 and 2.2). The interventions made at the end of July and in August 1995 meet with particular success. After the rally of the Japanese currency between the end of the year and January 1996, the Yen strengthens again in April, for no apparent reason; in May a sustained series of verbal interventions weaken the Yen again (Figure 2.3). During the summer and in October the Yen devalues to 114 without specific verbal interventions pushing it in that direction. At the beginning of November the Ministry of Finance (MoF) considers that the Yen has devalued sufficiently. From then on statements by its representatives are generally in favor of a strengthening of the Japanese currency, in a *crescendo* that culminates in December 1997 (Table 6.7).

From Table 6.6 we can see that the greatest number of statements is made by one of the MoF General Directors, Sakakibara (30). As mentioned above, the international financial press has assigned him the role of "Yen spokesman", calling him "Mr. Yen", especially in *Newsmetrics*' period of reference. When he intervenes, or releases some statement, any movement in the Yen is attributed to his action.

Notes

1 To be more precise, the majority of events are communicated to the public by means of press releases and direct statements to the media by policy-makers. In this sense, there cannot be a clear dividing line between events and statements. In *Newsmetrics* many events – especially in the older parts of the database – are reported in the form of headlines from the newspapers we have used as sources. For instance the third newsflash of 1995 (552) at the time of the official interviews following Berlusconi's resignation, "Beginning of the dialogue. The Polo: without Berlusconi only an electoral government", is considered and codified as an event in the database, but it certainly implies many statements to the media. On the other hand, many events in the newer part of the database, where article headlines are no longer the only source of news but also the texts of the articles are used (for instance 4896, 4897, 4941 in 1997), imply a press release or a statement. A final addendum: The policy statements reported here are a subset of the actual ones, they are only those which filter through the international press.

2 See, as an example, the two statements by the Hon. Gasparri and the Hon. Visco on

17 February, 1995, mentioned in section 2.5, first quarter. They conform a single news item to which two event codes are assigned: GOVDINI (for the events related to the action of the Dini Government) and FINPUBL (for the events related to the Italian public accounts).

3 In the part of econometric verification of the explicative power of unscheduled news collected in *Newsmetrics*, Chapter 7, the subdivision of statements is more subtle because it takes into account the separation of the global trading day in two parts. See section 7.3 and Table 7.11, which present the codes of the variables used to calculate the equations in this work.

4 Thus, while it would not be appropriate to attribute particular scientific rigour to this "exercise" of ours, it can be considered as an introduction to further analysis – in two stages – in which the entire text of the statement is used where possible, and in which content analysis tools are applied to the entire text of the intervention or statement in order to identify its objective with certainty. As a second stage in the analysis, one could statistically correlate the message identified in the first stage with the exchange rate or other asset price dynamics. We have performed in our study a first classification of events and a first overview of their distribution among various subjects. Chapter 7 contains a statistical verification and an analysis to measure the effect on the exchange rate of each type of news.

5 Tables 6.1, 6.3, 6.5 and 6.6 also contain a question mark indicating a third type of effect, i.e. when it is not possible to identify it as positive or negative.

6 In addition to the official sources of the various countries that have not been identified individually, we have other statements by representatives of France, the European Union, Belgium, Italy, the Netherlands and the United Kingdom. The French are Alphandery, Arhuis, Balladour, Chirac, Gerard, Giscard d'Estaing, Jospin, Juppé, Marchelli, Seguin, Strauss-Khan and Trichet. The representatives of the European Union are Santer, Thibauld de Silguy, Van Miert and Duisenberg, President of the European Monetary Institute, forerunner of the Central European Bank. The Belgian, Dutch, Italian and English statement issuers are respectively Dutch Republic President Verplaetse, Dini, Prodi, Russo and Blair.

7 See the series of statements regarding the need to raise interest rates in the presence of renewed inflation: Sievert begins on Tuesday, 2 September (4259, against an interest rate increase), followed by Tietmeyer (4265, in favour), Welteke (4297, against), Jochimsen (4298, against), Zeitler (4308, in favour), Issing (4315, in favour), Krupp (4316, against), Koebnick (4327, against), Tietmeyer (4342 and 4343, in favour), and Welteke (4370, in favour), the last one of this round, on Wednesday, 17 September. We have five statements in favour and five statements against an interest rate increase.

8 The German non-political statement issuers are Hax, Hausman, Scharping, Siebert, Stark, and Donges.

9 The other US statement issuers are Angel, Barshefsky, Bentsen, Clinton, Garten, Ginrich, Kantor, Mondale, Moskow, Rivlin and Yellen.

10 There are 18 interventions of this kind, i.e. 56% of the total interventions made by him contained in the database.

11 In fact, the interventions are fewer in 1995 compared to 1997. This may be because of the lower number of total news collected in that year (1076) compared to 1997 (2203). On this point it is better to consider the net balance between interventions in favour and against a devaluation of the Yen in 1995 (+11), compared to a similar net balance in 1997 (-14, i.e. interventions in favour of a revaluation of the Yen prevail).

Chapter 7

The Impact of News on Exchange Rates

7.1 Introduction

During the course of their daily work, investors and foreign currency traders receive an immense amount of information through multiple channels: news in general, economic data releases, market opinions and market rumours regarding political and economic policy events, market analyses prepared by the leading financial institutions, and other material. All this flow of information can be divided into two distinct categories, depending on the regularity with which it occurs: expected events (scheduled news) and unexpected events (unscheduled news). The former, also defined in this work as quantitative or macroeconomic news, consist mostly of announcements of quantitative economic data at scheduled times, although the actual values are not known in advance; the latter, also defined as qualitative news, are generally unpredictable both in terms of timing and of content.

Unscheduled news represent an economic or institutional event, a statement or a clarification that is either fully unexpected or, even if somehow expected, their timing is not known beforehand. The analysis of fresh information constitutes a large portion of the foreign currency trader's complex activity. This obsessive attention for the latest piece of news is in strident contrast with the usual price formation theories applied to finance, based as they are on stable and predictable relationships between "fundamentals" and prices. The latest results of behavioural finance theory (Thaler, 1993) indicate that traders devote more time to the decoding of the latest events than to forecasting future developments of the fundamental macroeconomic variables. In the final chapter, section 8.4, we suggest a behavioral model for the foreign currency markets that uses communication theory elements, from the information flow and the traders' decoding perspective.

Scheduled news relate to macroeconomic data published by governments or central banks. Among the four countries under study, the United States publish well in advance a fixed calendar of macroeconomic releases, complete with day and time. For a long time financial operators have concentrated their attention on the publication of the major macroeconomic indicators of the US economic situation, at 8:30 Eastern Standard Time (EST), in the days indicated by the calendar, thus causing volatility peaks in the financial markets open at that time.[1] For this reason, particular attention is devoted to the collection of USA data, as described in detail in Chapter 4. Japan too maintains a daily calendar for a good part of its economic indicators. This news has not been collected in *Newsmetrics* because of the greater interest of this database for Italian and German events, but they appear indirectly in market comments or in statements by the Japanese authorities. Germany has an approximate calendar that indicates only the week of publication of the data, often preceded by indiscretions or unofficial information, usually for unemployment data, when the markets' interest is particularly intense. Given the relative uncertainty of the time of publication, the effect of the German economic releases on the DM-$ exchange rate is much more limited than that produced by the American ones. We will return to this point when we comment on the exchange rate equations, in section 7.3.2.

The majority of empirical studies on the impact of unexpected events on the exchange rates have used the American macroeconomic releases.[2] The main novelty of this study is the prevailing use of unscheduled news, collected in *Newsmetrics*.

The empirical results thus obtained are described in the following paragraphs. A ranking by importance of the various families of news identified in this work is described in the next chapter, in section 8.3. Here we limit ourselves to the overall conclusions drawn from our analysis. Qualitative news (statements and policy news, events of the international financial markets) have always carried much greater weight than quantitative news (differences between expected and actual values of the major macroeconomic indicators). German quantitative news are never significant. This could be due to the absence of a precise calendar to communicate the major macroeconomic variables to the markets.[3]

7.2 A Taxonomy of Events in the Foreign Exchange Markets

The number of events that can influence financial markets is virtually unlimited. Thus selecting those that truly affect the currency markets has been quite a complex job, and the unscheduled events collected in *Newsmetrics* are the result of a series of intermediate controls, briefly described in footnote 7 of this chapter.

Our objective in this section is to attempt a general taxonomy of the events affecting the currency markets in order to be able to state that we have collected a representative sample of all the exchange rate moving events, and to provide a concise example of the news included in the news bank and used in the empirical estimates of this chapter.

Qualitative unscheduled events that move the currency markets can be classified under one of the following five categories:

a) market information and opinions regarding:
    a1) economic, political and economic policy events (primarily of monetary and fiscal policy) that move the market;

- a2) expected values or current fluctuation ranges of the exchange rates deriving, for instance, from technical situations of the market or from profit-taking;
- a3) unconfirmed rumors relative to market events, specific orientations of market key personalities, opinions deriving from studies prepared by the leading financial institutions or from interviews with market leaders and opinion leaders;
- a4) unconfirmed rumors on economic, fiscal, monetary and exchange rate policies, on the professional characteristics and the orientation of policy-makers (for instance more hawkish or more doveish attitudes) and particularly on orientation changes relative to previous behavior or to a well-established stereotype (for example "*Greenspan's new doveish attitude…*", according to a market-moving article in *Business Week*, in the summer of 1997).

b) Economic, political and economic policy news, describing the event in the official and technical form rather than the form in which the markets register this kind of news: the latter should be classified under (a) given that they produce a different market reaction.

c) Qualitative description of a quantitative event, with or without confidential or background information, with or without opinions by traders or estimations of the ultimate effect of the news.

d) Expressions of opinion or economic policy statements by the most influential political representatives, ministers and central bankers, either as free and "spontaneous" opinions or as planned interventions to inform or influence traders' expectations and opinions, or to move exchange rates and other asset prices (see also section 6.1).

e) Official and well-publicized interventions by the central banks in the foreign exchange markets.

Now let us look at some examples of each type of qualitative news contained in *Newsmetrics*.

The following could represent examples of news under (a1):

> Favourable economic data, increasing speculation of a forthcoming US interest rate rise and unstable conditions in Mexico helped to buoy dollar sentiment. *Financial Times*, FT, 4.1.1995.

> DM continued to rampage through the foreign exchanges: with numerous European countries beset by either financial or political problems, in some cases both, the DM is seen as a bastion of safety for risk-averse investors. FT, 24.2.1995.

> Government defeated twice in the Lower House. Dini forced to call for a confidence vote for the corrective measure. *Il Sole-24 Ore*, 16.3.1995.

> The Dollar rallied sharply as details emerged of a late agreement in Geneva between the US and Japan in their disputed car trade talks. The news surprised markets which had anticipated that the talks would fail. FT, 27.6.1995.

> News that Yeltsin had been admitted to hospital was sufficient to push the $ higher while putting a dampener on the DM. Political uncertainty in Russia traditionally weighs on the DM. FT, 11.7.1995.

> The Dollar rallied sharply on intensified speculation of a cut in German interest rates when Buba council meets on Thursday. FT, 27.11.1995.

> No success for the attempt at dialogue in the Lower House between Government and Rifondazione. Prodi Government edging closer to a crisis. The fate of the legislature could soon return into Scalfaro's hand. *Il Sole-24 Ore*, 7.10.1997.

The first example provides some background information on some of the causes determining the crisis of the Dollar in that period. We then have a news item that represents an important strength factor for the Deutschmark and a weakness factor for the Dollar, consisting of the political turmoil in Spain and Italy in February 1995 (we also have a news item on the latter and another one on the period of turmoil of the Lira caused by the mini-crisis of the Prodi Government in October 1996). The third news, regarding the famous trade dispute between the United States and Japan over the auto sector, is a factor strengthening the Dollar that day. The fourth example offers some information on a temporary strengthening of the US currency.

The following are examples of news on the technical position of the foreign exchange markets under (a2):

> The DM lost ground across the board as investors took profits following the recent sharp appreciation of the currency. FT, 1.3.1995.

> The Dollar continued its recent consolidation on the foreign exchanges, but opinion remains divided about whether it has reached a bottom. FT, 14.3.1995.

> The Dollar lost ground against the DM due to profit-taking in morning trading. FT, 22.10.1995.

The following are examples of news relative to rumours, indiscretions and opinions under (a3):

> The recent Dollar rally came to a grinding halt as worries about a US recession and rumors of a Mexican debt default hit sentiment. FT, 25.5.1995.

> The first boost for the DM came from forecasts by German research institutes that gross domestic product growth this year would be 1.5%, twice as high as previously forecast. FT, 29.10.1996.

An example of news under (a4) could be:

> The Dollar recovered with world asset markets as traders reassessed comments on Thursday night by Mr. Greenspan. FT, 9.12.1995.

In *Newsmetrics* there are plenty of qualitative economic and political news of type (b). The following are some examples:

> The national budget presented did not pass market test. Stock exchange and BTP drop. Lira at –1%. *Il Sole-24 Ore*, 29.9.1995.

> Germany said that it was raising its unemployment forecast for 1997. This hurts the country's chances to meet Maastricht criteria. FT, 11.5.1997.

> Weigel outlines proposals for revaluation of Buba gold reserves to support public finances. FT, 15.5.1997.

> France turns to the left in first round of elections and leaves the contest wide open. FT, 26.5.1997.

In the empirical part of this chapter we use quantitative news on twelve US economic indicators and four German indicators, comparing the official published data with the expected values, selected by MMS, according to the indications of the literature. In our estimates we usually use the quantitative representation of scheduled news, rather than the news under (c), unless the latter contains additional information. The following are examples of news under (c):

> In the morning $ enjoyed the continuing effects of a weakened DM against peripheral European currencies while a higher-than-expected producer price index in the same month gave $ a boost in the afternoon. FT, 11.5.1995.

> The US payrolls report was stronger than expected but the expectation of higher US short-term interest rates proved supportive of the Dollar. FT, 7.6.1996.

> $ surged versus DM after new figures confirmed the strength of the US economy. $ jumped after US stronger-than-expected US non-farm payrolls data for July, then briefly stumbled after an unexpected jump in the price component of July NAPM. FT, 1.7.1997.

Newsmetrics contains a significant number of statements, such as discourses and verbal interventions explicitly aimed at influencing the markets or simply rash statements, which are gathered under (d). In the empirical analysis of this chapter we have tried to measure the effects on the exchange rate of the new fashion of verbally intervening in the currency markets ("talking one's currency up or down"), consolidated in recent years especially among G3 monetary authorities. Some examples of this news:

> Tietmeyer was reported as saying in a Japanese paper: "If all the information is going in the right direction I am not excluding some room for manoeuvre in reducing interest rates. FT, 23.7.1995.

> Rubin said that he "strongly believed" in a stronger Dollar. FT, 6.10.1995.

> Sakakibara told senior traders at a meeting on Monday that he would be persisting in his efforts to weaken the Yen. FT, 12.9.1995.

> Greenspan hit stocks, bonds and the $ by warning that "irrational exuberance" could inflate asset prices. FT, 5.12.1996.

> Greenspan declared in a testimony: "The economy has been on an unsustainable track. If labor demand continues to outpace sustainable increases in supply, the question is surely when, not whether, labor costs will escalate more rapidly." WSJ, 7.10.1997.

The last type of events, under (e), is constituted by central bank interventions on foreign exchange markets, with currency sales or purchases. Given the type of events collected in *Newsmetrics*, we have considered only interventions announced by monetary authorities or recognised as such by traders. Some examples include:

> Fed intervened actively on the foreign exch. in an attempt to curb the continued fall of the $. According to market sources the intervention was broad rather than substantial. It had a negligible impact with the $ continuing to trade at pre-intervention level. FT, 3.4.1995.

> $ had a better day on the market following the intervention undertaken on Monday by the Fed. There was no follow-up but the threat of central bank support was sufficient to dissuade the market from selling the Dollar aggressively. FT, 4.4.1995.

> Currency speculators were left licking their wounds as an unexpected round of central bank support for the $ caught the market napping. With most European Central Banks selling DM to support the $ the German currency lost ground across the board. FT. 31.5.1995.

> Aggressive intervention by the Fed, Buba and the Bank of Japan prompted the biggest one-day surge in the $ for three years. The foreign exchange markets were caught off guard by the unexpected round of co-ordinated support for the $. "FT", 15.7.1995.

7.3 The Impact of News on the Exchange Rate

We have seen in the first chapter of this work that there is a vast body of empirical literature on this subject, primarily studying the effects on the exchange rate of scheduled macroeconomic news, mostly of US source. *Newsmetrics* significantly extends the number of news items that are potentially useful to explain the exchange rate dynamics.

At this point, we must test the statistical significance of the news we have collected and their explanatory power when they are introduced in exchange rate equations, so as to justify the selection we have made. An additional benefit of an econometric analysis of the news is that they can be measured, as described in section 8.3 – hence the name *Newsmetrics* given to our database.

7.3.1 Econometric Estimation Strategies

Our database gathers the news that is potentially useful to explain exchange rate fluctuations. In order to realise this potential, we must classify the events in categories that are as homogeneous as possible. The structure of the database is the result of this work, as described in the previous chapters. The verification of the explanatory power of the events thus collected is performed, in this chapter, through the calculation of daily exchange rate equations. The salient issues in achieving this objective are:

a) the econometric specification of equations calculated with daily data;
b) how to deal with the exchange rate market's particular feature of "round-the-clock" operations in the so-called global trading day (GTD);
c) how to quantify qualitative news;
d) how to compare the quantitative effects of variables measured on different scales;
e) which estimation techniques to use.

(a) The models from which the exchange rate equations (usually calculated with monthly or even less frequent data) have been derived, can be grouped under three fundamental schemes: the Keynesian Mundell-Fleming model, the monetary model and the portfolio balance model.[4] In the monetary model, exchange rates are explained, in short, by the differentials in monetary expansion, the differentials in output growth and, depending on the interest rate assumptions (nominal or real), either by the differentials in interest rates (long- or short-term) or by the differentials in inflation. In the Keynesian model, the exchange rate is a function of the differentials in output growth, inflation and interest rates. In the portfolio balance model the exchange rate is determined by the differential in interest rates and the relative levels of financial activity in the two countries.

As we know, all the macroeconomic variables used to calculate exchange rate equations are sampled on a monthly basis or with even less frequency. Only interest rates and a few other variables are available on a daily basis. It is therefore not surprising that the majority of daily models use auto-regressive techniques of one kind or another, multiple transformations of interest rates and, most importantly, news.

All the scheduled news refer generally to the fundamental economic variables that appear in the three families of exchange rate equations: (1) inflation (consumer or production prices); (2) output growth (represented directly by industrial production and by sample surveys on production trends such as the US NAPM or on business confidence climate such as the German IFO, or indirectly by variations in employment, retail sales, durable goods orders or in leading indicators of economic activity); (3) trade balance (in the portfolio balance model); and (4) monetary expansion differentials (not recorded in our database nor used in this analysis). In estimating models with daily data and in news models, all these macroeconomic variables are introduced into the equations not in terms of growth of actual values of the regressor, as in the traditional monthly or quarterly regression models,[5] but in terms of news consisting of the difference between the published value and the value expected by the markets (collected in our analysis by MMS).

Thus in our analysis the econometric specification of the exchange rate equation, in terms of macroeconomic determinants, as indicated in the Keynesian theory of reference, is restored in terms of news.

Our main objective in this chapter is to calculate daily exchange rate equations as a function of various types of event-variables. In order to quantify with precision the impact on the exchange rate of each family of events, we have preliminarily identified a base specification, without news, of a "statistical-fundamental-technical analysis" type. The base specification contains several interest rate calculations, taken individually or as differentials, and regressors that are representative of technical analysis filters, in the form of differences between the actual exchange rate values and moving averages of the values of previous days, together with lags of the dependent variable. For the sake of brevity, the extensive preliminary work of specification search of these models is not presented here. The equations shown in Tables 7.1 to 7.6 for the DM-$ and Yen-$ exchange rates and in Tables 7.7 and 7.8 for the Lira-DM exchange rate contain the functional forms that have given the best results.

b) The foreign exchange market operates over a 24-hour span. It opens a new daily trading phase in the Asian market and it continues in Europe, where activity begins approximately as the Tokyo markets close (although the Japanese news continues to flow in well beyond that time). The American market begins trading after the US federal government announcement of the macroeconomic indicators of the day, at 8:30 Eastern Standard or Daylight Time (EST or EDT). The European market remains active for approximately another three hours. The American market closes the trading day around 16:00 EST, which corresponds to 22:00 Central European Time (CET).

Table 7.1 ETZ, SURE and GARCH (1,1) estimates of the DM-$ and Yen-$ exchange rates. Full model. US long-term interest rate variation (Yen-$) and long-term interest rate differential variation (DM-$). German MMS variables: both specification (1)

A

Dependent variable is DGUEU, DM-$ Exchange Rate
726 observations: Jan. 4, 1995 – Dec. 30, 1997

	(1) T-Prob	(2) T-Prob	(3) T-Prob
K	.0533 [.054]	0549 [.048]	.0321 [.176]
DDIFGU	-.0580 [.019]	-.0595 [.017]	-.0720 [.002]
DJUUS(-1)	-.0430 [.111]	-.0443 [.101]	-.0423 [.101]
DGUEU(-1)	-.0689 [.004]	-.0671 [.005]	-.0599 [.026]
TGE	.0789 [.001]	.0778 [.001]	.0776 [.001]
INTERV	.0772 [.004]	.0772 [.004]	.0842 [.002]
GCPI	.0212 [.362]		
GUN	.0147 [.531]		
GM3	-.0210 [.370]		
GCPI3		.0237 [.310]	
GUN3		-.00537 [.824]	
GIFO3		-.00144 [.951]	
DGE	.246 [.000]	.247 [.000]	.271 [.000]
MGE	.439 [.000]	.438 [.000]	.492 [.000]
QUMIN	.186 [.000]	.186 [.000]	.214 [.000]
QGE	.0963 [.000]	.101 [.000]	.128 [.000]
Constant (2)			.00218 [.001]
E-SQ(- 1)			.0259 [.006]
H-SQ(- 1)			.969 [.006]
R-Sq.	.49051	.49037	.50003
R-Bar-Sq.	.48194	.48180	.49232
S.E.Reg.	.72005	.72015	.71280
Mean Dep.Var.	.10922	.10922	.10922
DW	2.0186	2.0189	2.0178
S.D.Dep.Var.	1.0004	1.0004	1.0004

B

Dependent variable is DJUEU, Yen-$ Exchange Rate
726 observations: Jan. 4, 1995 – Dec. 30, 1997

	(4) T-Prob	(5) T-Prob	(6) T-Prob
K	.00667 [.819]	.00679 [.816]	.0220 [.414]
DUSB1	.0411 [.115]	.0423 [.105]	.0390 [.135]
DGUUS(-1)	.0745 [.019]	.0751 [.018]	.0692 [.044]
DJUUS(-1)	-.109 [.002]	-.109 [.002]	-.102 [.006]
TJA	.00655 [.799]	.00662 [.797]	
INTERV	.0391 [.185]	.0392 [.184]	.0586 [.051]
DJAEU	.264 [.000]	.264 [.000]	.263 [.000]
MJAEUY	.421 [.000]	.421 [.000]	.471 [.000]
MJAEUD	.284 [.000]	.284 [.000]	.277 [.000]
Constant (2)			.297 [.077]
E-SQ(- 1)			.322 [.084]
H-SQ(- 1)			.223 [.155]
R-Sq.	.42340	.42340	.42331
R-Bar-Sq.	.41697	.41697	.41606
S.E.Reg.	.76378	.76378	.76437
Mean Dep.Var.	.014391	.014391	.014391
DW	2.0577	2.0579	2.0403
S.D.Dep.Var.	1.0003	1.0003	1.0003

(1) A P-Value is indicated after each SURE coefficient. For GARCH estimation, the bracketed coefficients refer to the asymptotic standard error.
(2) H-SQ stands for the conditional variance of the error term. E-SQ stands for the square of the error term.

The daily frequency of our analysis should make it necessary to use as dependent variables in our calculations the estimates of exchange rate variations relative to the previous 24 hours. But this would not enable us to adequately evaluate the impact of events taking place in the different time zones – Asia, Europe and America. We have therefore divided the 24 trading hours of the global trading day into two parts: a European trading zone, which goes from the closure of the New York foreign exchange market the previous day, at 16:00 EST (corresponding to 22:00 CET), to an "artificial" European closure at 14:15 CET. No market closes at this time, but this is when the main European central banks jointly fix the official parity of their currencies – and that of the Euro since the beginning of 1999 – hence the "artificiality" of the previous sentence. Fifteen minutes later, at 8:30EST or 14:30 CET, the US government announces almost every day its indicators of the current economic situation, usually generating some volatility in the foreign exchange markets, which is why we end the European zone period a

Table 7.2 ATZ, SURE and GARCH estimates of the DM-$ and Yen-$ exchange rates. Full model. Long-term interest rate differentials. MMS variables: both specifications (1)

A

Dependent variable is DGUUS, DM-$ Exchange Rate
726 observations: Jan. 4, 1995 – Dec. 30, 1997

	MMS:Expected (1) T-Prob	Less Actual (2) T-Prob	MMS:Current (3) T-Prob	Less Mov.Aver. (4) T-Prob
K	-.153 [.000]	-.166 [.000]	-.142 [.001]	-.153 [.000]
DDJ	.0792 [.001]	.107 [.000]	.0832 [.001]	.113 [.000]
DIFUG	.0781 [.003]	.0816 [.002]	.0720 [.006]	.0751 [.004]
M3GUUS1	-.0239 [.546]	-.0205 [.607]	-.0213 [.587]	-.0181 [.647]
DJUEU	.0734 [.022]	.0701 [.029]	.0674 [.032]	.0642 [.043]
DGUUS(-1)	-.0836 [.012]	-.0891 [.008]	-.0855 [.010]	-.0910 [.006]
INTERV	.0177 [.520]	.0180 [.516]	.0184 [.504]	.0187 [.499]
TGE	-.0201 [.381]	-.0202 [.380]	-.0189 [.404]	-.0189 [.404]
TUS	.0115 [.675]	.0115 [.675]	.0149 [.582]	.0143 [.599]
QGE	-.0290 [.216]	-.0293 [.210]	-.0293 [.213]	-.0297 [.206]
GCPI	.1934E [.993]	-.2439E [.991]	.0294 [.200]	.0291 [.204]
GUN	.0203 [.374]	.0205 [.369]	.0148 [.519]	.0150 [.514]
GM3	-.0150 [.510]	-.0151 [.508]	.0291 [.200]	.0293 [.198]
UCC	.1848E [.995]	-.00107 [.969]	-.00199 [.941]	-.00360 [.894]
UOC	.0677 [.018]	.0637 [.027]	.0737 [.010]	.0666 [.020]
UCPI	.00257 [.925]	.00616 [.823]	.0182 [.508]	.0241 [.383]
UDG	-.0243 [.372]	-.0226 [.408]	-.0280 [.303]	-.0250 [.360]
UW	.0623 [.023]	.0685 [.013]	.0525 [.060]	.0566 [.044]
UIPI	-.00639 [.815]	-.00488 [.859]	.0207 [.448]	.0223 [.415]
ULEAD	-.0181 [.512]	-.0183 [.510]	.0170 [.533]	.0154 [.574]
UNAPM	.0520 [.065]	.0452 [.109]	.0738 [.007]	.0689 [.013]
UPPI	-.0152 [.579]	-.0166 [.547]	-.0204 [.448]	-.0228 [.401]
URET	-.00948 [.729]	-.0102 [.710]	.0160 [.553]	.0187 [.491]
UTRB	.0272 [.318]	.0224 [.412]	.0150 [.580]	.0118 [.665]
UUN	.0405 [.154]	.0374 [.190]	.0631 [.026]	.0537 [.059]
DUSD	.206 [.000]	.206 [.000]	.204 [.000]	.204 [.000]
MUS	.408 [.000]	.407 [.000]	.408 [.000]	.407 [.000]
GRE	.111 [.000]	.111 [.000]	.109 [.000]	.109 [.000]
QMFIN	.281 [.000]	.201 [.000]	.288 [.000]	.206 [.000]
R-Sq.	.49252	.48691	.50047	.49471
R-Bar-Sq.	.47213	.46630	.48040	.47441
S.E.Reg.	.72702	.73102	.72130	.72545
Mean Dep.Var.	-.066457	-.066457	-.066457	-.066457
DW	1.9617	1.9782	1.9583	1.9741
S.D.Dep.Var.	1.0007	1.0007	1.0007	1.0007

B

Dependent variable is DJUUS, Yen-$ Exchange Rate
726 observations: Jan. 4, 1995 – Dec. 30, 1997

	MMS:Expected (5) T-Prob	Less Actual (6) T-Prob	MMS:Current (7) T-Prob	Less Mov.Aver. (8) T-Prob
K	-.514 [.043]	-.602 [.020]	-.498 [.050]	-.577 [.026]
DDJ		.0573 [.070]		.0611 [.054]
QMFIN	.162 [.000]		.169 [.000]	
DIFUJ	.0679 [.019]	.0763 [.010]	.0668 [.021]	.0741 [.012]
M3JUUS1	-.00767 [.841]	-.0169 [.662]	-.0101 [.792]	-.0191 [.623]
DGUEU	-.0395 [.258]	-.0339 [.343]	-.0402 [.252]	-.0351 [.328]
DJUUS(-1)	-.117 [.000]	-.124 [.000]	-.115 [.000]	-.123 [.000]
INTERV	.0227 [.476]	.0229 [.479]	.0218 [.497]	.0221 [.498]
TJA	-.7758E [.977]	-.6268E [.981]	-.2920E [.991]	-.1977E [.994]
TUS	.0143 [.642]	.0146 [.641]	.00521 [.865]	.00427 [.891]
UCC	.0234 [.441]	.0203 [.511]	.0297 [.330]	.0261 [.400]
UOC	.0596 [.062]	.0511 [.116]	.0762 [.018]	.0611 [.061]
UCPI	-.00479 [.875]	.00278 [.929]	.0175 [.573]	.0299 [.343]
UDG	-.0104 [.730]	-.00731 [.813]	-.0282 [.352]	-.0222 [.475]
UW	.0723 [.019]	.0844 [.007]	.0704 [.026]	.0783 [.015]
UIPI	.0209 [.497]	.0235 [.452]	.0213 [.492]	.0249 [.431]
ULEAD	-.0516 [.098]	-.0520 [.102]	-.0136 [.660]	-.0167 [.596]
UNAPM	.0347 [.270]	.0213 [.505]	.0166 [.590]	.00722 [.818]
UPPI	.0275 [.372]	.0247 [.431]	.00593 [.846]	.00129 [.967]
URET	-.0145 [.635]	-.0160 [.607]	.0267 [.382]	.0325 [.297]
UTRB	.0125 [.681]	.00300 [.923]	.00263 [.931]	-.00399 [.898]
UUN	.0397 [.214]	.0336 [.301]	.0666 [.039]	.0475 [.145]
DJAUS	.113 [.000]	.116 [.000]	.112 [.000]	.115 [.000]
DUSY	.122 [.000]	.124 [.000]	.126 [.000]	.128 [.000]
MJAUSY	.331 [.000]	.332 [.000]	.330 [.000]	.331 [.000]
MJAUSD	.275 [.000]	.270 [.000]	.277 [.000]	.272 [.000]
R-Sq.	.35415	.33106	.35415	.32982
R-Bar-Sq.	.33204	.30816	.33204	.30687
S.E.Reg.	.81704	.83152	.81704	.83229
Mean Dep.Var.	.057727	.057727	.057727	.057727
DW	2.0571	2.0820	2.0551	2.0821
S.D.Dep.Var.	.99970	.99970	.99970	.99970

(1) A P-Value is indicated after each SURE coefficient. The two jointly estimated SURE equations, are one below the other (e.g. equations number (1) and (5), etc.). The MMS variable symbols on the left are those referring to the expected less actual version.

little earlier. Thus the first artificial trading zone, defined as European, includes all of the Asian trading and the European morning trading.

The second trading zone, defined in our analysis as the American trading zone, begins at 8:30 EST or 14:30 CET. It covers the entire US trading day, unofficially ending at 16:00 EST and thus covering also the European afternoon trading (Chicago and California are still active after 16:00 EST, but generally the quotes do not differ from those of New York).

The partitioning of a continuous currency trading day enables us to establish more precisely the relationship between scheduled news and the exchange rate values that are most influenced by them. With regards to the unscheduled news, we have had to perform further studies[6] and, in some cases, to formulate assumptions.

c) The qualitative news of the type analysed in section 7.2 is introduced in the analysis as triple variables. They consist of a zero when the event to which they refer has not taken place, a –1 when the news item produces a revaluation of the exchange rate, and a +1 when it produces a devaluation.

Therefore, in our type of analysis we need to fix the sign of the effect of an event *a priori*. This is less arbitrary than it may appear and it is in any case strictly necessary in order to obtain reliable quantitative estimates of the

Table 7.3 ATZ and SURE restricted and unrestricted estimates of the DM-$ and Yen-$ exchange rates. Reduced model. Long-term interest rate differentials. MMS variables: expected less actual (1)

A

Dependent variable is DGUUS, DM-$ Exchange Rate
726 observations: Jan. 4, 1995 – Dec. 30, 1997

	(1) T-Prob	(2) T-Prob	(3) T-Prob
K	-.169 [.000]	-.159 [.000]	-.164 [.000]
DDJ	.111 [.000]	.0847 [.000]	.0872 [.001]
DIFUG	.0812 [.001]	.0782 [.002]	.0799 [.002]
DJUEU	.0751 [.001]	.0746 [.001]	.0766 [.001]
DGUUS(-1)	-.103 [.000]	-.0998 [.000]	-.0988 [.000]
UOC	.0637 [.026]	.0677 [.017]	.0585 [.026]
UW	.0677 [.013]	.0624 [.022]	.0714 [.005]
UNAPM	.0358 [.121]	.0358 [.121]	.0351 [.125]
UUN	.0379 [.181]	.0409 [.147]	.0369 [.159]
DUSD	.205 [.000]	.204 [.000]	.204 [.000]
MUS	.404 [.000]	.405 [.000]	.409 [.000]
GRE	.111 [.000]	.111 [.000]	.111 [.000]
QMFIN	.198 [.000]	.276 [.000]	.213 [.000]
R-Sq.	.48047	.48591	.48267
R-Bar-Sq.	.47173	.47726	N/A
S.E.Reg.	.72730	.72348	.71923
Mean Dep.Var.	-.066457	-.066457	-.066457
DW	1.9967	1.9820	1.9998
S.D.Dep.Var.	1.0007	1.0007	1.0007

B

Dependent variable is DJUUS, Yen-$ Exchange Rate 726 observations: Jan. 4, 1995 – Dec. 30, 1997			
	(4) T-Prob	(5) T-Prob	(6) T-Prob
K	-.556 [.028]	-.480 [.054]	-.575 [.022]
DDJ	.0532 [.085]		.0872 [.001]
QMFIN		.157 [.000]	
DIFUJ	.0713 [.013]	.0641 [.024]	.0732 [.011]
DJUUS(-1)	-.131 [.000]	-.120 [.000]	-.130 [.000]
UOC	.0490 [.130]	.0573 [.072]	.0585 [.026]
UW	.0802 [.010]	.0699 [.022]	.0714 [.005]
UUN	.0341 [.290]	.0400 [.208]	.0369 [.159]
DJAUS	.115 [.000]	.112 [.000]	.112 [.000]
DUSY	.127 [.000]	.125 [.000]	.126 [.000]
MJAUSY	.329 [.000]	.329 [.000]	.330 [.000]
MJAUSD	.270 [.000]	.276 [.000]	.271 [.000]
R-Sq.	.32316	.34531	.32189
R-Bar-Sq.	.31369	.33616	N/A
S.E.Reg.	.82818	.81452	.82266
Mean Dep.Var.	.057727	.057727	.057727
DW	2.0820	2.0601	2.0800
S.D.Dep.Var.	.99970	.99970	.99970

(1) A P-Value is indicated after each SURE coefficient. The two jointly estimated SURE equations, are one below the other (e.g. equations number (1) and (4), etc.). The coefficients of MMS variables in equations (3) and (6) are restricted.

effect of a qualitative event. First of all, we have performed an extensive preliminary statistical analysis[7] and, over time, a long series of interviews with various currency traders to determine the effects of the markets' most frequent news. In addition, an *a priori* determination of the effect of an event is necessary: since each event can have positive or negative effects on the exchange rate, the use of a standard binary variable (0, 1) may produce parameters that are not relevant because the effects of the various events cancel each other out over time.

d) The variables we use in the calculation of exchange rate equations are expressed in different units: dummies of the (+1, 0, -1) type, rates of change, and percentage rates. In order to render the coefficients of the estimates comparable within the equation and across equations, we have standardized all the variables so as to obtain beta coefficients.

e) For the empirical estimates two alternative techniques have been used. First we have used a SURE estimation for the DM-$ and Yen-$ equations, in each of the two trading zones, and for the Lira-DM equations in both trading zones. In fact it can be reasonably assumed that, for DM-$ and Yen-$, the error terms of the equations referring to currencies traded at the same time are strongly correlated. In addition, the consistency of SURE makes it possible to accurately evaluate the statistical significance of the news-variables. This attention to the significance of news is also made necessary by our estimation strategy. First we have built a part based on fundamentals, on statistical regularity and, when possible, on technical analysis, which has enabled us to explain currency fluctuations, which are systematic to some extent, leaving a residual part still to be interpreted. Then we have tried to explain the residual part with news. With such a procedure it is essential to verify the statistical significance in order to be able to state with some certainty that a given family of events contributes to explaining the anomalous fluctuations of exchange rates.

Table 7.4 ATZ and SURE restricted and unrestricted estimates of the DM-$ and Yen-$ exchange rates. Reduced model. Long-term interest rate differentials. MMS variables: current less moving average (1)

A

Dependent variable is DGUUS, DM-$ Exchange Rate
726 observations: Jan. 4, 1995 – Dec. 30, 1997

	(1) T-Prob	(2) T-Prob	(3) T-Prob
K	-.121 [.002]	-.113 [.004]	-.114 [.003]
DDJ	.111 [.000]	.0854 [.000]	.0875 [.001]
DIFUG	.0457 [.046]	.0456 [.046]	.0431 [.057]
DJUEU	.0716 [.002]	.0713 [.002]	.0723 [.001]
DGUUS(-1)	-.0994 [.000]	-.0961 [.000]	-.0958 [.000]
GCPI3	.0318 [.157]	.0321 [.153]	.0327 [.142]
GIFO3	.0274 [.224]	.0272 [.226]	.0293 [.190]
UOC3	.0678 [.017]	.0756 [.008]	.0649 [.013]
UW3	.0565 [.042]	.0532 [.054]	.0618 [.016]
UNAPM3	.0650 [.004]	.0652 [.004]	.0638 [.005]
UUN3	.0539 [.057]	.0638 [.024]	.0506 [.053]
DUSD	.204 [.000]	.204 [.000]	.204 [.000]
MUS	.406 [.000]	.407 [.000]	.411 [.000]
GRE	.109 [.000]	.109 [.000]	.110 [.000]
QMFIN	.204 [.000]	.286 [.000]	.217 [.000]
R-Sq.	.48707	.49312	.48927
R-Bar-Sq.	.47697	.48313	N/A
S.E.Reg.	.72368	.71940	.71463
Mean Dep.Var.	-.066457	-.066457	-.066457
DW	1.9980	1.9826	2.0000
S.D.Dep.Var.	1.0007	1.0007	1.0007

B

Dependent variable is DJUUS, Yen-$ Exchange Rate
726 observations: Jan. 4, 1995 – Dec. 30, 1997

	(4) T-Prob	(5) T-Prob	(6) T-Prob
K	.0678 [.030]	.0819 [.007]	.0645 [.037]
DDJ	.0522 [.092]		.0875 [.001]
QMFIN		.169 [.000]	
DJUUS(-1)	-.126 [.000]	-.115 [.000]	-.125 [.000]
UOC3	.0584 [.072]	.0747 [.020]	.0649 [.013]
UW3	.0734 [.021]	.0670 [.031]	.0618 [.016]
UUN3	.0418 [.196]	.0621 [.052]	.0506 [.053]
DJAUS	.116 [.000]	.113 [.000]	.114 [.000]
DUSY	.128 [.000]	.125 [.000]	.127 [.000]
MJAUSY	.329 [.000]	.328 [.000]	.329 [.000]
MJAUSD	.276 [.000]	.282 [.000]	.277 [.000]
R-Sq.	.31890	.34429	.31744
R-Bar-Sq.	.31034	.33605	N/A
S.E.Reg.	.83021	.81458	.82535
Mean Dep.Var.	.057727	.057727	.057727
DW	2.0736	2.0543	2.0726
S.D.Dep.Var.	.99970	.99970	.99970

(1) A P-Value is indicated after each SURE coefficient. The two jointly estimated SURE equations, are one below the other (e.g. equations number (1) and (4), etc.). The coefficients of MMS variables in equations (3) and (6) are restricted.

With the information obtained from the SURE estimations, we have calculated reduced (i.e. with fewer regressors) GARCH (1,1) models[8] for both exchange rates in the two trading zones. The objective of adding a GARCH estimation to a SURE estimation is threefold: 1) to confirm the statistical significance of the "surviving" news-variables with a heteroscedastic technique suited to highly volatile variables such as the exchange rates; 2) to test the significance of news in explaining the dependent variable mean and the conditional volatility in the same exchange rate equation;[9] (3) to study the conditional volatility of exchange rates over time.

Once again, all the variables have been standardized so that it is possible to compare the coefficients of news-variables within the same equation and across equations.

Table 7.5 ATZ and SURE estimates of the DM-$ and Yen-$ exchange rates. Full and reduced model. Short-term interest rate differentials. MMS variables: expected less actual, except German CPI and IFO (1)

A

Dependent variable is DGUUS, DM-$ Exchange Rate
726 observations: Jan. 4, 1995 – Dec. 30, 1997

	(1) T-Prob	(2) T-Prob	(3) T-Prob	(4) T-Prob
K	-.455 [.000]	-.413 [.001]	-.452 [.000]	-.402 [.001]
DDJ	.104 [.000]	.110 [.000]	.107 [.000]	.109 [.000]
DIF3UG	.0807 [.001]	.0731 [.003]	.0793 [.001]	.0702 [.003]
M3GUUS1	-.0171 [.667]	-.0152 [.700]	.0760 [.001]	.0737 [.001]
DJUEU	.0673 [.035]	.0618 [.050]	-.104 [.000]	-.102 [.000]
DGUUS(-1)	-.0929 [.006]	-.0944 [.004]		
INTERV	.0184 [.504]	.0186 [.500]		
TGE	-.0184 [.421]	-.0174 [.441]		
TUS	.0163 [.552]	.0186 [.492]		
QGE	-.0302 [.197]	-.0299 [.203]		
GCPI	-.4859E [.983]	.0281 [.219]		
GUN	.0191 [.402]	.0138 [.549]		
GM3	-.0180 [.430]	.0281 [.216]		
UCC	-.7980E [.998]	-.00219 [.935]		
UOC	.0655 [.022]	.0673 [.019]	.0655 [.022]	.0690 [.015]
UCPI	.00509 [.853]	.0240 [.383]		
UDG	-.0228 [.402]	-.0260 [.341]		
UW	.0698 [.011]	.0572 [.042]	.0688 [.011]	.0574 [.038]
UIPI	-.00258 [.925]	.0238 [.383]		
ULEAD	-.0178 [.520]	.0156 [.567]		
UNAPM	.0464 [.099]	.0670 [.015]	.0357 [.122]	.0630 [.006]
UPPI	-.0182 [.507]	-.0245 [.364]		
URET	-.0123 [.654]	.0164 [.544]		
UTRB	.0211 [.439]	.00961 [.724]		
UUN	.0388 [.174]	.0536 [.059]	.0393 [.164]	.0557 [.048]
DUSD	.207 [.000]	.205 [.000]	.206 [.000]	.205 [.000]
MUS	.406 [.000]	.407 [.000]	.404 [.000]	.405 [.000]
GRE	.113 [.000]	.111 [.000]	.112 [.000]	.110 [.000]
QMFIN	.201 [.000]	.206 [.000]	.198 [.000]	.204 [.000]
GCPI3				.0307 [.169]
GIFO3				.0264 [.239]
R-Sq.	.49091	.49776	.48408	.49004
R-Bar-Sq.	.47046	.47759	.47540	.48000
S.E.Reg.	.72817	.72325	.72477	.72158
Mean Dep.Var.	-.066457	-.066457	-.066457	-.066457
DW	1.9902	1.9825	2.0079	2.0060
S.D.Dep.Var.	1.0007	1.0007	1.0007	1.0007

B

Dependent variable is DJUUS, Yen-$ Exchange Rate 726 observations: Jan. 4, 1995 – Dec. 30, 1997	(5) T-Prob	(6) T-Prob	(7) T-Prob	(8) T-Prob
K	-.759 [.035]	-.723 [.045]	-.706 [.046]	-.686 [.053]
DDJ	.0535 [.090]	.0571 [.072]	.0488 [.113]	.0520 [.093]
DIF3UJ	.0630 [.022]	.0608 [.028]	.0592 [.029]	.0579 [.033]
M3JUUS1	-.0217 [.575]	-.0239 [.539]	-.132 [.000]	-.131 [.000]
DGUEU	-.0336 [.347]	-.0344 [.339]		
DJUUS(-1)	-.124 [.000]	-.123 [.000]		
INTERV	.0186 [.564]	.0178 [.583]		
TJA	-.00375 [.889]	-.00322 [.905]		
TUS	.0194 [.535]	.0101 [.746]		
UCC	.0210 [.497]	.0287 [.355]		
UOC	.0521 [.109]	.0603 [.065]	.0499 [.122]	.0579 [.074]
UCPI	.3627E [.991]	.0283 [.369]		
UDG	-.00790 [.799]	-.0223 [.471]		
UW	.0838 [.007]	.0776 [.016]	.0803 [.009]	.0740 [.019]
UIPI	.0254 [.416]	.0269 [.396]		
ULEAD	-.0456 [.150]	-.0140 [.655]		
UNAPM	.0241 [.448]	.00733 [.816]		
UPPI	.0234 [.454]	.00158 [.959]		
URET	-.0190 [.544]	.0314 [.314]		
UTRB	-.00178 [.954]	-.00930 [.765]		
UUN	.0303 [.350]	.0429 [.186]	.0315 [.328]	.0435 [.177]
DJAUS	.117 [.000]	.116 [.000]	.116 [.000]	.116 [.000]
DUSY	.124 [.000]	.129 [.000]	.128 [.000]	.129 [.000]
MJAUSY	.330 [.000]	.328 [.000]	.326 [.000]	.327 [.000]
MJAUSD	.271 [.000]	.272 [.000]	.271 [.000]	.272 [.000]
R-Sq.	.33233	.33098	.32422	.32342
R-Bar-Sq.	.30947	.30807	.31476	.31396
S.E. of Reg.	.83073	.83157	.82754	.82802
Mean of Dep.Var.	.057727	.057727	.057727	.057727
DW	2.0867	2.0861	2.0861	2.0839
S.D.Dep.Var.	.99970	.99970	.99970	.99970

(1) A P-Value is indicated after each SURE coefficient. The two jointly estimated SURE equations, are one below the other (e.g. equations number (1) and (5), etc.).

7.3.2 DM-$ and Yen-$ Equations

All the equations estimated in this chapter have the same characteristics. They are all estimated to logarithmic first differences – with the exception of news-variables, stationary by definition, and of exchange rate differentials, stationary in our case – because all the unitary root tests, not shown here for the sake of brevity, have indicated the non-stationary nature of exchange rates and of most exchange rate moving averages.

We would like to highlight from the outset that the first differences of exchange rates do not refer to the previous day (t-1) but to the end-of-period exchange rate in the previous trading zone, according to the scheme adopted in this chapter (see section 7.3.1).

All the equations consist of two parts: the base specification, i.e. what we have already defined as "statistical-fundamental-technical analysis", and a second part that includes the news-variables.

Table 7.6 GARCH (1,1) estimates of the DM-$ and Yen-$ exchange rates. ETZ and ATZ. Reduced models. Interest rate variations, differentials and differential variations. US MMS variables: current less moving average (1)

A

European time zone

726 observations: Jan. 4, 1995 – Dec. 30, 1997

DEP. VAR.	DGUEU (1) T-Prob	DGUEU (2) T-Prob	DJUEU (3) T-Prob
K	.0220 [.608]	.0321 [.176]	.0220 [.414]
DIFGU	-.00803 [.749]		
DDIFGU		-.0720 [.002]	
DUSB1			.0390 [.135]
DGUUS(-1)			.0692 [.044]
DJUUS(-1)	-.0460 [.076]	-.0423 [.101]	-.102 [.006]
DGUEU(-1)	-.0659 [.015]	-.0599 [.026]	
TGE	.0817 [.001]	.0776 [.001]	
INTERV	.0845 [.002]	.0842 [.002]	.0586 [.051]
DGE	.276 [.000]	.271 [.000]	
MGE	.496 [.000]	.492 [.000]	
QUMIN	.223 [.000]	.214 [.000]	
QGE	.134 [.000]	.128 [.000]	
DJAEU			.263 [.000]
MJAEUY			.471 [.000]
MJAEUD			.277 [.000]
Constant (2)	.00245 [.001]	.00218 [.001]	.297 [.077]
E-SQ(- 1)	.0266 [.006]	.0259 [.006]	.322 [.084]
H-SQ(- 1)	.968 [.006]	.969 [.006]	.223 [.155]
R-Sq.	.49450	.50003	.42331
R-Bar-Sq.	.48672	.49232	.41606
S.E.Reg.	.71672	.71280	.76437
Mean Dep.Var.	.10922	.10922	014391
DW	2.0284	2.0178	2.0403
S.D.Dep.Var.	1.0004	1.0004	1.0003

B

American Time Zone

726 observations: Jan. 4, 1995 – Dec. 30, 1997

DEP. VAR.	DGUUS (4) T-Prob	DGUUS (5) T-Prob	DJUUS (6) T-Prob	DJUUS (7) T-Prob
K	-.0976 [.018]	-.456 [.001]	-.426 [.083]	-.355 [.135]
DDJ	.0542 [.023]	.0523 [.028]	.0446 [.114]	
QMFIN				.173 [.000]
DIFUG	.0572 [.020]			
DIF3UG		.0866 [.001]		
DIFUJ			.0587 [.037]	.0523 [.054]
DGUUS(-1)	-.0985 [.000]	-.102 [.000]		
DJUUS(-1)	-.120 [.000]	-.101 [.002]		
UOC3	.0841 [.001]	.0857 [.001]	.0758 [.011]	.0916 [.002]
UW3	.0657 [.011]	.0669 [.009]	.0986 [.002]	.0920 [.003]
UUN3	.0640 [.005]	.0645 [.005]	.0567 [.057]	.0803 [.005]
DUSD	.235 [.000]	.234 [.000]		
MUS	.486 [.000]	.485 [.000]		
GRE	.178 [.000]	.181 [.000]		
QMFIN	.310 [.000]	.310 [.000]		
MJAUSY			.355 [.000]	.352 [.000]
MJAUSD			.340 [.000]	.344 [.000]
DJAUS			.114 [.000]	.108 [.000]
DUSY			.137 [.000]	.128 [.000]
Constant	.0351 [.013]	.0346 [.013]	.116 [.081]	.0858 [.050]
E-SQ(- 1)	.115 [.029]	.114 [.029]	.0850 [.027]	.0855 [.024]
H-SQ(- 1)	.811 [.049]	.812 [.048]	.736 [.147]	.777 [.098]
R-Sq.	.49439	.49806	.32777	.35170
R-Bar-Sq.	.48588	.48961	.31645	.34079
S.E.Reg.	.71749	.71488	.82652	.81167
Mean Dep.Var.	-.066457	-.066457	.057727	.057727
DW	1.9146	1.9238	2.0844	2.0772
S.D.Dep.Var.	1.0007	1.0007	.99970	.99970

(1) A P-Value is indicated after each GARCH. For the volatility part of the GARCH model, the square bracketed coefficients refer to the asymptotic standard error.
(2) H-SQ stands for the conditional variance of the error term. E-SQ stands for the square of the error term.

The first part of our equations is composed of interest rate differentials, a variation in the other exchange rate (i.e. the DM-$ in the Yen-$ equation and vice versa) lagged one period, a moving average filter of the exchange rate that appears as a dependent variable, also lagged one period, and the lagged dependent variable. The second part of the equation is composed of news, scheduled and unscheduled.

The entire equation (the "whole model" in the headings of our tables, as opposed to the "reduced model" obtained by leaving out all the less relevant variables) of the two exchange rates, in the two trading zones used in this study, is presented in Table 7.1 (for the European zone) and 7.2 (for the American zone).

Part A of Table 7.1 contains two versions – (1) and (2) – of the same DM-$ base specification for the European zone. In both versions the first part – the

Table 7.7 ETZ (A) and ATZ (B), SURE estimates of LIT-DM exchange rate. Full model. Long- and short-term interest rates (1)

A

Dependent variable is DIGEU, LIT-DM Exchange Rate in ETZ
910 observations: Apr. 5, 1994 – Dec. 30, 1997

	(1) T-Prob	(2) T-Prob	(3) T-Prob	(4) T-Prob
K	.00010 [.518]	.00010 [.522]	.00011 [.494]	00010 [.508]
DIF33GI	-.167 [.000]			
DIF3GI		-.238 [.000]		
M3E3GF			.0163 [.504]	
M3E3IT			.189 [.000]	
M3GEB				-.113 [.000]
M3ITB				.288 [.000]
M3GUEU	-.530 [.000]	-.513 [.000]	-.528 [.000]	-.510 [.000]
DIGUS(-1)	-.198 [.000]	-.237 [.000]	-.200 [.000]	-.238 [.000]
DIGEU(-1)	-.124 [.000]	-.157 [.000]	-.137 [.000]	-.158 [.000]
M2PCC	.0196 [.399]	.0182 [.423]	.0216 [.350]	.0188 [.408]
DU17EU	.234 [.000]	.235 [.000]	.231 [.000]	.236 [.000]
PCEU	.0831 [.000]	.0752 [.001]	.0824 [.000]	.0763 [.001]
CPEU	.105 [.000]	.101 [.000]	.0974 [.000]	.0992 [.000]
CGEU	.0654 [.006]	.0521 [.024]	.0644 [.006]	.0507 [.028]
CIEU	.130 [.000]	.105 [.000]	.131 [.000]	.106 [.000]
VEEU	.0819 [.003]	.0766 [.004]	.0890 [.001]	.0744 [.006]
FPEU	.108 [.000]	.0937 [.000]	.105 [.000]	.0927 [.000]
GDEU	.220 [.000]	.198 [.000]	.219 [.000]	.197 [.000]
MAEU	.103 [.000]	.0992 [.000]	.102 [.000]	.0985 [.000]
SCEU	.0444 [.058]	.0407 [.074]	.0419 [.072]	.0393 [.085]
P96EU	.0945 [.000]	.0821 [.000]	.0879 [.000]	.0817 [.000]
GPREU	.0614 [.009]	.0545 [.019]	.0628 [.007]	.0563 [.015]
RIFEU	.0446 [.061]	.0423 [.069]	.0455 [.054]	.0424 [.068]
QUMEU	.0857 [.000]	.0814 [.000]	.0861 [.000]	.0813 [.001]
R-Sq	.47015	.48385	.47669	.48479
R-Bar-Sq.	.45884	.47283	.46492	.47320
S.E Reg.	.73271	.72318	.72858	.72293
Mean Dep.Var	.0013632	.0013632	.0013632	.0013632
DW	1.8737	1.8285	1.8574	1.8246
S.D.Dep.Var.	.99602	.99602	.99602	.99602

B

Dependent variable is DIGUS, LIT-DM Exchange Rate in ATZ 910 observations: Apr. 5, 1994 – Dec. 30, 1997	(5) T-Prob	(6) T-Prob	(7) T-Prob	(8) T-Prob
K	.00022 [.465]	.00023 [.436]	.00022 [.463]	.00022 [.448]
DIF33GI	-.0924 [.002]			
DIF3GI		-.180 [.000]		
M3E3GF			-.0254 [.347]	
M3E3IT			.0924 [.002]	
M3GEB				-.119 [.000]
M3ITB				.218 [.000]
M3GUUS	-.584 [.000]	-.586 [.000]	-.584 [.000]	-.586 [.000]
M3IGUS1	-.486 [.000]	-.563 [.000]	-.489 [.000]	-.560 [.000]
TIT	-.00000 [.793]	-.00000 [.891]	-.00000 [.742]	-.00000 [.870]
DU17US	.207 [.000]	.209 [.000]	.207 [.000]	.210 [.000]
PCUS	.0398 [.129]	.0402 [.124]	.0388 [.139]	.0390 [.136]
CPUS	.139 [.000]	.137 [.000]	.138 [.000]	.138 [.000]
CGUS	.0553 [.036]	.0471 [.074]	.0553 [.036]	.0466 [.077]
CIUS	.0418 [.118]	.0409 [.126]	.0423 [.115]	.0402 [.132]
VEUS	.0762 [.007]	.0746 [.009]	.0779 [.006]	.0758 [.008]
FPUS	.113 [.000]	.108 [.000]	.113 [.000]	.109 [.000]
GDUS	.245 [.000]	.243 [.000]	.245 [.000]	.243 [.000]
MAUS	.0615 [.019]	.0649 [.014]	.0621 [.018]	.0655 [.013]
SCUS	.0926 [.000]	.0903 [.000]	.0923 [.000]	.0895 [.000]
P96US	.111 [.000]	.104 [.000]	.112 [.000]	.104 [.000]
GPRUS	.0479 [.064]	.0479 [.063]	.0477 [.065]	.0478 [.064]
RIFUS	.0198 [.445]	.0208 [.421]	.0199 [.443]	.0200 [.441]
QUMUS	.124 [.000]	.123 [.000]	.124 [.000]	.123 [.000]
R-Sq	.36969	.36136	.36900	.36195
R-Bar-Sq.	.35695	.34846	.35553	.34833
S.E.Reg.	.80273	.80801	.80361	.80809
Mean Dep.Var.	.00439	.00439	.00439	.00439
DW	1.8721	1.8528	1.8727	1.8538
S.D.Dep.Var.	1.0010	1.0010	1.0010	1.0010

(1) A P-Value is indicated after each SURE coefficient.

one containing the "non-news" basic exchange rate determinants – has a rate differential (more precisely a variation of the differential, DDIFGU), a lagged Yen-Dollar exchange rate (DJUUS, i.e. the variation in the American zone for the previous day) and a lagged dependent variable. The news part begins with two variables, one related to variations in the German official rates (TGE), and the other related to central bank interventions (INTERV). We thus have some German scheduled variables from the MMS: in the form of differences between actual and expected values, GCPI, GUN, GM3, equation (1); in the form of differences between the last actual value of the macroeconomic variable and a moving average of the three previous values, GCPI3, GUN3, GIFO3, equation (2); and four qualitative variables that refer to statements by Bundesbank council members and by German government officials (DGE), to events and information on the foreign exchange market (MGE), to issues related to the launch of the European Monetary Union that are particularly relevant to the DM-$ (QUMIN), and to important German macroeconomic events (QGE).

Part B of Table 7.1, equation (4), contains the Yen-$ base specification for the European zone. The interest rate differential between Yen- and Dollar-denominated financial instruments has not turned out to be significant in any

Table 7.8 ETZ (A) and ATZ (B), GARCH (1,1) estimates of LIT-DM exchange rate. Reduced model. Long- and short-term interest rates (1) (2)

A

Dependent Variable: DIGEU, LIT-DM Exchange Rate in ETZ 910 observations: Apr. 5, 1994 – Dec. 30, 1997		
	(1) T-Prob	(2) T-Prob
K	.0250 [.202]	.0404 [.035]
DIF33GI	-.0959 [.000]	
DIF3GI		-.205 [.000]
M3GUEU	-.305 [.000]	-.283 [.000]
DIGUS(-1)	-.204 [.000]	-.251 [.000]
DIGEU(-1)	-.0665 [.024]	-.106 [.000]
DU17EU	.321 [.000]	.338 [.000]
PCEU	.0772 [.032]	.0755 [.025]
CPEU	.104 [.000]	.102 [.000]
CGEU	.0665 [.001]	.0495 [.011]
CIEU	.0959 [.000]	.0700 [.002]
VEEU	.0260 [.253]	.0249 [.222]
FPEU	.0595 [.001]	.0477 [.004]
GDEU	.191 [.000]	.149 [.000]
MAEU	.0837 [.041]	.0837 [.041]
P96EU	.104 [.000]	.0884 [.000]
GPREU	.0611 [.000]	.0512 [.001]
RIFEU	.0555 [.000]	.0506 [.000]
QUMEU	.0896 [.000]	.0819 [.000]
Cost.(2)	00504 [.003]	.00430 [.003]
E-SQ(- 1)	.0738 [.024]	.0813 [.030]
H-SQ(- 1)	.918 [.027]	.913 [.034]
R-Sq.	.41047	.42574
R-Bar-Sq.	.39788	.41348
S.E.Reg.	.77288	.76280
Mean Dep.Var.	.00136	.00136
DW	1.9069	1.8952
S.D.Dep.Var.	.99602	.99602

B

Dependent Variable: DIGEU,LIT-DM Exchange Rate in ATZ 910 observations: Apr. 5, 1994 – Dec. 30, 1997		
	(3) T-Prob	(4) T-Prob
K	-.0320 [.137]	-.0253 [.234]
DIF33GI	-.00695 [.777]	
DIF3GI		-.0673 [.019]
M3GUUS	-.362 [.000]	-.356 [.000]
M3IGUS1	-.278 [.000]	-.309 [.000]
DU17US	.170 [.001]	.168 [.001]
PCUS	.0252 [.385]	.0950 [.000]
CPUS	.0946 [.000]	
CGUS	.0450 [.049]	
CIUS	.0322 [.242]	
VEUS	.0209 [.329]	.0192 [.368]
FPUS	.0582 [.003]	.0520 [.008]
GDUS	.186 [.000]	.198 [.000]
MAUS	.0531 [.178]	.0539 [.176]
SCUS	.0773 [.122]	.0793 [.101]
P96US	.0973 [.000]	.932 [.001]
GPRUS	.0393 [.037]	.0406 [.029]
QUMUS	.115 [.000]	.115 [.000]
Cost.(2)	.00261 [.002]	.00199 [.002]
E-SQ(- 1)	.0574 [.023]	.0532 [.019]
H-SQ(- 1)	.939 [.025]	.944 [.020]
R-Sq.	.35747	.35786
R-Bar-Sq.	.34449	.34709
S.E.Reg.	.81047	.80886
Mean Dep.Var.	.00439	.00439
DW	1.9771	1.9976
S.D.Dep.Var.	1.0010	1.0010

(1) A P-Value is indicated after each GARCH. For the volatility part of the GARCH model, the square bracketed coefficients refer to the asymptotic standard error.

(2) H-SQ stands for the conditional variance of the error term. E-SQ stands for the square of the error term.

of the various equations estimated;[10] our interest rate regressor is the American long-term interest rate variation (DUSB1) of the first part of the equation. Other regressors in this part of the equation are similar to those seen for the DM-$ equation. The variable capturing the effect of variations in Japanese official rates – which is never significant due to the reduced number of Bank of Japan interventions on this variable in the period under examination – is followed by statements by Japanese policy makers (DJAEU) and political events, of economic and market policy, of two types:

those that concern the Yen and the Japanese economy (MJAEUY) and those that concern the Dollar and the US economy (MJAEUD).

In part A of Table 7.2 the variables appearing in the four equations indicate the DM-$ base specification for the American zone.[11] The first part of this equation is much more articulated than that for the European zone, almost presenting "structural" features, in the sense attributed to the term in studies in which exchange rate equations are estimated on the basis of monthly or quarterly data. Here we have two important regressors: the Dow Jones index variation (DDJ) and the differential between American and German long-term interest rates (DIFUG). This first part is complemented by a regressor that captures the effect of a technical analysis with moving averages (M3GUUS1), the variation in the Yen-$ exchange rate in the European zone (DJUEU), then lagged by one period, and the displaced dependent variable. The news part of this equation begins with variations in the German and American official interest rates (TGE, TUS) and with the official interventions variable (INTERV); it continues with the same three quantitative news regarding the German economy[12] seen in the European zone, and with twelve quantitative news referring to the US economy,[13] ending with four qualitative variables that relate to: statements by US policy makers, in the regular trading hours, and by German policy makers, generally in the European afternoon (DUS); US political, economic policy and market events (MUS); statements by Fed Governor Greenspan (GRE), which are grouped in a separate variable relative to DUS because our preliminary analysis (footnote 7) indicated a differential impact with respect to DUS; and, finally, strong variations in the Wall Street stock indices, which exert a particularly strong effect on the Dollar (QMFIN).

The Yen-$ base specification for the American zone, equations (5) to (8) in part B of Table 7.2, is similar to that of the DM-$: the first part has two regressors linked to Wall Street – the DDJ plus a news-variable that includes only extreme movements of the US stock indices, QMFIN, used alternatively – a US-Japan long-term interest rate differential, a lagged technical analysis variable on the Yen-$ (M3JUUS1) and a lagged dependent variable. The news part of this equation is similar to that of the DM-$ as well: it has variations in the Japanese and American official rates (TJA, TUS), the interventions variable (INTERV), the same 12 US macroeconomic variables and four qualitative news-variables. The latter refer to: a) statements by Japanese policy makers, the effects of which are seen also in the American trading (DJAUS), and statements by US counterparts on the Yen and on the Japanese economy and economic policy, DUSY; b) economic, political and economic policy events relating to Japan or to the Yen, MJAUSY, or relating to the Dollar and the US economy but with consequences on the bilateral Yen-$ exchange rate, MJAUSD.

7.3.2.1 The European Trading Zone

The SURE equations for the two exchange rates are found in Table 7.1; the GARCH equations for the same rates are found in Tables 7.1 and 7.6.

We have carried out several tests to identify the best functional form to introduce interest rates in the exchange rate equations: different formulations of individual interest rates,[14] differentials on the rates, variations on these differentials (day by day and between moving averages over three days) and variations of domestic and foreign interest rates, both short- and long-term, which at the same time represented variations in yield and capital gains. From Table 7.1 we can see that calculations on long-term interest rates are significant both in the DM-$ and in the Yen-$ equations, even if to different extents. In the DM-$ equation, part A of the table, we have variations of the interest rate differentials with a negative sign, which is correct. In the Yen-$ equation, in part B of the table, the interest rate differentials have turned out to be non-significant. Only the variation of the US long-term interest rate has shown a marginal significance, which could be due to the opposite effects of yield and capital gain prompted by a variation in yield on a long-term financial instrument, as well as possible distortions created by the long-term interest rate data chosen – as observed in a previous note.

The coefficients of the lagged dependent variables (in the peculiar formulation indicated above) in the two equations are negative, indicating a mean-reverting behavior of exchange rates, consistent with the literature and with traders' experience. The lagged variation of the other exchange rate in each of the two equations (the Yen-$ in the DM-$ equation and vice versa) is another important dynamic term in our equations. As it refers to a lagged variable it may, as a rule, carry both signs. In the Yen-$, part B, the effect of the other exchange rate is positive and stronger than in the DM-$, where the effect is negative and only marginally significant. This is reasonable, given that the Deutschmark is less traded in the Asian market while it is obviously more traded than the Yen in the European market.

Both DM-$ and Yen-$ equations include a variable for central bank interventions in the foreign exchange market (INTERV) and one or two official interest rate variables (TJA, TGE). The INTERV variable is a triple variable, constructed in the same way as all the other qualitative variables in this chapter, the positive or negative values (+1, -1) of which are determined by the explicit objectives of the intervention: to strengthen or weaken the Deutschmark or the Yen against the Dollar. Also the variables relating to variations in the three official interest rates considered in this study are of a triple nature, their sign (+ or -) indicating the standard effect (devaluation or revaluation) that such a measure can have on the exchange rate to which it directly applies. The sign of their coefficients, therefore, is always positive. Only the effect of a variation in the German official interest rates is significant in the corresponding equation. This is reasonable given that there have only been two variations in Japanese interest rates in the entire sample, while the German ones have been much more frequent, often with an appreciable effect on the exchange rate.

Now we examine the effect of scheduled news. The DM-$ in Table 7.1, part A, contains some German quantitative variables: the preliminary estimates of the variations in the consumer price index (GCPI, GCPI3); the monthly unemployment value adjusted for seasonality (GUN, GUN3); the M3 variation rate (GM3) and the value of the popular IFO business confidence index calculated by the Munich institute (GIFO3). All these variables refer to Germany as a whole and their "surprise" or news element is given, in equation (1), by the difference between actual and expected values calculated by MMS, or alternatively in equation (2) by the difference between current value and a moving average of the three previous values of the variable. None of these variables has ever resulted significant.

Now we make a brief digression on the scheduled news nature of the German macroeconomic variables, trying to understand why they are never significant in the DM-$ equations. As mentioned earlier, Germany does not publish a calendar of macroeconomic releases with day and time like the US, but rather it indicates the week during which the value of a certain indicator will be published. This can explain why these variables are never significant in the DM-$ in the European zone, and they are only marginally significant in the American zone. This result is consistent with those of Almeida-Goodhart-Payne (1998), who finds a contained reaction of the Deutschmark to short-term economic announcements during the European trading, attributing this fact to the weekly calendar.

This study has not taken into account macroeconomic variables for the Yen-$.

The qualitative news, constituting the greater part of *Newsmetrics*, statements by monetary authorities and government officials, events, comments, and foreign exchange market indiscretions (see the preceding section 7.2 and the preceding chapters in this work), are by far more significant and have a greater explanatory power.

The main results of the SURE estimations are confirmed by the GARCH (1,1) estimations in Tables 7.1 and 7.6. The GARCH models have a lower number of explanatory variables compared to the SURE models, because we have eliminated the non-significant variables or those that are explanatory only to a small degree.[15] It should be remembered that one of the main reasons for running GARCH estimations is to confirm the relevance of news-variables using also technique that explicitly takes into account the exchange rate volatility.

The GARCH estimations produce two additional results: they allow the testing of the significance of certain news-variables as factors that influence the conditional volatility of exchange rates; they also allow a graphical representation, by estimating the parameters that model such volatility without the news-variables. In this manner it is possible, on the one hand, to see whether the news that is significant on average is also significant in variance and with which sign, and on the other hand, to examine whether the conditional volatility of the exchange rates is influenced, and to what extent, by the various phases of the international financial markets and by the events described in Chapter 2 and collected in *Newsmetrics*.

With regards to the first result, it has not always been possible to obtain data of the highest reliability in the estimate of some coefficients of the news in variance because it was not possible to reach the optimum point in the estimate's iterative process.[16] The results of these estimates for the DM-$ and Yen-$ equations are presented in Table 7.9.

From part A of Table 7.9, related to the estimates in the European zone, we see that the news considered are not significant, with the exception of MJAEUD, which would tend to reduce the volatility while positively and significantly influencing the Yen-$ average. Also the other coefficients are mostly negative but not significant.

7.3.2.2 The United States Trading Zone

The greatest trading intensity occurs in the morning of the US market, since the European market is still open for a few hours after 14:15 CET while the US market starts after the almost daily publication of the major macroeconomic indicators at 8:30 EST (14:30 CET). The literature described in the first chapter makes ample use of the American short-term economic indicators, and so have we. We have supplemented this substantial volume of information with the vast collection of economic, political and market news gathered in this work. In addition, the use of long- and short-term rates and their differentials has turned out to be more practical. In short, we can state that the results obtained on the US market are much more interesting than those obtained on the European market.

The SURE and GARCH estimations of the two exchange rates in this zone are presented in Tables 7.2 to 7.6. The SURE equations using long-term interest rate differentials are found in Tables 7.2, 7.3 and 7.4; those that use short-term interest rate differentials are in Table 7.5; GARCH (1,1) equations using both types of rates are in Table 7.6. Once again, the symbols of the regressors used are in Table 7.11.

Let us begin by examining in Table 7.2 the non-restricted estimates of the two exchange rate equations. We have a first part consisting of fundamentals, technical analysis and statistical regressors (the first five regressors, excluding the intercept, in part A, and the first six in part B); we then have all the German and American quantitative economic news from the tenth to the twenty-fourth regressor, for the DM-$, in part A, and from the tenth to the twenty-first regressor with US news only, for Japan, in part B; the last part contains the qualitative variables developed in this work. Quantitative variables have been used in the form of news, as before: as differences between the actual and expected values, equations (1), (2), (5) and (6), and as differences between current values and a moving average of the three previous actual values, equations (3), (4), (7) and (8).

The German macroeconomic news in the DM-$ equation, in part A of Table 7.2, are not significant, even if the situation improves relative to the estimates in the European zone. Among the US macroeconomic news, only those referring to the labour market are always significant in their various specifications: the creation of employment in the non-agricultural sector, the variation in the hourly earnings rate and the unemployment rate relative to the entire economy. No financial markets expert would be surprised by this result, even though one could expect more significance from other important indicators. The popular industrial activity index prepared by NAPM is only marginally significant in SURE, but it fails the second test of the GARCH estimations and therefore does not appear in Table 7.6.

The trade balance is never significant in the SURE estimations in Table 7.2.[17] This is not entirely surprising because the market comments between 1995 and 1997 very rarely refer to a US trade balance problem. The parameters estimated using this and all the other US macroeconomic variables remain consistently immaterial in the estimates shown in Table 7.2, both for the Deutschmark and for the Yen. Therefore in subsequent SURE estimations of reduced models, in Tables 7.3 and 7.4, we have kept only the three labour market variables (UOC, UW, UUN) plus the NAPM index.

The qualitative news (DUSD, MUS, GRE, QMFIN) are always highly significant and the magnitude of the respective coefficients is much greater than that of other variables. The qualitative events captured by these variables have indeed produced substantial jumps in the two exchange rates examined.

The SURE results obtained for the Yen-$ – Table 7.2, part B – are similar to those obtained for the DM-$.

With regards to the use of interest rates in our equations, we have estimated for both exchange rates models that replicate those in Table 7.2 using short-term interest rates. The results are shown in Table 7.5 and can be compared with those in Table 7.2, or at least to those estimated with short-term variables in the form of actual value minus expected value. Equations (1) and (2) in Table 7.5, part A, are comparable to equations (1) and (2) in Table 7.2, part A. Equations (3) and (4) in the same part A of Table 7.5 are reduced relative to equations (1) and (2) in Table 7.2, and their parameters are therefore comparable to the equivalent ones in Table 7.3, part A. The same goes for the estimates of Yen-$ equations in part B of Tables 7.5, 7.2 and 7.3.

A reduced model for the two exchange rates is presented in Tables 7.3 and 7.4. Having eliminated all the variables that are not significant, or that are significant only to a limited extent, we have estimated with SURE the parameters of the four surviving US economic news that are common to both exchange rates (UOC, UW, UUN, UNAPM), in free form (equations (1), (2), (4), (5), Tables 7.3 and 7.4) or in restricted form (equations (3) and (6), Tables 7.3 and 7.4). The restricted estimates have not rejected the implicit assumption that the US variables indicated above have the same effect on both exchange rates in the American zone. The orders of magnitude of the parameters arc thus confirmed.

The same reduced models have been used for the GARCH (1,1) estimations, with a few changes, and shown in Table 7.6, where we use long- and short-term interest rate differentials. These variables are significant in the DM-$, and a little less in the Yen-$. All the coefficients of the other news-variables have approximately the same magnitude and significance as those obtained with the SURE estimations.

In Table 7.9, part B, which contains the coefficients of some news-variables introduced in variance in the two exchange rate equations, we continue to observe this curious negative sign in many of the qualitative news-variables. These are statistically significant in the currency market events (MUS, MJAUSY, MJAUSD) and in the variable relating to Governor Greenspan's statements (GRE). This result seems to indicate that the reaction of the exchange rate to the event represented by these news-variables, which exists always given that the same variables are highly significant in the mean, exhausts the "trauma" represented by this event and therefore the volatility later decreases.

We can observe that the news relating to the labor market has a positive volatility coefficient, which in two cases is significant. Given that this news has a coefficient much smaller on average than that of qualitative variables, some of which, as we have seen, seem to reduce the exchange rate volatility, one could assume that on average the US labor market news does not exhaust their effect, leaving behind a residual volatility. On this last point it is worth noting that these short-term variables also have a great impact on the US long-term securities markets and on the stock market: it is therefore possible that the exchange rate volatility remains also due to this effect; moreover, there could also be some distortion from the simultaneity of our estimates.

7.3.3 Lira-DM Equations

The Lira-DM exchange rate equations also contain a first part referring to the macroeconomic fundamentals, represented here by the differentials in interest rates and by the consumer inflation dynamics in Italy, and to statistical-technical analysis type of variables. The second part of the equation contains the news-variables. Also these equations are estimated first in SURE and then in GARCH and for the two time zones of this study. There is a difference relative to the Dollar equations: here the SURE estimation is performed only on the Lira-DM exchange rate in both time zones, in the assumption that any errors in the Lira exchange rate equations are correlated in the two parts, as they contain the entire trading span (the global trading day).

The base specification of the Lira-DM exchange rate equation is found in parts A and B of Table 7.7 for the European and the American zone respectively. We have not estimated reduced equations in SURE, eliminating the non-significant variables, like we have done for the Dollar equations, primarily because they turned out to be very few; however, we have estimated directly in GARCH equations from which we have omitted the few non-significant variables that were present in the SURE estimations in Table 7.7 (Table 7.8).

The first six explanatory variables, after the intercept, in the equations in Table 7.7 are composed of long- and short-term interest rate levels and differentials. Four additional variables complete the first part of the equation, that of the fundamentals. After an inflation variable (M2PCC, consisting of the difference between the current inflation rate and a moving average of the two previous values), there is a dummy (DU17, in the two versions EU and US) that captures the strong devaluation of the Lira on the apparently unexplainable "Black Friday" of 17 March, 1995, and the equally strong rally of the following two days. Then follow the news-variables of this equation.

The Lira-DM exchange rate equation contains several combinations of interest rate variables. This is due to the fact that these interest rate variables are highly significant and their sign, at separate levels, (3), (7) and (4), (8), Table 7.7, and in differential, (1), (5) and (2), (6), in both the long term – (2), (6) and (4), (8) – and the short term – (1), (5) and (3), (7) – is systematically opposite to the expected one. This situation had to be explored further. We have tried several formulations of the interest rate differential, and they have all confirmed the result indicated above. In Table 7.7 the base formulation of the interest rate variables, both in differential form and separately, consists of an interest rate variation relative to a moving average of the three preceding values. From the point of view of consistency and statistical significance this particular representation of the interest rate variable has always given the best results. Using daily data this does not come as a surprise. The use of specific interest rates, that is with daily interest rate differentials or with variations in the daily differentials, has yielded substantially worse results, although in any case consistent with those presented here.

In equation (1) DIF33GI is a differential on the three-month Euro-Lira and Euro-Deutschmark interest rate variations relative to a moving average of the three previous values. In equation (2) DIF3GI is a differential on 10-year German and Italian securities rates, calculated as the previous one. For M3E3GF and M3E3IT, equation (3), and M3GEB and M3ITB, equation (4), the same transformations have been performed on the three-month and the ten-year rates: in these equations, then, the interest rates are entered separately.

The fundamental variables that complete the first part of the equation are represented primarily by the DM-$ exchange rate, which during the greater part of the period of fluctuation of the Lira has been the main explanatory variable for its fluctuations against the Deutschmark.[18] M3GUEU is constructed as a variation between the current value of the DM-$ exchange rate and a moving average of the three previous values. This is followed by a variation on the Lira-DM exchange rate in the American zone in the previous day, DIGUS, and the lagged variable.

The variable relative to the discount rate variations is usually communicated once the European markets are closed and for this reason it is inserted in the Lira-DM exchange rate equation for the American zone, Table 7.7, part B. This variable has never resulted significant, and understandably so, given that the Italian discount rate variation generally ratifies what has already happened in the money market.

The news-variables in this equation are those amply described in Chapter 3: we want to test their statistical significance[19] and their relative weight in explaining the fluctuations of the Lira. The codes for these variables are shown in Table 7.11.[20] We have strictly political news – CP (conflicts among the Polo), CG (judiciary conflict), CI (institutional conflict), VE (electoral victories), MA (events of ex-Minister of Justice Mancuso), SC (political clarifications in 1995), P96 (political events in the first quarter of 1996), GPR (events of the Prodi Government), RIF (action by Rifondazione Comunista) – and news of a primarily economic or economic-political content, PC (inflation news), FP (public finance news), GD (economic policy action of the Dini Government), and QUM (news on EMU of interest for the Lira).

As indicated above, all the interest rate variables (from the second to the seventh in Table 7.7) enter with a highly significant coefficient but with a systematically wrong sign, according to a theoretical reference of the Mundell-Fleming or Keynesian[21] type. This sign can be justified by a situation of particularly high levels in the Italian public debt, whereby an increase in interest rates is perceived by the financial markets as an increase in the likelihood of default on the debt, with the resulting increase in the risk premium on Lira-holding financial activities. This result is confirmed by preliminary results of construction of vectors of news (those mentioned in two previous notes), according to which increases in BOT interest rates in the twice-monthly auctions produce a devaluation of the Lira on the same day, and by other empirical studies with daily Italian data: Tivegna (1996 and Fornari-Monticelli-Pericoli-Tivegna (1999).

We see both in parts A (European zone) and B (American zone) of Table 7.7 that the negative sign of the Germany-Italy rate differential in equations (1), (2), (5) and (6) is confirmed by the signs and the magnitude of the coefficients in equations (3), (4), (7) and (8), in which the interest rates enter individually. Again one should remember that the individual interest rates are considered as the difference relative to the performance in the three previous days, and therefore the interest rate differentials are really differentials on interest rate variations.

In equation (3), the positive coefficient of the Italian short-term interest rate (M3E3IT) is much greater than the non-significant coefficient of the German short-term interest rate (M3E3GF). In equation (4), which contains long-term interest rates, the coefficient of the German interest rate (M3GEB) has a negative and significant sign, indicating the prevalence of capital gains over the simple interest rate differential, but the coefficient of the Italian interest rate (M3ITB) is also almost three times greater and it is highly significant. These results indicate consistently that an increase in long- and short-term Italian interest rates cause a devaluation of the Lira against the Deutschmark. These results for the European zone are confirmed, with some negligible differences, by those for the American zone.

Moving on to the SURE news coefficients, we immediately see that the one on inflation (M2PCC) – a variable that is the result of the percentage variation of ISTAT's flash estimate of inflation for the current month relative to a moving average of two immediately preceding periods of the same index – is never significant. On the contrary, the news on inflation expressed in qualitative form – with regressor values of 0, +1, -1 – are always significant in the European zone (PCEU), and a little less significant in the American zone (PCUS). We must underline that the latter contain news relative to very strong and unexpected variations in consumer prices, which have had particular exposure in the specialized media, in addition to several other events that are relevant to inflation (for instance particularly "generous" contract renewals, tensions on raw material prices, etc.). All of this may indicate that only variations in prices that are strong and unexpected exert an effect on the exchange rates.

We then have twelve regressors relative to political news (CP, CG, CI, VE, SC, MA, P96, GPR, RIF) and economic policy news (FP, GD, QUM). Here we merely comment (because we will talk about this later) that in the European zone (Table 7.7, part A) these variables are all significant, with the exception of the political clarifications during the Dini Government (SC), which are only moderately significant; in the American zone (part B, same Table) the events related to the action of Rifondazione Comunista (RIFUS) are not significant, and somewhat less significant are those events related to institutional conflict (CIUS), to Minister Mancuso (MAUS), and to the action of the Prodi Government (GPRUS).

In Table 7.8, parts A and B, we find the GARCH (1,1) estimations for the Lira-DM equation in both trading zones.[22] We can immediately observe that the coefficients of the part relating to the mean of the equations in the table are smaller than those relative to the SURE estimations, because of the GARCH (1,1) estimations of the parameters of the exchange conditional volatility, which are always significant. This indicates the benefit of integrating the SURE and the GARCH estimations. The statistical significance of the surviving variables after having eliminated the very few

Table 7.9 GARCH(1,1) coefficients of some news variables in volatility. DM-$ and Yen-$ exchange rates (1)

	Long-term Interest Rate Differential		Short-term Interest Rate Differential	
A European Time Zone				
DM/$				
DGE		-.0007		
MGE		-.0074		
QUMIN				
QGE		.0023		
Yen/$				
DJAEU		-.0148		
MJAEUY		-.0298		
MJAEUD		-.0701*		
B American Time Zone				
DM/$	**A – E**	**A – M(3)**	**A – E**	**A – M(3)**
UOC	-.0023	.0020		.0031
UW	.0181**	.0068	.0057	
UUN	.0126	.0103**		.0107**
DUSD	.0045	.0053	.0047	.0054
MUS	-.0242**	-.0290*	-.0240*	-.0287*
GRE	-.0185*	-.0185**	-.0189**	-.0187**
QMFIN	-.0173	-.0174	-.0164	-.0162
Yen/$				
UOC		.0332*		.0397
UW				-.0518
UUN				-.0368
MJAUSY	-.0701*	-.0682*	-.0694*	-.0677*
MJAUSD	-.0172	.0392*	-.0435	.0397**
DJAUSD				-.0200
DUSY				-.0297

(1) The scheduled news variables in volatility are expressed as differences between actual values of the variable (A) less expected values (E) or less three-term moving averages of the preceding actual values (M(3)).
(*) Significant at 95%
(**) Significant at 99%

non-significant variables of the SURE estimations is confirmed, with some exceptions: the news on electoral results (VEEU and VEEUS), the Mancuso-related events (MAEU, MAUS) and the various political clarifications (SCUS).

As noted earlier, the GARCH estimations enable us to evaluate the significance of the news-variables also in variance, as well as in median, and to have a graphical image of the conditional volatility.

As for the first result, it has not always been possible to obtain results of the highest reliability for many news-variables because the optimum point in the iterative estimate point has not been reached. The results of the introduction in variance of the Italian news are shown in Table 7.10. From the table we see that the only significant news in the European zone are

Table 7.10 GARCH(1,1) coefficients of some news variables in volatility. LIT-DM exchange rate

	Long-term Interest Rate Differential	Short-term Interest Rate Differential
A European Time Zone		
LIT/DM		
PCEU		.0106**
CPEU		.0043
CGEU		
CIEU		.0298**
VEEU		-.0089
FPEU	.0055	.0096
GDEU	-.0891**	-.1026**
MAEU		.0474
SP96EU		-.0073
GPREU		.0037
RIFEU		-.0053
QUMEU		.0061
B American Time Zone		
LIT/DM		
PCEU		
CPEU		.0129**
CGEU		
CIEU		
VEEU		
FPEU	.0010	.0009
GDEU	-.0389	
MAEU	-.0045	
SP96EU	.0141	.0147
GPREU	.0074	.0082
RIFEU		
QUMEU		

(*) Significant at 95%
(**) Significant at 99%

those on inflation (PCEU), with a positive sign, and those on the action of the Dini Government (GDEU), with a negative sign. While it is not difficult to understand why inflation news increase volatility, it is harder to understand why the often traumatic events of the Dini Government decrease it. A possible interpretation – noting that the coefficient in median of GDEU is positive, significant, and of relevant magnitude while the coefficient in variance is negative, significant, and roughly half the size – may be that the occurrence of the event exhausts the GDEU effect on the exchange and perhaps brings the expectations of traders back into balance: this reduces the fluctuations after the original event.

Table 7.11 List of variables in tables 7.1 – 7.10

CGEU:	Italy, judicial conflicts, ETZ
CGUS:	Italy, judicial conflicts, ATZ
CIEU:	Italy, institutional conflicts, ETZ
CIUS:	Italy, institutional conflicts, ATZ
CPEU:	Italy, conflicts inside the Polo coalition, ETZ
CPUS:	Italy, conflicts inside the Polo coalition, ATZ
DDIFGU:	Variation of long-term int. Rate differential, Germany-USA
DDJ:	Log-variation of Dow Jones
DGE:	Statements by members of Bundesbank and German Gov. in ETZ
DGUEU:	Log-variation of DM-$ in day t in ETZ w.r.t. t-1 in ATZ
DGUUS:	Log-variation of DM-$ in day t in ATZ w.r.t. t in ETZ
DIF33GI:	3-month interest rate differentials between Germany-Italy in day t
DIF3GI:	Long-term interest rate differentials between Germany-Italy in day t
DIF3UG:	3-month interest rate differentials between Germany-USA in day t
DIF3UJ:	3-month interest rate differentials between USA-Japan in day t
DIFGU:	Long-term interest rate differentials between Germany-USA in day t
DIFUG:	Long-term interest rate differentials between USA-Germany in day t
DIFUJ:	Long-term interest rate differentials between USA-Japan in day t
DIGEU:	Log-variation of Lit-DM in day t in ETZ w.r.t. t-1 in ATZ
DIGUS:	Log-variation of Lit-DM in day t in ATZ w.r.t. t in ETZ
DJAEU:	Statements by Policy-maker of Japan on Yen in ETZ
DJAUS:	Statements by Policy-maker of Japan on Yen in ATZ
DJUEU:	Log-variation of Yen-$ in day t in ETZ w.r.t. t-1 in ATZ
DJUUS:	Log-variation of Yen-$ in day t in ATZ w.r.t. t-1 in ETZ
DU17EU:	Italy, dummies of "Black Friday" March 17 1995, ETZ
DU17US:	Italy, dummies of "Black Friday" March 17 1995, ATZ
DUSB1:	Log-variation of 10-Year US int. rate in day t w.r.t. t-1
DUSD:	Statements by US and German policy-makers in ATZ
DUSY:	Statements US Policy-maker on Yen in ATZ
FPEU:	Italy, public finance news, ETZ

FPUS:	Italy, public finance news , ATZ
GCPI:	Monthly datum of consumer price Germany: actual less expected
GCPI3:	Monthly datum of consumer price Germany: actual less Moving average 3 month
GDEU:	Italy, policies of Dini Gov., ETZ
GDUS:	Italy, policies of Dini Gov., ATZ
GIFO3:	Monthly datum IFO index for Germany: actual less Moving average 3 month
GM3:	Monthly datum of M3 variation in Germany: actual less expected
GPREU:	Italy, policies of Prodi Gov., ETZ
GPRUS:	Italy, policies of Prodi Gov., ATZ
GRE:	Statements by Alan Greenspan
GUN:	Monthly datum of unemployment in Germany: actual less expected
GUN3:	Monthly datum of unemployment in Germany: actual less Moving average 3-month
INTERV:	Public interventions by Central Banks in the foreign exchange market
M2PCC:	Moving average 2-month CPI in Italy
M3E3GF:	Moving average 3-month German interest rate 3 month
M3E3IT:	Moving average 3-month Italy interest rate 3 month
M3GEB:	Moving average 3-month long-term rate (10 years) Germany
M3GUEU:	Moving average 3-month variation log. DM-$, ETZ (DGUEU)
M3GUUS:	Moving average 3-month variation log. DM-$, ATZ (DGUUS)
M3GUUS1:	Moving average 3-month DM-$ in ATZ (DGUUS) lagged one period
M3IGUS1:	Moving average 3-month Lit-DM in ATZ (DIGUS) lagged one period
M3ITB:	Moving average 3-month long-term rate (10 years) Italy
M3JUUS1:	Moving average 3-month Yen-$ in ATZ (DJUUS) lagged one period
MAEU:	Italy, Minister Mancuso action, ETZ
MAUS:	Italy: Minister Mancuso action, ATZ
MGE:	Political and market events having an impact on DM-$ in ETZ
MJAEUD:	Political and market events on $ having an impact on Yen-$ in ETZ
MJAEUY:	Political and market events on Yen having an impact on Yen-$ in ETZ
MJAUSD:	Political and market events on $ having an impact on Yen-$ in ATZ
MJAUSY:	Political and market events on Yen having an impact on Yen-$ in ATZ
MUS:	Political and market events having an impact on DM-$ in ATZ
P96EU:	Italy, political events in the first quarter of 1996, ETZ
P96US:	Italy, political events in the first quarter of 1996, ATZ
PCEU:	Italy, news on inflation, ETZ
PCUS:	Italy, news on inflation, ATZ
QGE:	Qualitative description of German economic events
QMFIN:	Strong variations of US stock indexes
QUMEU:	Italy, events and statements concerning EMU relevant for the Lira, ETZ
QUMIN:	Events and statements concerning EMU relevant for DM-$
QUMUS:	Italy, events and statements concerning EMU relevant for the Lira, ATZ
RIFEU:	Italy, political action by Rifondazione Comunista, ETZ
RIFUS:	Italy, political action by Rifondazione Comunista, ATZ
SCEU:	Italy, political appeasement during Dini Gov., ETZ

SCUS:	Italy, political appeasement during Dini Gov., ATZ
TGE	Official interest rate change from Bundesbank
TIT:	Official interest rate change from Bank of Italy
TJA:	Official interest rate change from Bank of Japan
TUS	Official interest rate change from the Federal Reserve
UCC:	Monthly datum USA, consumer confidence: actual less expected
UCC3:	Monthly datum USA, consumer confidence: actual less expected 3M Mov.Av.
UCPI:	Monthly datum USA, CPI: actual less expected
UCPI3:	Monthly datum USA, CPI: actual less expected 3M Mov.Av.
UDG:	Monthly datum USA, durable goods orders: actual less expected
UDG3:	Monthly datum USA, durable goods orders: actual less expected 3M Mov.Av.
UIPI:	Monthly datum USA, industrial production: actual less expected
UIPI3:	Monthly datum USA, industrial production: actual less expected 3M Mov.Av.
ULEAD:	Monthly datum USA, leading indicators: actual less expected
ULEAD3:	Monthly datum USA, leading indicators: actual less expected 3M Mov.Av.
UNAPM:	Monthly datum USA, NAPM: actual less expected
UNAPM3:	Monthly datum USA, NAPM: actual less expected 3M Mov.Av.
UOC:	Monthly datum USA, non-farm payrolls: actual less expected
UOC3:	Monthly datum USA, non-farm payrolls: actual less expected 3M Mov.Av.
UPPI:	Monthly datum USA, PPI: actual less expected
UPPI3:	Monthly datum USA, PPI: actual less expected 3M Mov.Av.
URET:	Monthly datum USA, retail sales: actual less expected
URET3:	Monthly datum USA, retail sales: actual less expected 3M Mov.Av.
UTRB:	Monthly datum USA, trade balance: actual less expected
UTRB3:	Monthly datum USA, trade balance: actual less expected 3M Mov.Av.
UUN:	Monthly datum USA, unemployment rate: actual less expected
UUN3:	Monthly datum USA, unemployment rate: actual less expected 3M Mov.Av.
UW:	Monthly datum USA, hourly wage change: actual less expected
UW3:	Monthly datum USA, hourly wage change: actual less expected 3M Mov.Av.
VEEU:	Italy, election victories, ETZ
VEUS:	Italy, election victories, ATZ

Notes

1 See studies that base their empirical analysis on intra-daily exchange rates, for instance Ederington-Lee (1993, 1995); Goodhart-Hall-Henry-Pesaran (1993); Almeida-Goodhart-Payne (1998).

2 The majority of the studies quoted in the first chapter use this source.

3 This is what is suggested in Almeida-Goodhart-Payne (1998).

4 See Baillie-McMahon (1989, especially Chapters 3 and 8); Hallwood-Macdonald (1994, Chapters 5, 8, 9 and 10); Copeland (1994, Chapters 5, 6 and 7).

5 For a survey, see Baillie-McMahon (1989, Chapter 7).

6 For this study we have used "Business Briefing", the database of all the communications Reuters enters into its system (indicating day, hour and minute), which

was kindly made available to us by the Italian office.

7 Preliminary tests on the explanatory power of each qualitative variable have been conducted according to the following steps: 1) all the events of a particular type were gathered together; 2) those events most likely to produce a positive effect (exchange rate appreciation) were separated from those with an opposite sign; 3) binary variables (0, 1) were built both for news with a likely positive effect and for news with a likely negative effect; 4) using the variables thus constructed, multiple regressions on the exchange rates were performed so that the calculation process determined the sign, the intensity and the significance of each category of events; 5) an analysis of the coefficients and the residuals of the regressions under (4) was performed in order to identify individual events that have a weaker effect on the day's exchange rate variation and therefore of a more uncertain or even opposite sign; 6) based on (5) modify the vectors of events, with some shifts, and then repeat steps (3) to (5) until all the controversial sign assignments are eliminated.

8 Our base references are Bollerslev (1986, 1987, 1990); Bollerslev-Chou-Kroner (1992); Bollerslev-Engle-Nelson (1994).

9 This is possible with GARCH models. Many works on the impact of the news devote particular attention to the measurement of their effects on the conditional volatility. See, for example, Fornari-Monticelli-Pericoli-Tivegna (1999).

10 This could be due to the fact that we use interest rate variables polled in London, even though these instruments are traded continuously, almost like currencies, and therefore the same rates are quoted also on the Japanese market.

11 The different parameters of the two pairs of equations – (1), (2) and (3), (4) – of Table 7.2, part A, are due to the different specifications of the Yen-$ equations with which they are simultaneously estimated in the SURE model, in part B of the table.

12 Here too they are specified in the form of differences between the actual and the expected values – GCPI, GUN, GM3, equations (1) and (2) – and between current values and a running average of the three previous values – GCPI3, GUN3, GIFO3, equations (3) and (4). We will later indicate why we have tested also for the American zone the explanatory power of German quantitative indicators announced at the beginning of the European trading, the effect of which, therefore, should already be included in the US opening quotes.

13 For an accurate description of these indicators see Chapter 4 and Table 7.11.

14 We have observed above that, with daily data, it may be necessary to use interest rates not as an actual value but as the difference between the current value of the rate and a moving average of the previous values, in order better to capture the modus operandi of analysts who, in the very short-term, base their own decisions more on trends than on the day's values.

15 We have checked that these variables, not significant in SURE, would maintain this quality also in the GARCH model, but we have not reproduced the results.

16 These estimates have been obtained by introducing news-variables individually in average and variance modes, adding them to the part of the equation relating to the "fundamentals". For the sake of brevity the complete results of these estimates have not been reproduced here. Tables 7.9 and 7.10 show only the parameters of the news-variables in variance and an indication of their statistical significance.

17 Hardouvelis obtains a different result but in a different period, the one following the sharp revaluation of the Dollar in the mid-1980s.

18 See Tivegna (1996).

19 It should also be noted that for the news-variables relating to the Lira-DM exchange rate we have followed a pre-selection procedure similar to that already described in note 7 of this chapter.

20 One should remember that Chapter 3 uses the *Newsmetrics* classification codes that appear in the database containing the texts of the news. For easier reading, in Table 7.11 this news contains a double code: that used in Tables 7.1 and 7.9 and that used in the

database and presented in its entirety in the database.

21 It is however true that this sign, which we qualify as “wrong”, is consistent with what theory should demand from an exchange rate equation of a monetary type; however, the theoretical basis of our equations is not of this kind as they never contain differentials of monetary expansion or of related news. In addition, the empirical exchange rate equations of a monetary type generally have a “Keynesian sign” too, and therefore a “wrong” sign, according to their own theoretical basis. See Baillie-McMahon (1989), Chapter 8, and the many studies quoted there.

22 For the sake of brevity we have not reproduced the GARCH results of equations in which the interest rates enter separately, (3), (4), (7) and (8) in Table 7.7.

Chapter 8

Events and Foreign Exchange Markets

8.1 Introduction

In this last chapter we draw some conclusions from the results of this work, highlighting also some aspects of our analysis that we have not treated before. An important result is that this is the first attempt in the international literature at making an inventory of the events that are relevant to foreign exchange traders and gathering them in a single source.

At the beginning of this work, in the first quarter of 1995, any event related to nature (for instance the Kobe earthquake), to economics and finance (nearly all), to politics (potentially all, but in reality just a few), and to any indiscretion, opinion or statement without geographical limitations appeared to us potentially useful to explain exchange rate fluctuations. This belief was reinforced by the wealth of recurring news communicated by journalistic sources exclusively dedicated to trading, such as Reuters, Bloomberg, Radiocor, Bridge and Ansa. Consequently, we have extended the collection of events beyond the Italian borders, to the point that now the majority of the events in *Newsmetrics* come from abroad.

One of the results of our analysis is that we have limited the span of news that is relevant to an understanding of the exchange market dynamics, albeit within a wide and constantly evolving range, in Chapters 3, 4, 5, 6 and section 7.2.

Having identified a universe of events that determines price formation in the foreign exchange market, we have selected a vast sample that could replicate all its characteristics, the main one obviously being the ability to explain exchange rate fluctuations. Therefore an extended empirical analysis was performed, with estimates of the exchange rate equations containing the news thus selected and grouped in homogeneous categories according to a taxonomy of events, Chapter 7. The next section, 8.2, illustrates the main novelties of this study.

This quantitative analysis has enabled us to achieve one of our main objectives, i.e. the development of a metric of news, identifying a hierarchy among them depending on their explanatory contribution to the exchange rate dynamics. This is discussed in section 8.3.

In addition to the economic and financial literature reviewed in Chapter 1, we could not leave out the identification of the communication model apparently used by traders, whether explicitly or implicitly. The information received from traders has determined to a significant extent many of the contents of *Newsmetrics*. The model that is emerging from the analysis of events and economic data does not appear to belong explicitly to an economic theory, which comprises various aspects of expectation formation theory, but it certainly will appear familiar to scholars of communication theory. This is described in section 8.4, as a further clarification of the criteria followed in the construction of the database.

The various categories of news, therefore, have their own "specific weight", estimated with a fixed coefficient dictated by the econometric techniques that we have used, along the sample horizon of our study, from 1994 to 1997. The reaction of the markets to events, however, is not constant; it varies depending on market sentiment and on the cyclical phases of the markets themselves and of the economies within which they operate, at times giving way to phenomena of market polarisation. This is well known to traders and quite visible in our historical reconstruction of the markets during the period covered by our study, Chapter 2. Section 8.5 contains a few considerations on this subject.

The identification of market sentiment is more an art than a science. Although our intent was to write a "scientific" book, based primarily on theoretical analysis, empirical verification and on economic and financial literature, we have at least tried to describe the basic ingredients that underpin this "art": the statistical regularity that connects fundamentals and news to exchange rate dynamics, the weight of news in the explanation of exchange rates, a model to decode events, an awareness of the various phases experienced by the markets and the role of the prevailing market sentiment. In section 8.6 we illustrate some operational applications of the results of this study, which could lead to further analysis.

8.2 Novelties

This study brings essentially two main innovative elements:

1) the identification of a methodology to assemble events that are relevant to foreign exchange markets; and
2) the consequent expansion of the empirical literature on news and exchange rates.

The identification of selection criteria for the events that are relevant to a systematic explanation (to the extent possible) of exchange rate fluctuation, has been a laborious trial-and-error process. The interviews with the traders, the readings of financial newspapers and the in-depth examination of news-flashes communicated by the most respected trading systems (e.g. Reuters, Bloomberg, etc.) often leave a sense of lack of definition. This is determined primarily by two factors: on one hand one feels the need to explain the unexplainable, with the traditional economic and financial analysis tools and with the experience accumulated until a few hours earlier, on the other hand some *ad hoc* explanations may take on a consensus status, at least for some time.

This situation compels the providers of primary information to communicate a substantial amount of base information, with minimal selectivity in terms of relevance, from which quite a vast range of event interpretations develops. This was the starting point when we first tried to put together a limited number of events – out of a vast universe – capable of explaining the exchange rate dynamics.

The criteria for assembling the news have their origin in the historical reconstruction of the period, Chapter 2, and in an interactive selection process of micro-events that, on the one hand, are consistent with market trends and, on the other hand, contribute to identify new ones. At the base of this procedure is a gradual empirical verification of the ability of events to explain the exchange rate variations, according to the methodology described in note 4 of section 7.3. In the econometric estimates of Chapter 7 there is a final verification of the explanatory power of the individual categories of events, ordered according to a taxonomy of the news described in section 7.2 and to the adjustments for the economic, financial, political and institutional framework of the four countries considered, Chapters 3, 4, 5 and 6.

The very structure of *Newsmetrics* is a model to identify criteria for assembling a database of events that are relevant to explain exchange rate fluctuations for other currencies, in different contexts and different time periods.

As we have often repeated, the literature of reference of this study uses almost exclusively scheduled macroeconomic news. Our empirical verification increases the existing knowledge because it extends the list of news variables which can explain exchange rate fluctuations.

The majority of the qualitative or (almost equivalently) unscheduled news in this study, remain within the stochastic error term of equations estimated using only scheduled quantitative news, and therefore permits an extension of the interpretations of the factors that produce fluctuations and, even more importantly, turning points in exchange rates. The latter are often determined by a deep alteration of the market sentiment, which is often the result of new perspectives on the economic policies, revealed by statements by the major policy makers. These changes in direction generally originate in new or unexpected macroeconomic developments, but they are generally determined by a series of elements that take place in a longer time span rather than by the publication of the latest statistical fact. They may even include the short-term macroeconomic developments of another country.

In short, then, we believe that having a wider range of political and market news adds multiple elements for understanding the exchange rate dynamics, producing a substantial leap forward in our knowledge of this subject.

The empirical part of this study seems to indicate that the relationship between news and exchange rate dynamics is substantially different in the European and the American parts of the global trading day.

8.3 The Metrics of News

The econometric results contained in Tables 7.1 to 7.8 may be used to define, as a rule, the order of importance of each of the news appearing as a regressor in the equations estimated there. These variables have been standardized and therefore the corresponding coefficient, estimated by SURE and by GARCH models, is comparable within the equation or across equations. Given the trinal nature of the variables representing news, this comparability is greater among the variables of the same nature, which consist of: qualitative – or unscheduled – news that have a (+1, 0, -1) nature; quantitative – or scheduled – news that consist of zeros in the absence of an event, and by positive or negative values, resulting from the differences between actual and expected values (or moving averages representing expected values); and, lastly, economic and financial variables that have different readings in each day. An evaluation of the news metrics used in this study is provided in Tables 8.1, 8.2 and 8.3, which show the coefficients of the news and of the main economic and financial variables in some of the equations estimated in Chapter 7.

Tables 8.1 and 8.2 contain, for the two trading zones and for SURE and GARCH estimates, the coefficients of some economic variables and of news relative to the DM-$ and Yen-$ exchange rates. From the table we see at first glance that qualitative news have by far the greatest weight for both currencies. We see that there is a significant coincidence of quantitative results with the two estimation techniques where the ranking of the news is concerned, while the value of the coefficients changes only slightly.

In the DM-$, monetary policy and market news (MGE and MUS, in the equations and database codes) have the greatest weight. These are followed, in the European trading zone, by statements by policy makers (DGE) and then by the other news (EMU events, QUMIN, and German current economic news, QGE). In the American zone they are followed by news on the US stock market, QMFIN,[1] by general statements (DUSD) and by Greenspan's statements (GRE), Tables 8.1 and 8.2. This last result appears unusual but it is not wholly unexpected given that the impact of Greenspan's statements on the Dollar is felt through the US financial market and that their effect on the exchange rate and on the stock trends often carries the opposite sign.[2]

In the European zone the news relative to the publication of current macroeconomic indicators have proven not to be material in explaining DM-$ variations (Table 8.1), and in the American zone (Table 8.2) they are represented only by labour market news (employment, UOC3, hourly

Table 8.1 Relative weight of news variables in some DM-$ and Yen-$ equations in ETZ (*)

DM – Dollar				
		(1)	(2)	(3)
Long-term Diff. Change	(DDIFGU)	-.0580	-.0595	-.0720
Lagged Yen-Dollar	(DJUUS(-1)	-.0430	-.0443	-.0423
Lagged DM-Dollar	(DGUEU(-1)	-.0689	-.0671	-.0599
German Discount Rates	(TGE)	.0789	.0778	.0776
Central Banks Interv	(INTERV)	.0772	.0772	.0842
German Statements	(DGE)	.246	.247	.271
DM-$ MKT News	(MGE)	.439	.438	.492
EMU DM-$ News	(QUMIN)	.186	.186	.214
German Economic News	(QGE)	.0963	.101	.128
Yen – Dollar				
		(4)	(5)	(6)
US Long-term Variation	(DUSB1)	.0411	.0423	.0390
Lagged DM-Dollar	(DGUUS(-1)	.0745	.0751	.0692
Lagged Yen-Dollar	(DJUUS(-1)	-.109	-.109	-.102
Japanese Statements	(DJAEU)	.264	.264	.263
Yen-related Policy News	(MJAEUY)	.421	.421	.471
$-related Policy News	(MJAEUD)	.284	.284	.277

(*) The symbols of the variables used in econometric estimates in Chapter 7 are in parentheses. For a better understanding see Table 7.11

(1) SURE Equation n. 1 Tab. 7.1 (4) SURE Equation n. 4 Tab. 7.1
(2) SURE Equation n. 2 Tab. 7.1 (5) SURE Equation n. 5 Tab. 7.1
(3) GARCH Equation n. 3 Tab. 7.1 (6) GARCH Equation n. 6 Tab. 7.1

earnings, UW3, and unemployment rate, UUN3). These news are quantitatively less relevant than qualitative news; the most prominent among them is the variation in unemployment, followed by variations in earnings and unemployment rate. The weight of quantitative news seem to be comparable – sometimes more, sometimes less – to that of the micro-financial variables appearing in Table 8.2.

Also for the Yen-$ the weight of market and economic policy news in general (relative to the Japanese economy and the Yen, MJAEUY and MJAUSY, or to events that concern the Dollar, MJAEUD and MJAUSD) is more prominent, followed by statements news (DJAE, DJAUS, DUSY) and by quantitative news, similar to those of the DM-$, with a prominence of the hourly earnings variables. See Tables 8.1 and 8.2. Here too, the current situation news have a weight comparable to the macroeconomic ones.

Table 8.3, illustrating the weight of the news on the Lira-Deutschmark exchange rate, presents a parallel structure. The main differences in the explanatory relationships of the Lira exchange rate relative to the DM-$ and Yen-$ are given by the absence of significant current macroeconomic news and the hierarchical inversion between the news and the other explanatory variables: the main fundamental variables explaining the Lira-DM are those related to the DM-$ exchange rate, as well as the interest rate variable, the

Table 8.2 Relative weight of news variables in some DM-$ and Yen-$ equations in ATZ (*)

DM – Dollar

		(1)	(2)	(3)	(4)
Dow Jones Variation	(DDJ)	.111	.0854	.0875	.0542
DM-$ LT Int. Rate Diff.	(DIFUG)	.0457	.0456	.0431	.0572
Lagged Yen-Dollar	(DJUEU)	.0716	.0713	.0723	
Lagged DM-Dollar	(DGUUS(-1)	-.0994	-.0961	-.0958	-.0985
Employment Variat.	(UOC3)	.0678	.0756	.0649	.0841
Hourly Rate Variat.	(UW3)	.0565	.0532	.0618	.0657
Unemployment Rate	(UUN3)	.0539	.0638	.0506	.0640
US Policy Statements	(DUSD)	.204	.204	.204	.235
DM-$ MKT News	(MUS)	.406	.407	.411	.486
Greenspan Statements	(GRE)	.109	.109	.110	.178
Wall Street News	(QMFIN)	.204	.286	.217	.310

Yen – Dollar

		(5)	(6)	(7)	(8)	(9)
Dow Jones Variation	(DDJ)	.0522	.0875	.0446		
Wall Street News	(QMFIN)		.169			.173
Yen-$ LT Int. Rate Diff.	(DIFUJ)					.0523
Lagged Yen-Dollar	(DJUUS(-1))	-.126	-.115		-.125	-.101
Employment Variat.	(UOC3)	.0584	.0747	.0649	.0758	.0916
Hourly Rate Variat.	(UW3)	.0734	.0670	.0618	.0986	.0920
Unemployment Rate	(UUN3)	.0418	.0621	.0506	.0567	.0803
Japanese Yen-related Stat.	(DJAUS)	.116	.113	.114	.114	.108
US Yen-related Stat.	(DUSY)	.128	.125	.127	.137	.128
Yen Political, MKT News	(MJAUSY)	.329	.328	.329	.355	.352
$ Political, MKT News	(MJAUSD)	.276	.282	.277	.340	.344

(*) The symbols of the variables used in econometric estimates in Chapter 7 are in parentheses. For a better understanding see Table 7.11

(1) SURE Equation n. 1 Tab. 7.4
(2) SURE Equation n. 2 Tab. 7.4
(3) SURE Equation n. 3 Tab. 7.4
(4) GARCH Equation n. 4 Tab. 7.6
(5) SURE Equation n. 4 Tab. 7.4
(6) SURE Equation n. 5 Tab. 7.4
(7) SURE Equation n. 6 Tab. 7.4
(8) GARCH Equation n. 6 Tab. 7.6
(9) GARCH Equation n. 7 Tab. 7.6

Table 8.3 Relative weight of news variables in some LIT-DM equations in ETZ and ATZ (*)

Europen Time Zone

		(1)	(2)	(3)	(4)
Short Int. Rate Diff	(DIF33GI)	-.167		-.0959	
Long Int. Rate Diff.	(DIF3GI)	-.238		-.205	
DM-$ Moving Ave.	(M3GUEU)	-.530	-.513	-.305	-.283
Lagged DM-$ in ATZ	(DIGUS(-1))	-.198	-.237	-.204	-.251
Lagged DM-$ in ETZ	(DIGEU(-1))	-.124	-.157	-.0665	-.106
Lira Black Friday	(DU17EU)	.234	.235	.321	.338
Italy Consumer Prices	(PCEU)	.0831	.0752	.0772	.0755
Conflicts in the Polo	(CPEU)	.105	.101	.104	.102
Judicial Conflicts	(CGEU)	.0654	.0521	.0665	.0495
Institutional Conflicts	(CIEU)	.130	.105	.0959	.0700
Election Victories	(VEEU)	.0819	.0766	.0260	.0249
Italy Public Finance	(FPEU)	.108	.0937	.0595	.0477
Dini Government	(GDEU)	.220	.198	.191	.149
Minister Mancuso	(MAEU)	.103	.0992	.0837	.0837
Political Appeasement	(SCEU)	.0444	.0407		
Political News in 1996	(P96EU)	.0945	.0821	.104	.0884
Prodi Government	(GPREU)	.0614	.0545	.0611	.0512
PRC Action	(RIFEU)	.0446	.0423	.0555	.0506
Lira EMU News	(QUMEU)	.0857	.0814	.0896	.0819

American Time Zone

		(5)	(6)	(7))
Short Int. Rate Diff.	(DIF33GI)	-.0924		-.00695
Long Int. Rate Diff.	(DIF3GI)		-.180	
DM-$ Moving Ave.	(M3GUUS)	-.584	-.586	-.362
LIT-DM Moving Ave.	(M3IGUS1)	-.486	-.563	-.278
Lira Black Friday	(DU17US)	.207	.209	.170
Italy Consumer Prices	(PCUS)	.0398	.0402	.0252
Conflicts in the Polo	(CPUS)	.139	.137	.0946
Judicial Conflicts	(CGUS)	.0553	.0471	.0450
Institutional Conflicts	(CIUS)	.0418	.0409	.0322
Election Victories	(VEUS)	.0762	.0746	.0209
Italy Public Finance	(FPUS)	.113	.108	.0582
Dini Government	(GDUS)	.245	.243	.186
Minister Mancuso	(MAUS)	.0615	.0649	.0531
Political Appeasement	(SCUS)	.0926	.0903	.0773
Political News in 1996	(P96US)	.111	.104	.0973
Prodi Government	(GPRUS)	.0479	.0479	.0393
PRC Action	(RIFUS)	.019	.208	
Lira EMU News	(QUMUS)	.124	.123	.115

(*) The symbols of the variables used in econometric estimates in Chapter 7 are in parentheses. For a better understanding see Table 7.11

(1) SURE Equation n. 1 Tab. 7.7
(2) SURE Equation n. 2 Tab. 7.7
(3) GARCH Equation n. 1 Tab. 7.8
(4) GARCH Equation n. 2 Tab. 7.8
(5) SURE Equation n. 5 Tab. 7.7
(6) SURE Equation n. 6 Tab. 7.7
(7) GARCH Equation n. 3 Tab. 7.8

sign of which is opposite to what is expected, as discussed in section 7.3.3. Among the news variables, only those related to the violent fluctuations of the Lira, around the "Black Friday" on 17 March, 1995, and, more rarely, to the actions of the Dini Government, have generally more weight than the "fundamental" explanatory variables.

The ranking results obtained for the Lira in the European zone and the American zone are comparable but there are some differences.

The Dini Government news have higher coefficients, while public finance news have slightly lower coefficients. The news of conflicts within the Polo during the Berlusconi Government always have relatively high coefficients, as do news on EMU that are relevant for the Lira. The Prodi Government news and those relating to the action of Rifondazione Comunista during this last government have very low coefficients. The reasons are easy to see: the Lira stabilizes with the beginning of the Prodi Government in May 1996, and with its re-entry into the ERM at the end of November the Lira volatility is drastically reduced.

The metrics results of the news relating to the Lira have primarily a historical value. They underscore the important role of the political and economic policy turmoil during the Berlusconi and the Dini governments (codes GOVDINI, CONPOLO, and FINPUBL) and the later tension with regards to the Euro (code QUM). Public finances are the main common denominator of these results. This is explicit during the Dini Government, in 1995. But also the subsequent difficulties of the Lira, especially between September 1996 – with France's and the Bundesbank's opposition to its re-entry into the ERM and above all to Italy's participation in the initial phase of the EMU, section 2.6 – and May 1997 – with the event of the Bundesbank's gold reserves revaluation and with the victory of the Left in the French elections, section 2.7 – are always tied to the political credibility of our country's budget policy.

The metrics results of the Dollar indicate a prevalence of that vast aggregate of monetary and market policy events that appear in the database under the codes MGE, MUS and MJA. Unlike those of the Lira, these results maintain their validity and may be used, with the necessary adjustments and updates, to measure the impact of the introduction of the Euro on the international volatility of exchange rates.

Why should we encourage more news metrics research? Because ours are the first results. Their validity must be confirmed and evaluated with an appropriate sensitivity analysis of the estimated coefficients by introducing and excluding certain news. It will also be necessary to refine the estimation techniques with an in-depth study of the simultaneity present in the markets considered and in the formation of the monetary policy direction contained in policy-makers' statements. Lastly, confirmation of the relative weight of each class of events will require extended simulations with a small econometric model consisting of the exchange rate equations estimated in Chapter 7, with the possible addition of other equations for the Dow Jones index and for the long-term US and European securities.

8.4 A Communication Model

The *modus operandi* of the foreign exchange markets represents the meeting point of economic theory, financial theory and behavioural models in which the theory of communications plays an important role.

The exchange rate dynamics has solid macroeconomic foundations, especially in the monetary, Mundell-Fleming and the portfolio balance models mentioned in section 7.3.1.[3] Currency traders refer largely to these models and follow more closely the variables that constitute their basic elements: economic activity, monetary dynamics, inflation, interest rates, trade balances and financial activities, all in relative terms. They naturally follow with even greater attention the formation of those economic policy orientations more likely to influence the dynamics of these macro-variables.

Given that the greater part of international investment activity occurs in the foreign exchange markets, traders are also very alert to the determinants of the stock and bond markets. Here there are many price formation theories but they all find a common denominator in the same group of macroeconomic data that underlies the foreign exchange dynamics.

The macroeconomic relationships governing the phenomena mentioned above are stable enough, at least in the short and medium term, but they still retain a stochastic nature, with the presence of an error term that communication theory experts call "noise". The almost daily flow of information is subject to an interpretation activity that consists of eliminating from the economic datum factors that are incidental, that is, in communication theory terms, of filtering the "signal" from the "noise".

While economic and financial theory constitutes the primary term of reference in the explanation of the exchange rate dynamics in the short and medium term, understanding their daily fluctuations requires an analytical-conceptual structure that goes beyond economic theory. The ways in which traders decode political, economic and market information can be usefully analysed within a communication theory framework.[4] Communication theory has been of great help in the choice of information included in *Newsmetrics*, and for a better understanding of how traders select, how analyse and transform information into actions.

Figure 8.1 outlines the process whereby traders obtain, select, interpret or decode, organise and use information in their decisions. The diagram is drawn from two primary contributions: Umberto Eco's semiotic-informational model[5] and Shannon Weaver's model (1947), which is at the base of mathematical information theory, and which has influenced a great number of communication models[6] including ours.

The box at the far left in Figure 8.1 shows the "Source of information", which consists mainly of the macro financial system that generates it, and listed below we find the sources of scheduled and unscheduled information.

Up to this point we have the raw information and the mechanisms that generate it. Between the source and the users we find the producers of "organised information", in our case the agencies of the specialized press (Dow Jones, Reuters, Bloomberg, Associated Press, Ansa, Radiocor, etc.), the major economic and financial dailies (*Il Sole-24 Ore*, *Financial Times*, *Wall Street Journal*, etc.), the specialized providers of information to the financial markets operators (Bloomberg, Reuters, Bridge, DBC, Tenfore, etc.).

The amount of information thus arranged is still enormous. This is where the information "decoding" processes performed by traders themselves come into play, together with the supporting analytical and research structures (central part of Figure 8.1). In this phase the input information is still plentiful and often discordant: this calls for a selection process that uses the tools of economic and financial analysis but also incorporates Fisher Black's "noise" (1993), through the variously heterogeneous processes to decode the political context, the market climate and market rumours determined by expectations at the time. At certain times there is a uniformity of interpretation that produces monotonous movements in the exchange rates for a certain period with resulting variations that, in the end, can be quite sensitive. This is the phenomenon known as market polarization.

Occasionally there are events or political turning points that are not necessarily expected or of particular momentum and yet gather a certain interpretative consensus, resulting in behaviours that can generate otherwise unpredictable turning points and an acceleration of trends already at work. This in turn attracts flows of speculative funds that strongly reinforce the phenomenon.

At the end of the decoding or interpretation process, we obtain "processed information" ready for the foreign exchange markets' consumption. This information may take the form of internal documents or of the thousands of publications produced by leading financial institutions for their clients. Naturally the most frequent result is the production of buy or sell orders that are passed to traders.

Since traders usually enjoy ample margins for manoeuvre, there are also psychological and propensity factors at work tied to the market sentiment at the time that can still produce exchange movements not immediately consistent with the "organized information" and the "processed information" received by the trading desk. We believe that the outline in Figure 8.1 represents with sufficient accuracy the ways in which currency traders use political, economic and financial primary information. This introduces the last two sections of this final chapter: the role of market sentiment and polarization in the foreign exchange dynamics, and the practical applications of *Newsmetrics* and similar foreign exchange market information systems.

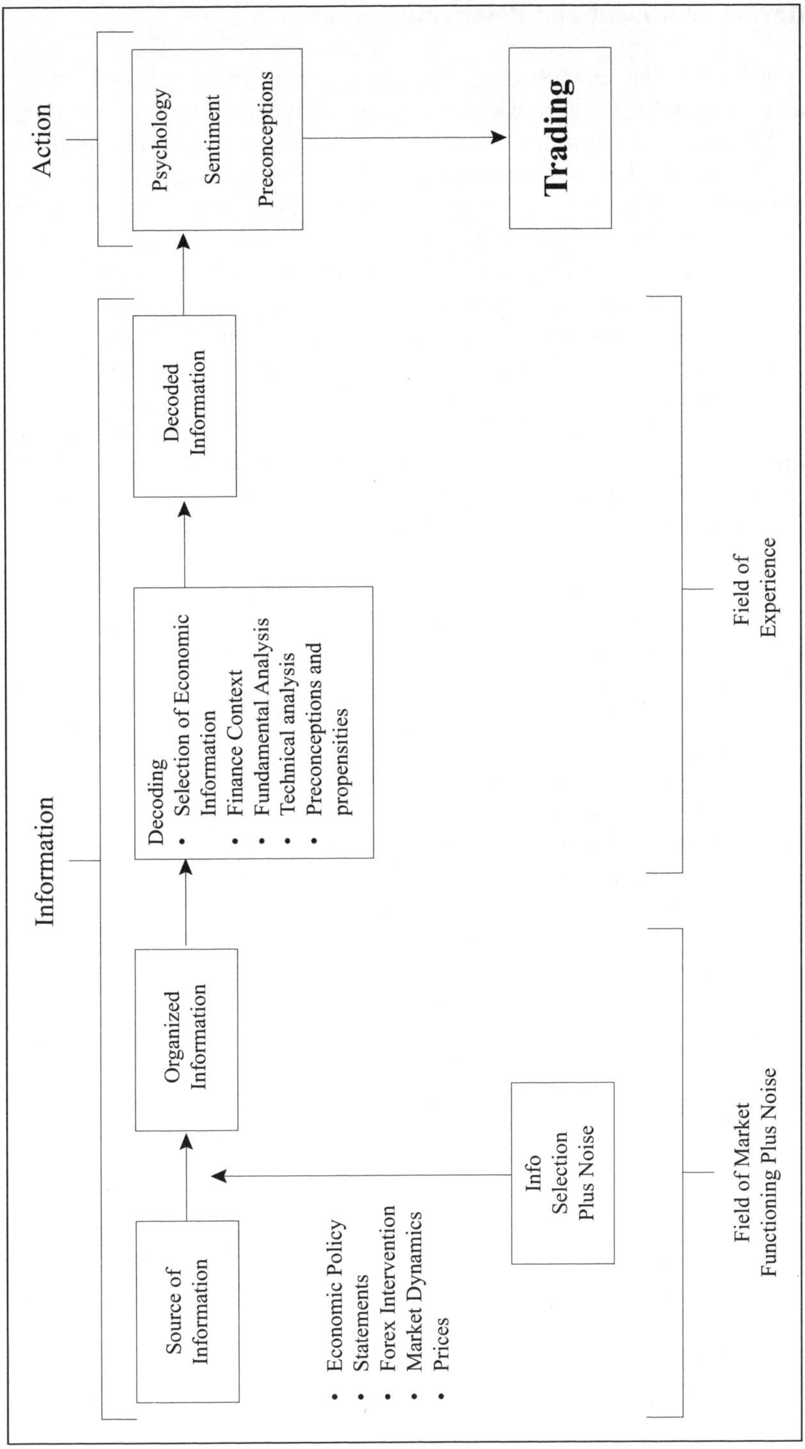

Figure 8.1 Traders in the foreign exchange market

8.5 Market Sentiment and Polarization

From Figure 8.1 we can observe that there are sources of noise in the fundamental statistical relationships between the macroeconomic variables, among the financial variables,[7] and among the latter and policy-makers' reactions to events. This source of noise, inherent to the way the economic and financial systems work, is joined by another one, present in the collection of the base information and its transformation in "organized information". This latter source of noise, probably much less intense than the first one, includes the selection of the information, its presentation, its revision and, above all, the possible distortion of statements by policy-makers or other influential market gurus. All of this occurs within the context defined as "Market operation plus noise" in Figure 8.1.

Therefore, by the time it arrives to the area of "experience" and to "decoding" and "action" stages, the "organized information" is already substantially affected by noise (Figure 8.1). At this stage the noise is filtered, inevitably generating further noise as described earlier.

In this study we have tried to further organize the "organized information" and then we have estimated the statistical relationships between this information and exchange rate dynamics. The econometric results indicate that this information "reduction process" is valid, but some margins of error remain in the explanation of the exchange rate fluctuations that justify the amplitude of the noise produced by the processing of information and by the action of traders.

The perception of market sentiment and the phenomena of micro- and macro-polarization are probably the factors that produce the greatest noise.

In our database we have a few examples of exchange rate dynamics that can be attributed to a specific market climate and to polarisation phenomena. Evidently, the attribution of the episodes that we will examine next to these two causes is subjective. We should specify, in addition, that there we have not used other attribution criteria for phenomena that have a substantial degree of conceptual and statistical proximity.

The following are examples of polarization:

a) the strong devaluation of the Dollar in February 1995;
b) the collapse of the Lira in the final phases of the approval of the "second corrective measure" in March 1995;
c) the impetuous revaluation of the Lira in the final phases of the pension reform negotiation between the Dini Government and union representatives;
d) the weakness of the Dollar and its inability to rally back, despite the various interventions, in March-April-May 1995; and
e) the weakening of the Deutschmark in July-August 1997 with the general sentiment that the Euro would be weak from the outset.

a) The strong depreciation of the US currency in February 1995 is a polarisation episode because every event is read as Dollar-bearish. Starting from an objective weakness of the American economy, all the episodes affecting currencies at international level represent an "excuse"[8] to sell greenbacks: from the Mexican crisis, to the European currency turbulence, to the union militancy of the German IG Metall.[9]

b) The devaluation of the Lira in the last phases of the approval of the second corrective measure by the Dini Government in March 1995 (section 2.5, first and second quarters) is a polarisation episode, especially in the meteoric ascent of the Lira on the "Black Friday" of 17 March, after the approval of the measure with the vote of confidence.

c) We also propose as an example of polarization the strong rally of the Lira between the defeat of the Polo at the administrative elections, on 23 April, 1995 and the completion of the negotiations over the pension reform, on 8 May. See section 2.5, second quarter.

d) The Dollar fluctuation at extremely depressed values in March-April-May 1995, despite the support interventions of G3 central banks and the numerous statements to the same purpose (section 2.1), also constitutes an example of the impact of market climate on the exchange rate. An additional confirmation of the negative attitude of the markets relative to the Dollar is given by the marked appreciation of the US currency in the first half of May, even after positive events, and the subsequent depreciation in the last ten days of the month in correspondence with news of little weight in the overall metrics of events constructed in this study.

e) In early July 1997 the Deutschmark initiates a devaluation phase that follows Minister Weigel's questionable proposal to use the Bundesbank's gold reserves to resolve the German balance problems and the victory of the Left in the French elections in May-June of that year. The market consensus has now consolidated expectations of a weak Euro. See section 2.7, third quarter. The climate is therefore unfavorable to the German currency, which in that period loses approximately 10 pfennings. This episode is therefore a good example of exchange rate dynamics being influenced by market climate.

8.6 Practical Applications and Further Research

The characteristics. The heading of this last section indicates the two key characteristics of this research: 1) the essentially practical implications for trading and for the development of economic policy measures to counter an excessive exchange rate volatility; and 2) the fact that it constitutes a first step towards expanding our understanding of what can influence the exchange rate dynamics in the short term, daily and weekly.

The practical objective of our work is self-evident, first of all because it questions "what happens, why it happens, whether it happens for a reason, and how long it will last". As it does not take into account the "consequences of what happens", nor does it extend its scope beyond the short and very short term, it has less relevance for economic policy and for the understanding of the medium-long term of exchange rate dynamics.

This is not to mean, however, that the results are irrelevant or of little interest. In the world of modern finance the medium and long term pricing appear increasingly more as a succession of short periods; this makes a return to exchange rate "long-term values" compatible with economic theory fundamentals or with policy-makers' desires, a lengthy, unpredictable and often undefinable proposition. All of this can be seen from the experience of the Dollar in our three-year period: the marked devaluation in early 1995 was reabsorbed only two years later, with the continuous series of short-term shocks described in Chapter 2 and easily identifiable in Figures 2.1 to 2.6.

This introduces a second consideration. The nature and the timing of statements and of monetary policy measures are highly influential in exchange rate short-term dynamics. They may obtain the desired results, but only after having been filtered by the markets' decoding process. Therefore, achieving the desired objectives presupposes a correct decoding; at the same time the deliberation of measures can benefit from a correct interpretation of the prevailing market sentiment. The interventions in the foreign exchange markets by central banks now occur following this procedure: they reinforce the market's spontaneous trends and they no longer try to contrast them as they did in the past.[10]

Ours is the first attempt at collecting the events to which the markets seem to react, describing their taxonomy and testing their explanatory power. Ours is not just "an" attempt but the "first" attempt and will therefore require further interaction with traders and with the leading economists in this field.[11] The major difficulty that we see in achieving this objective is the assimilation of a massive amount of events, of relationships among events and of the consequences of events contained in this study. The subjective nature of some interpretations does not help, but it cannot be eliminated; for instance, all else being equal, there is no specific theoretical support to explain the markets' exaggerated reactions, or lack of reactions, to the same type of statements or announcements of measures; similarly, there is no explanation to why the Dollar reactions to variations, or expected variations in interest rates are sometimes felt in the stock markets and some times not.

An agenda for research. Our research agenda depends first of all on the interest that this study may elicit and in any case it will require solid operating and scientific alliances. During the development of this methodology (section 8.3) several technical improvements have been identified: (a) a better treatment of simultaneity – which we do not think will substantially change the cognitive results of this work but may improve its operating results, (b) a sensitivity analysis on the estimates of the variations in the news included in the existing categories, and (c) the creation of new categories – already initiated and developed to a small extent, resulting in an appreciable stability of the estimates.

Another improvement could come from the construction and simulation of multi-equation models, by trading zones and by currencies, with various techniques: the traditional multi-equation models (FIML, simple and iterative MQ3S, etc.), VAR techniques (with and without error correction), heteroscedastic vectorial techniques such as, for instance, the GARCH vectorial models.[12]

An interesting line of research concerns the effects of event decoding processes, which here are only studied "downstream", see Figure 8.1. This would be a research on the microstructure of foreign exchange markets, using questionnaires or the analysis of various "trading patterns" of a representative sample of traders in response to the flow of news. It is in this kind of task that a solid operating alliance with one or more institutions would be most useful. But equally useful would be a scientific alliance for the development of questionnaires with statisticians of the social sciences, and almost certainly for the analysis of the "discordant semiotics" that would result from it.

Practical applications. The analysis in this study can enrich the large set of tools already used in foreign exchange trading and speculative activity, along two dimensions: a) the construction of an information system for monitoring and identifying recent cyclical phases of the markets that are similar to the current ones; b) the expansion and refinement of the econometric structure of this study in order to evaluate the markets' reaction to the news and to trace the impulsive dynamic response of the exchange rate to certain events that are particularly relevant.

Some among the most aggressive international hedge funds have informative systems that are conceptually similar to ours, which are used to identify the market situation most favorable to a speculative attack on a currency or on any other asset by evaluating whether the market climate and the consensus of traders may produce behaviours reinforcing their speculative initiative.

Newsmetrics has a remarkable potential to facilitate the construction of an information system because it provides a model and a checklist of requirements to identify the contents best suited for it.

This monitoring activity can benefit from the construction of a small daily econometric model[13] based on equations estimated for the two trading zones of this study, or for analogous trading zones, in order to: 1) build normality thresholds that can be used to evaluate the reaction of exchange rates to scheduled and unscheduled (but in any case possible or somehow expected) news; 2) to estimate impulse response functions in correspondence with a range of possible scheduled or unscheduled news; and 3) to draw exchange rate dynamics profiles after their occurrence.

Notes

1 It should be noted that the US stock market enters the Dollar exchange rate equations in two ways: through the daily variation of the Dow Jones (DDJ) and through the US stock market qualitative news (QMFIN), with entries that correspond to very strong variations in the stock indices and to events that are considered particularly relevant by the media.

2 A statement implying a possible increase in the US interest rates can be positive for the exchange rate but negative for the stock market and, therefore, negative also for the value of the Dollar. See the frequent examples shown in the database entries relative to Greenspan's statements (GRE) and the considerations in the various sections of Chapter 2, for instance those relative to the third quarter 1995, section 2.1.

3 It is worth remembering here that the relationship between exchange rate variations and variations in the two explanatory variables, output growth rate and interest rates, could have opposite signs depending on whether reference is made to a monetary model or to a Mundell-Fleming model (see section 7.3).

4 A brief and exhaustive source in Italian can be found in Morcellini-Fratelli (1996). The number of references in English is huge. The authors have drawn great benefits from re-reading SHANNON-WEAVER (1949) and from summary statements of the theory (e.g. WINDHAL-SIGNITZER-OLSON (1992)) and from a historical survey of communication theory, ROGERS (1994).

5 Eco and others(1965).

6 Morcellini-Fratelli (1996, Chapter 4).

7 The error terms of the equations in the macro-econometric and macro-financial models, in addition to those already existing in the asset pricing micro-operating models.

8 This term is by now a classic in that particular lexicon describing international financial markets phenomena. There are frequent examples: the video interviews in international financial channels (examples include CNBC and Bloomberg), market comments by leading financial and non-financial dailies, agency news flashes, and interviews with traders.

9 See section 2.1, first quarter, and the references to *Newsmetrics* items contained therein.

10 As an example we can mention the strong resistance opposed by the Bank of England to the devaluation of the pound in 1967 or, more recently, the defence of parity of the Lira with the pound in 1992, before it had to leave the ERM.

11 Our research activity has already had external contacts: an internal presentation to Olsen and Associates in Zurich, in April 1996; an international seminar at the Faculty of Economics of the University of Rome "Tor Vergata" in November 1996 (Tivegna, 1996); a presentation to the university of Venice, in February 1997; the preparation of a joint research (Fornari-Monticelli-Pericoli-Tivegna, 1999) with members of the Bank of Italy Research Centre, which was later presented to the Link seminar in Rio de Janeiro in September 1998.

12 An example is provided by Fornari-Monticelli-Pericoli-Tivegna (1999).

13 The availability of intra-daily data can significantly improve the precision of these valuations, permitting an automatic and continuous update of the equations' intercept, so that they are lined-up even in the minute immediately preceding the news.

Bibliography

Agmon, T. and Findlay, C., (1992) 'Domestic Political Risk', *Financial Analysts Journal*, **38** , pp. 74-7.

Allen, H.L. and Taylor, M.P., (1990) 'Charts, noise and fundamentals in the foreign exchange market', *Economic Journal*, **45** (March), pp.49-59.

Allvine, F.C. and D. O'Neil, E., (1980) 'Stock market returns and the Presidential election cycle. Implications for market efficiency', *Financial Analysts Journal*, **36,** pp. 49-56.

Almeida, A., Goodhart, C. and Paine, R., (1998) 'The effects of macroeconomic 'news' on high frequency exchange rate behaviour', *Journal of Financial and Quantitative Analysis*, **33**, pp. 1-47.

Almekinders, G. and Rovers, M., (1994) 'Are floating exchange rates driven by news?', *Konjunkturpolitik*, **40**, pp. 27-42.

Annunziato, P. and Malgarini, M., (1994) 'La previsione della produzione industriale con indagini quantitative: l'indagine rapida del Centro Studi Confindustria', in Banca d'Italia, '*Ricerche quantitative per la politica economica 1993*', Banca d'Italia.

Baestaens, D.J.E. and Van den Bergh, W.M., (1996) 'Money market headline newsflashes, effective news and the DEM-USD swap rate: an intraday analysis in operational time', Erasmus University, Mimeo.

Baillie, R.T., and McMahon, P.C., (1989) 'The foreign exchange market: theory and econometric evidence', *Cambridge University Press*.

Balduzzi, P., Elton, E.J. and Green, T.C., (1998) 'Economic News and the Yield Curve: Evidence from the U.S. Treasury Market', New York University Salomon Center, *Working Paper S-98-5*.

Becker, K.G., Finnerty, J.E. and Kopecky, K.J., (1995) 'Domestic macroeconomic news and foreign exchange rates', *Journal of International Money and Finance*, **14**, pp. 763-783.

Bera, A.K. and Higgins, M.L., (1993) 'ARCH models: properties, estimation and testing', *Journal of Economic Surveys*, **7**.

Black, F., (1993) 'Noise', in *Advances in behavioural finance*, R.H.Thaler (ed.), Russel Sage Foundation, New York.

Bollerslev, T., (1986) 'Generalized Autoregressive Conditional Heteroskedasticity', *Journal of Econometrics*, **31**, pp. 307-27.

Bollerslev, T., (1987) 'A Conditionally Heteroskedastic Time-Series Model for Security Prices and Rates of Return Data', *Review of Economic Studies*, **69**, pp. 542-7.

Bollerslev, T., (1990) 'Modelling the Coherence in Short-run Nominal Exchange Rates: A Multivariate Generalized Arch Model', *Review of Economics and Statistics*, **72**, pp. 498-505.

Bollerslev, T., Chou R. and Kroner, K. (1992) 'ARCH Modeling in Finance: A Review of the Theory and Empirical Evidence', *Journal of Econometrics*, **52**, pp. 5-59.

Bollerslev, T., Engle, R. and Nelson, D., (1994) 'ARCH Models', in McFadden (ed.), *Handbook of Econometrics*, **Volume 4**.

Bomhoff, E.J. and Korteweg, P., (1983) 'Exchange rate variability and monetary policy under rational expectations. Some Euro-American Experience 1973-1979', *Journal of Monetary Economics*, **11**, pp. 169-206.

Branson, W.H., (1983) 'Macroeconomic determinants of real exchange risk', in Herring R.J. (ed.), *Managing Foreign Exchange Risk*, Cambridge, Cambridge University Press.

Buiter, W.H. and Marston, R.C., (1985) 'International economic policy coordination', Cambridge, MA, Cambridge University Press.

Campbell, J.Y., Lo, A.W. and MacKinlay, A.C., (1997) 'The econometrics of financial markets', Princeton University Press.

Catte, P., Galli, G. and Rebecchini, S., (1992) 'Gli interventi concertati e il dollaro: un'analisi dei dati giornalieri', in '*Il sistema monetario internazionale tra crisi e riforme*', Kenenn, P.B., Papadia, F. and Saccomanni, F., Il Mulino.

Chiofi, G. and Tivegna, M., (1996) 'Una banca dati di news per lo studio del tasso di cambio Lira-DM', Universita' di Roma "Tor Vergata", Mimeo.

Cifarelli, G., (1986) 'Exchange rates, market efficiency and news. Model specification and econometric identification', *Quaderni del Dipartimento di Economia politica*, **55**, Università di Siena.

Cifarelli, G., (1990) 'Sulle determinanti degli errori di previsione a termine del mercato dei cambi', *Quaderni del Dipartimento di Economia Politica*, **99**, Università di Siena.

Copeland, L.S., (1994) 'Exchange rates and international finance', Addison-Wesley.

Copeland, L.S., (1984) 'The Pound Sterling/US dollar exchange rate and the news', *Economic Letters*, **15**, pp. 109-14.

Cornell, B., (1983) 'The money supply announcement puzzle: review and interpretation', *The American Economic Review*, **83**, pp. 644-657.

Cutler, D.M., Poterba, J.M. and Summers, L.H., (1993) 'What moves stock prices?', in *Advances in behavioural finance*, R.H.Thaler (ed.), Russell Sage Foundation, New York.

Davidson, J., (1985) 'Econometric modelling of the sterling effective exchange rate', *Review of Economic Studies*, **211**.

Deravi, M.K., Gregorowicz, P. and Hegji, C.E., (1988) 'Balance of trade announcements and movements in in exchange rates', *Southern Economic Journal*, **55**, pp. 279-87.

Diamonte, R.L., Liew, J.M. and Stevens, R.L., (1996) 'Political risk in emerging and developed markets', *Financial Analysts Journal*, **52**, pp. 71-6.

Dominguez, K., (1993) 'Does central bank intervention increase the volatility of foreign exchange rates', *NBER Working Paper*, **4532**.

Dominguez, K. and Frankel, J.A., (1993) 'Does foreign exchange intervention work?', Institute for International Economics, Washington D.C.

Dornbusch, R., (1980) 'Exchange rate economics: where we stand?', *Brooking Papers and Economic Activity*, pp. 143-185.

Doukas, J. and Lifeland, S., (1994) 'Exchange rates and the role of trade balance account', *Managerial Finance*, **20**, pp. 67-78.

Dunis, C. and Feeny, M., (1989) 'Exchange rate forecasting', Woodhead-Faulkner, London.

Eco, U., Fabbri, P., Giglioli, P., Lumach, F., Seppilli, T. and Tinacci Mannelli, G., (1965) 'Prima proposta per un modello di ricerca interdisciplinare sul rapposrto televisione-pubblico', Istituto di Etnologia e Antropologia Culturale, Mimeo, Perugia.

Ederington, L.H. and Lee, J.H., (1993) 'How markets process information: news releases and volatility', *Journal of Finance*, **48**, pp. 1161-91.

Ederington, L.H. and Lee, J.H., (1995) 'The short-run dynamics of the price adjustment to new information', *Journal of Financial and Quantitative Analysis*, **30**, pp.117-34.

Ederington, L.H. and Lee J.H., (1996) 'The Creation and Resolution of Market Uncertainty: The Impact of Information Releases on Implied Volatility', *Journal of Financial and Quantitative Analysis*, **31**, pp. 513-39.

Edison, H.J., (1996) 'The reaction of exchange rates and interest rates to news releases', Board of Governors of the Federal Reserve System, *International Finance Discussion Paper*, **570**.

Edwards, S., (1982) 'Exchange rates and 'news': a multicurrency approach', *Journal of International Money and Finance*, **1** pp. 211-24.

Edwards, S., (1983) 'Floating Exchange rates, expectation and new information', *Journal of Monetary Economics*, **36**, pp. 321-36.

Elmendorf, D.W., Hirschfeld, M.L. and Weil, D., (1996) 'The effects of news on bond prices: evidence from the United Kingdom, 1900-1920', *Review of Economics and Statistics*.

Engel, C. and Frankel, J.A., (1984) 'Why interest rates react to monetary announcements: an explanation from the foreign exchange market', *Journal of Monetary Economics*, **13**, pp. 31-39.

Erb, C.B., Harvey, C.R. and Viskanta, T.E., (1986) 'The influence of political, economic and financial risk on expected fixed-income returns', *Journal of Fixed Income*, **6**, pp. 7-30.

Fiorentini, R., (1994) 'Exchange rates and news: the case of the Italian Lira', *Quaderni del Dipartimento di Scienze Economiche dell'Università di Padova*, **32**.

Flood, R.P. and Rose, A.K., (1993) 'Fixing exchange rates: a virtual quest for fundamentals", NBER W.P., **163**.

Fornari, F., Monticelli, C., Pericoli, M. and Tivegna, M., (1999) 'The impact of news on the Lira exchange and long-term interest rates', to be published on '*Temi di Discussione*' by the Bank of Italy.

Frenkel, J.A., (1981) 'Flexible exchange rates, prices and the role of 'news': lessons from the 1970's', *Journal of Political Economy*, **89**, pp. 665-705.

Frumkin, N., (1994) 'Guide to Economic Indicators', Second Edition, M.E. Sharpe.

Giovannetti, G., (1992) 'Survey of recent empirical tests of the purchasing power parity hypothesis', *BNL Quarterly Review*, **180**.

Goodhart, C.A.E., Hall, S.G., Henry, S.G.B. and Pesaran, B., (1993) 'News effects in a high-frequency model of the sterling-dollar exchange rate', *Journal of Applied Econometrics*, **8**, pp. 1-13.

Goodhart, C.A.E. and Smith, R.G., (1985) 'The impact of news on financial markets in the United Kingdom', *Journal of Money Credit and Banking*, **17**, pp. 507-511.

Hallwood, C.P. and MacDonald, R., (1994) 'International money and finance', Second Edition, Blackwell, pp. 251-2.

Hardouvelis, G., (1987) 'Macroeconomic information and stock prices', *Journal of Economics and Business*, **39**, pp. 131-140.

Hardouvelis, G., (1988) 'Economic news, exchange rates and interest rates', *Journal of International Money and Finance*, **7**, pp. 23-5.

Harvey, J.T., (1993) 'Daily exchange rate variance', *Journal of Post-keynesian economics*, pp. 515-540.

Hin Hock Lee, J., (1995) 'News and the volatility of the foreign exchange market', in Bos, T. and Fetherson, T.A. (eds.) *Advances in Pacific Basin Financial Markets*, JAI Press, Greenwich Conn., pp. 113-130.

Hobbs, G.R. and Riley, W.B., (1984) 'Profiting from a Presidential election', *Financial Analyst Journal*, **40**, pp. 46-52.

Hoffman, D.L. and Schlagenhauf, D.E., (1985) 'The impact of news and alternative theories of exchange rate determination', *Journal of Money Credit and Banking*, **17**, pp. 328-346.

Hogan, K., Melvin, M. and Roberts, D.J., (1991) 'Trade balance news and exchange rates: is there a policy signal?', *Journal of International Money and Finance*, **10**, pp. 590-99.

Isard, P., (1976) 'How exchange rates respond to the news', in Frenkel, J.A. and Johnson, H.G. (eds) '*The monetary approach to the balance of payments*', Allen & Unwin , London, pp.19-56.

Isard, P., (1995) 'Exchange rate economics', Cambridge University Press.

Irwin, D., (1989) 'Trade deficit announcements, interventions and the dollar', *Economics Letters*, **31**, pp. 257-62.

Ito, T. and Roley, V., (1988) 'News from the US and Japan: which moves the Yen-Dollar exchange rate', *NBER Working Paper*, **1853**.

Jones, C.M., Lamont, O. and Lumsdaine, R., (1998) 'Macroeconomic news and bond market volatility', *Journal of Financial Economics*, **47**, pp. 315-337.

Johnson, G. and Schneeweis, T., (1994) 'Jump-diffusion processes in the foreign exchange markets and the release of macroeconomic news', *Computational Economics*, **7**, pp. 309-329.

Karfakis, C. and Kim, S.J., (1995) 'Exchange rates, interest rates and current account news: some evidence from Australia', *Journal of International Money and Finance*, **14**, pp. 575-595.

Keil, M.W., (1993) 'A model of speculative efficiency with 'news' error component', *Applied Economics*, **25**, pp. 1293-1300.

Li, L. and Hu, Z.F., (1998) 'Responses of the Stock Market to Macroeconomic Announcements Across Economic States', International Monetary Fund, *Working Paper*, **79**.

MacDonald, R., (1983a) 'Some test of rational expectation hypothesis in the foreign exchange market', *Scottish Journal of Political Economy*, **30**.

MacDonald, R., (1983b) 'Test of efficiency and the impact of news in three foreign exchange markets', *Bullettin of Economic Research*, **35**, pp. 123-44.

Macdonald, R. and Milbourne, R., (1991) 'Recent developments on monetary theory', in D. Greenaway, M. Bleaney e I. Stewart (eds), *Companion to Contemporary Economic Thought*, London, Routledge.

MacDonald, R. and Taylor, M.P., (1992) 'Exchange rate economics: a survey', *International Monetary Fund Staff Papers*, **39**, pp. 1-57.

McQueen, G. and Roley, V., (1993) 'Stock Prices, news and business conditions', *Review of Financial Studies*, **6**, pp. 683-707.

Meese, R.A. and Rogoff, K., (1983) 'Empirical exchange rate models of the seventies: do they fit out of sample?', *Journal of International Economics*, **14**.

Mitchell, M. and Muhlerin, J., (1994) 'The impact of public information on the stock market', *Journal of Finance*, **49**, pp. 923-50.

Morcellini, M., Fatelli, G., (1996) 'Le scienze della comunicazione: modelli e percorsi disciplinari', *La Nuova Italia Scientifica*.

Mussa, M., (1979) 'Empirical regularities in the behavior of exchange rates and theories of the foreign exchange market', in K. Brunner, A.H. Meltzer (eds.) '*Policies for employment, prices and exchange rates*', Carnegie-Rochester Conference Series on Public Policy, **Vol. 11**, North-Holland, Amsterdam.

Pagan, A.R., (1984) 'Econometric issues in the analysis of regressions with generated regressors', *International Economic Review*, **25**, pp. 221-247.

Pearce, D.K. and Roley, V.V., (1985) 'Stock prices and economic news', *Journal of Business*, **58**, pp. 49-67.

Pentecost, E.J., (1993) 'Exchange rate dynamics. A modern analysis of exchange rate: theory and evidence', Cambridge University Press, Cambridge.

Peruga, R., (1996) 'Learning and exchange rate: exchange rate responses to money announcements in the early eighties', *Journal of International Money and Finance*, **15**, pp. 167-190.

Roley, V.V., (1983) 'The response of short-term interest rates to weekly money announcements', *Journal of Money Credit and Banking*, **15**, pp. 344-354.

Roley, V.V. and Walsh, C.E., (1985) 'Monetary policy regimes, expected inflation, and the response of interest rates to money announcements', *Quarterly Journal of Economics*, **100**, pp. 1011-1039.

Shannon, C.E. and Weaver, W., (1949) 'The mathematical theory of communication', University of Illinois Press, Urbana.

Smith, R.G. and Goodhart, C.A.E., (1985) 'The relationship between exchange rate movements and monetary surprises: results for the United Kingdom and the United States compared and contrasted', The Manchester School, **53**, pp. 2-22.

Svenson, L.E.O., (1992) 'Recent Research on Exchange Rate Target Zones: An Interpretation', *Journal of Economic Perspectives*.

Taylor, M., (1995) 'The economics of exchange rates', *Journal of Economic Literature*, **33**, pp. 13-47.

Thaler, R.H. (ed.), (1993) 'Advances in behavioural finance', Russell Sage Foundation, New York.

Tivegna, M., (1996) 'Economic and political news in the fluctuations of the Lira: the recent experience, March 28 1994 – December 29 1995', *Rivista di Politica Economica*, **86**, pp. 317-59.

Tivegna, M., (1996a) 'Analisi infragiornaliera del cambio Lira-Marco in periodi di particolare turbolenza: Gennaio 1995-Gennaio 1996', (Infra-daily analysis of the Lira-Mark exchange rate in particularly turbulent periods between January 1995 and February 1996), University of Rome "Tor Vergata", Mimeo.

Tivegna, M., (1999) 'News and Dollar exchange rate dynamics', VIII Conferenza finanziaria dell'Universita' di Roma 'Tor Vergata' su '*Financial crises, risk management and growth*'.

Urich, T.J. and Wachtel, P., (1981) 'Market response to the weekly money supply announcements in the 1970's', *Journal of Finance*, **36**, pp. 1063-1072.

Webb, S., (1989) 'Hyperinflation and stabilisation in Weimar Germany', Oxford University Press, New York.

Index